Family Psychology

Family Psychology

Theory, Research, and Practice

John W. Thoburn and Thomas L. Sexton

 PRAEGER™

An Imprint of ABC-CLIO, LLC

Santa Barbara, California • Denver, Colorado

Library of Congress Cataloging-in-Publication Data

Thoburn, John W.
   Family psychology : theory, research, and practice / John W. Thoburn and Thomas L. Sexton.
     pages cm
   Includes bibliographical references and index.
   ISBN 978-1-4408-3072-3 (hardback) — ISBN 978-1-4408-3076-1 (paperback) —
ISBN 978-1-4408-3073-0 (ebook)
I. Sexton, Thomas L., 1953–   II. Title.
RC488.5.T493   2016
616.89'156—dc23   2015027510

ISBN: 978-1-4408-3072-3 (cloth)
     978-1-4408-3076-1 (paper)
EISBN: 978-1-4408-3073-0

20 19 18 17 16   1 2 3 4 5

This book is also available on the World Wide Web as an eBook.
Visit www.abc-clio.com for details.

Praeger
An Imprint of ABC-CLIO, LLC

ABC-CLIO, LLC
130 Cremona Drive, P.O. Box 1911
Santa Barbara, California 93116–1911

This book is printed on acid-free paper ∞

Manufactured in the United States of America

Some portions of this book have been revised and expanded with permission from the following:

Sexton, T. L., Ridley, C. R., & Kleiner, A. J. (2004). Beyond common factors: Multilevel-process models of therapeutic change in marriage and family therapy. *Journal of Marital and Family Therapy, 30*(2), 131–149.

Sexton, T. L., Gilman, L., & Johnson-Erickson, C. (2005). Evidence-based practices. In T. P. Gullotta & G. R. Adams (Eds.), *Handbook of adolescent behavioral problems.* Springer.

Sexton, T. L., Hanes, C. W., & Kinser J. C. (2010). Translating science into clinical practice. In J. C. Thomas & M. Hersen (Eds.), *Handbook of clinical psychology competencies.* Springer.

Sexton, T. L. & Datchi, C. (2014). The development and evolution of family therapy research: Its impact on practice, current status, and future directions. *Family Practice, 53*(3), 415–433.

Thoburn, J. W., Hoffman-Robinson, G., Shelly, L. J., & Hagen, A. J. (2009). Clinical practice in family psychology. In J. H. Bray & M. Stanton (Eds.), *Wiley-Blackwell handbook of family psychology.* Wiley-Blackwell.

This book is dedicated to:

- Suzanne Thoburn, who has taught me more about love and healthy family life than any book ever did (JT).
- Astrid van Dam/Sexton, my partner, colleague, and inspiration (TS).

Contents

Illustrations xi

Preface: Looking through the Systemic Lens xiii

Acknowledgments xix

Section I: Family Psychology: Theory, Research, and Practice

Chapter 1. What Is Family Psychology? 3

  Defining Family Psychology 5
  The "Praxis" of Family Psychology 11
  Becoming a Family Psychologist 13
  Conclusions: What Is Next? 19

Chapter 2. The Systemic Epistemology of Family Psychology 21

  Revolution and Evolution: From the Individual
  to the System 24
  Systems Epistemology: The Core of
  Family Psychology 27
  Structures and Processes of Relational Systems 28
  Every System Is More Than the Sum of the Parts 31
  Importance of Context: The Place of Culture and
  Diversity in Systemic Thinking 35
  Unifying Threads of Family Psychology 40
  Conclusions: What Is Next? 44

Chapter 3. Through the Systemic Lens: Families,
            Problems, and Change   45

            The Role of Theories   46
            The Pioneering Theories of Family Psychology   47
            Relational Family Systems: Systemic Perspectives
            on Families' Relational Systems   51
            A Systemic View of Clinical Problems   54
            Conclusions: What Is Next?   59

Chapter 4. The Scientific Foundations of Family Psychology   61

            Science and the Scientific Method   62
            Domains of Family Psychology Research   64
            Types of Family Psychology Research   65
            What Is Good Family Psychology Research?   68
            What Do We Know about What We Do?   71
            Support for the Epistemological Perspective   71
            Do Family Psychology Clinical Interventions
            Work?   74
            Being a Scientist-Practitioner-Based Family
            Psychologist   78
            The Research-Practice Dialectic   81
            Conclusions: What Is Next?   83

Section II: The Clinical Practice of Family Psychology

Chapter 5. Mapping the Territory of Clinical Practice   87

            Mapping the Territory of Therapeutic Change
            in Family Psychology   88
            Clinical Interventions in Family Psychology   99
            Process of Change   104
            Conclusions and What Is Next?   106

Chapter 6: Case Planning and Clinical Assessment   109

            The Role of Clinical Assessment and Clinical
            Case Planning   111
            What This All Means and What Is Next?   123

Chapter 7: Family-Focused Clinical Intervention Models   125

            Theoretically Based Models   127
            Evidence-Based Clinical Intervention Models   134
            Conclusions: What Is Next?   148

Chapter 8. Couple-Focused Clinical Intervention Models   149

Theoretically Based Models   152
Evidence-Based Approaches   165
Thoughts, Comments, and What's Next?   173

Section III: The Professional Context of Family Psychology

Chapter 9. Specialty Areas of Family Psychology   177

Sex Therapy   177
International Family Psychology   181
Collaborative Health Care   184
Family Forensic Psychology   188
Conclusions: What Is Next?   189

Chapter 10. Training, Supervision, and Ethics in
Family Psychology   191

Training in Family Psychology   193
Supervision in Family Psychology   198
Ethics in Family Psychology   204
Conclusions and Reflections   210

Epilogue: The Art of Science, Practice, and Theory in
Family Psychology   213

References   217

Index   249

Illustrations

FIGURES

1.1	Core domains of family psychology (research, practice, and theory)	12
2.1	Unifying threads of family psychology	41
4.1	Research domains	65
4.2	Intervention research components	67
4.3	"Working the hyphen"	82
5.1	Components of clinical change	90
5.2	Levels of evidence and intervention in family psychology	98

TABLE

4.1	Levels of Evidence for Family Interventions	80

Preface
Looking through the Systemic Lens

I can't go back to yesterday because I was a different person then.
—Carroll, 2009

In the 1950s, a systems psychology developed from general system theory (von Bertalanffy, 1969), a new and revolutionary epistemology that directly competed with the Platonic and Aristotelian paradigms that had defined much of Western thought for centuries. Systems psychology developed as a reaction to the dominance of the Aristotelian-based medical model of psychology represented by psychoanalytic, cognitive behavioral, and humanistic psychologies. The medical model was characterized as individualistic (a focus on intrapsychic phenomena), dualistic (mind/body split), reductionistic (reducing phenomena down to discrete categories), and radically objective (accepting only objective data as scientifically valid). The systemic model, on the other hand, was characterized as relational (pathology and health are relationship oriented), holistic (the whole is greater than the sum of its parts), ecological (there is a reciprocal relationship between the biopsychosocial elements of being human), and subjective (the ideographic must be considered alongside the nomothetic).

I know who I WAS when I got up this morning, but I think I must have been changed several times since then.
—Carroll, 2009

Much as Alice's journey through the looking glass changed her perspective on everything, so too has systemic epistemology changed the way we, and the whole of psychology, view people as "persons in relationship." Viewing people systemically moves the individual and the individual mind to the background while the foreground shifts to the spaces between people, where meeting-of-minds occurs. This shift from individual mind to the relationship between minds offers a unique perspective on what comprises the basic elements of psychology. Within the space between are patterned pathways of relational interactions that shape individual emotion, meaning, and human value. For example, the new epistemology has impelled us to consider the impact of attachment relationships on neuronal and synaptic development in novel ways (Schore, 2012). Suddenly, in light of this new epistemology, relationships have come to the fore, and relationship characteristics are now viewed as vital mechanisms for change.

The promulgators of this new approach to psychology hailed from such diverse fields as sociology, psychology, anthropology, philosophy, and psychiatry. The movement was punctuated by the development of a new mental health discipline, marriage and family therapy, which focused primarily on interventions for interpersonal relationships (Shields, Wynne, McDaniel, & Gawinski, 1994). However, much of the early research in family therapy was done by psychologists, and ultimately these family-oriented psychologists who practiced and conducted research in the areas of family medicine, child psychology, social psychology, family therapy, and family education recognized the need to organize under the umbrella of psychology through the American Psychological Association (Thoburn, Jones, Cecchet, Oliver, & Sanchez, 2011; Thomas & McKenzie, 1986).

Family psychologists had distinguished themselves from marriage and family therapy as early as 1958 by creating an organization within the American Psychological Association designated the Academy of Psychologists and Marriage, Family and Sex Therapy. In 1984, the organization coalesced into a new APA division now called the Society for Couple and Family Psychology.

Family psychology quickly established itself as a viable field, and in 1990, the American Board of Professional Psychology recognized family psychology as a specialty and began awarding board certification in couple and family psychology. In 2002, APA approved the recognition of family psychology as a specialty, and as such, it joined 10 other specialized fields determined to have a unique set of training competencies, a unique knowledge base, and a unique and solid foundation of research. In the late 1980s, family psychologists founded the International Academy of Family Psychology, recognizing that most non-Western regions of the world practice a family systems-based psychology. Japan is a prime example, where family psychology carries greater weight as a specialty than does clinical psychology. The premier *Journal of Family Psychology* made its debut in 1987 and quickly established itself as one of the most popular of APA's offerings (Levant, 1997). The Society has two new journals, *Family Psychology: Research & Practice* and *The Journal of Couple and Family Psychology* as well as a membership bulletin, *The Family Psychologist*.

"No, no! The adventures first," said the Gryphon (to Alice) in an impatient tone: "explanations take such a dreadful time."

—Carroll, 2009

In the early days, the treatments that emerged from the new family systems way of thinking seemed magical, unique, and sometimes outrageous. Today, the ideas of systemic thinking have matured, developed, and evolved to found the field of family psychology. This book is about the world that opens up when one looks systemically at the relationships between people and the impact of a systemic perspective on viewing the clinical change process, on conducting research methods, and on theoretical speculation.

"Where should I go?"—Alice. "That depends on where you want to end up."—The Cheshire Cat.

—Carroll, 2009

Most books like this one focus on couple or family therapy, reviewing the various theories and approaches, describing the organizations, training, and ethics of the profession. While we cover all of the above ground, we have taken a decidedly different path overall. This book is the first to articulate a truly systemic view of the field of family psychology. Rather than beginning with theory, we start with the epistemological foundations from which theory, research, and practice are derived. As a result, this book fills an important gap and is one of the few that provide a systemic perspective for the three "legs" of the profession: research, theory, and practice. The book builds on the important work done by Stanton and Welsh (2012), who were the first to describe the competencies that make up the specialty of family psychology. Our book also carries forward the seminal work embodied in the *Wiley-Blackwell Handbook of Family Psychology* (Bray & Stanton, 2009), which was the first comprehensive review of the various elements of the specialty of family psychology.

I'm not strange, weird, off, nor crazy, my reality is just different from yours.

—Carroll, 2009

The authors are family psychologists, treatment model developers, family and couple clinicians, and educators. Though we have taken differing paths, our journeys mirror one of the core concepts of family psychology—equifinality, or "there are many roads to the same end." TS is a traditional family therapist who has spent his career working with troubled youth, researching the outcomes of effective family interventions, and who has cocreated one of the most highly respected evidence-based treatment approaches in family psychology, functional family therapy. JT, trained specifically to be a family psychologist, has spent over 30 years providing treatment to couples and families and has been educating clinical psychology students for decades in how to think about psychology systemically. While taking different paths, we have come to the same point today. . . . We are dyed-in-the-wool family psychologists who cannot think about the human condition from any other than a systems perspective.

If I had a world of my own, everything would be nonsense. Nothing would be what it is, because everything would be what it isn't And contrary wise, what is, it wouldn't be. And what it wouldn't be, it would. You see?

—Carroll, 2009

In sharing a systemic view on the profession, we embrace the complexities of theory, research, and practice and, along with other researchers, theorists, and clinicians, have struggled to rectify and bring together the various threads that unite these domains. Our unique experiences have led each of us to understand there is more to excellence in the field than research, science, or sound clinical wisdom—excellence comprises a whole greater than the sum of these parts. In fact, the whole is more defined by the linkages of these areas than anything else. The domains of research, theory, and practice are linked together by the conceptual threads of ecology, dialectic, function, systems, and development. These conceptual threads are akin to tendons in the body, anchoring research, theory, and practice to the family systems skeleton, providing a scaffold for understanding how to do effective work in the various domains of family psychology.

ORGANIZATION OF THE BOOK

"Curiouser and curiouser!" cried Alice.

—Carroll, 2009

Section I: Family Psychology: Research, Practice, and Theory. We'll begin Chapter 1 with a discussion on what is family psychology. Chapter 2 will take us into the world of systemic epistemology, which provides the anchor for the unique way of thinking that is at the heart of family psychology. Chapter 3 provides an overview for thinking systemically about individuals, couples and families, their problems, and course of change. The section is rounded out by Chapter 4, which provides a discussion about the scientific foundations of family psychology.

Section II, The Clinical Practice of Family Psychology, begins with Chapter 5, which maps the territory of clinical practice. Chapter 6 provides a description of clinical assessment and treatment planning from a family psychology perspective, and Chapters 7 and 8 offer a palate of both traditional contemporary family- and couple-based intervention models.

Section III, The Professional Context of Family Psychology, focuses on specific specialty areas of practice described in Chapter 9, while Chapter 10 discusses family psychology training, ethics, and supervision. The book ends with an epilogue on the motive creative force behind the *research, theory, and practice* of family psychology.

"Give your evidence," said the King; "and don't be nervous, or I'll have you executed on the spot." Thus grew the tale of Wonderland.

—Carroll, 2009

Acknowledgments

No worthy endeavor is the work of one or two people alone. We are indebted to our editor Debbie Carvalko for her patient guidance and to our copy editor Sivakumar Vijayaraghavan. We also want to acknowledge the copy editing work of Jessa Carlile, Noel Clark, Heather Lucas, Fiona Kurtz, Sadie Olson, Ryan Hamman, Jeff Holguin, Chris Keller, Sam Rennebohm and Jyssica Seebeck.

Section I

Family Psychology
Theory, Research, and Practice

Chapter 1

What Is Family Psychology?

All is connected . . . no one thing can change by itself.

—Paul Hawken

It might be easy to think of family psychology as merely clinical psychology with more than one person, such as a couple or family. It is true that family psychology often works with various constellations of the family in family and couple treatments. Yet to define family psychology simply in terms of population is to miss the most central, unique, and special aspects of the field. Family psychology is a specialization within the larger field of psychology that is founded on a unique way of understanding and intervening to change human behavior. Rather than looking at each individual, it views the connection between people as the core unit of analysis and avenue for change. Sexton (2010) suggested that it is the "space between" people that provides the necessary context within which to understand how and why individuals, couples, and families think, feel, and behave as they do. *Contextuality* is grounded in the principles of systems psychology—often called systems thinking.

The systemic and contextual foundations of family psychology represent an epistemological revolution that developed in reaction to a lens or way of thinking about clients and problems in a linear, individualistic, and radically objective fashion. Traditional psychological approaches identified internal mechanisms as the primary focus of attention, breaking down cognition, affect, and behavior into discrete units of measure within a person. By contrast, systems thinking brought a multisystemic perspective where the whole was seen to be "more than the sum of parts" and where the relationship between an individual, others, and the environment, the "space between," takes center stage. Thus, individuals are always embedded in a context of relationships, as couples, families, and members of extended family groups and communities. This pivotal idea of the *context of systems* brought into focus a whole new way of doing research and therapy, and it brought a new set of principles upon which to build theoretical models. It is this uniquely *contextual* lens through which we view multiple systems in search of helping clients with clinical issues that is family psychology.

Why did it take a revolution for these ideas to emerge? In all fields of knowledge, there is the development and evolution of new and unique ideas followed by periods of stabilization and solidification. Stable periods are resting points between revolutions, and revolution is really just one step in the ongoing evolution of constantly developing and refining and reorganizing ideas that comprise the next new way of thinking. Systems thinking developed as a result of what could not be fully explained by traditional Aristotelian and Platonic categories of thought. Aristotelian categories, which are linear and reductionistic, simply do not adequately explain the summative and holistic outcome of relational systems and their influence on human behavior. Systems thinking contributed to the development of ideas by suggesting that systems are the basic unit of analysis, not the individual, and that patterns of interlocking relational behaviors develop their own sets of rules and expectations that have a significant impact on individuals, both promoting certain behaviors and limiting others.

The unique ideas of systems thinking were represented by a group of early pioneers of family psychology who were much like Western cowboys, brilliant, special, and charismatic, yet in many ways as uncivilized as the Wild West. Personalities such as Minuchin, Whitaker, Bateson, Haley, and Erickson, to name just a few, were ideological gunslingers, firing off ideas that were rarely tested under the microscope of research, but brilliant in their structure and difficult to refute in the face of anecdotal charismatic declamation. The days of these early progenitors were unique in that their ideas were creative, exciting, and at the same time unstructured, nonspecific, and difficult to understand and replicate. Thus, it was difficult to pass along, refine, and evolve the earliest ideas of systems thinking. The field is now in somewhat of a post revolution phase with the exciting, cutting-edge infancy given way to a professional maturing. Family systems thinking developed into the field of family therapy, then further evolved into the specialty of family psychology and is now well defined with a theoretical knowledge base, a repository of clinical wisdom, and a scientific foundation to direct practice, research, and training.

As with any dynamic system, family psychology will continue to be pulled in a constant tension between the forces of stability and maturity and the need for evolution and change. The field wrestles with creativity, change, and reification where answers are often clear, but adaptation and growth are stifled. Such tensions between oppositional forces are referred to as *dialectic*. Dialectic consists of components that are oppositional, creating a positional thesis and antithesis. By holding the oppositional elements in dynamic tension, the thesis is sublated or absorbed by the antithesis, creating a synthesis wherein the elements combine to form a new transcendent insight or idea (Pinto, 2001). To understand family psychology, one needs to understand the tensions inherent in the dialectic of systems thinking that gives the profession its innovative and creative approach.

Our goal in this chapter is to present the broad landscape of family psychology upon which later chapters of the book will build. More than a theory or clever clinical intervention, family psychology is a comprehensive way to think and systematically work—the book and this chapter reflect that ideal. Our discussion will attempt to represent the core design elements of the profession as well as the tensions and debates that keep the field in flux, constantly shaking up the status quo, reshaping ideas to present an ever-emerging profession. The rest of this chapter will focus on the foundational elements of the profession. As with other applied psychological professions, family psychology has theoretical, clinical, and research foundations. These three domains are like three legs of a stool—each contributing something unique and bringing with them necessary stability and balance.

DEFINING FAMILY PSYCHOLOGY

As mentioned earlier, it is not that family psychologists treat populations different from those seen by other professional psychologists. Nor is it even that a family psychologist's client presents with vastly different issues. It is, rather, the epistemology of the family psychologist that differentiates him or her from the more traditionally trained professional psychologist. Whether the client is a family, a couple, or a single member of a family, to the extent that the client's presenting issue intersects with family or systemic functioning, a specialized conceptual model and related interventions are required. Consequently, a specialization in family psychology provides a unique perspective and approach to working with many of the same populations and problems treated by psychologists from other specialties. The differences are in how family psychology thinks about health and pathology and how that thinking affects clinical treatment.

Family psychology is unique in its core epistemology, a systems paradigm from which flow focused theoretical and clinical practice models. Epistemology is the study of knowledge; more specifically, it is a concern for the *nature* of knowledge and its limits. A systems perspective that recognizes the reciprocal interlocking relationships between biology, psychology, and sociality defines family psychology's core epistemology (Nutt & Stanton, 2008).

Consider the following metaphor: A king asked six blind wise men to determine what an elephant looked like by feeling different parts of the elephant's body. One blind man felt the elephant's leg and declared, "the elephant is like a pillar"; another grabbed the elephant's tail asserting, "the elephant is like a rope"; one blind man felt the trunk saying, "the elephant is like a tree branch"; the one who felt the elephant's ear remarked that "the elephant is like a hand fan"; the one who felt the elephant's belly emphatically stated, "the elephant is like a wall"; and the one who felt the tusk stated that "the elephant is like a spear." An exasperated king cried, "You foolish wise men, you are all correct and you are all wrong. I wish that you had hands that were like eyes that could truly see" (Jain Stories, retrieved August 29, 2006).

Like the metaphor mentioned earlier, a systemic perspective would suggest that we look beyond two-dimensional biopsychosocial modal integration, with approaches that are either/or categorical. Instead, systemic thinking promotes both/and thinking, where tensions are reconciled in some cases and simply embraced in others. Taking a systems perspective is difficult; in fact, as gleaned from the blind men metaphor, not only is it difficult to see beyond what you "have in hand," but it is also difficult to take a broad-enough perspective and at the same time be specific enough to maintain an identity.

When the various components of the field of family psychology are brought together, there will be tensions between factors. Dichotomous factors include (but are not limited to) the mind/body split, resulting in divided values between psychiatry and psychology, the gap between research and practice, the long-standing argument regarding the impact of nature or nurture, the split between cure and care, the tension between focusing on strengths and resources as opposed to pathology, and the uneasy relationship between process and content in psychotherapy. Recent research advances in neuroscience, genetics, and evidence-based treatment have brought to the fore the interactive relational aspects of these dichotomous factors. For example, we now know that nature influences genetic expression via nurture (Ridley, 2003), that medication and talk therapy together provide the basis for the most efficacious treatment of psychopathology (Hollon et al., 2014), that palliative care is vital in the curative process, that a local clinical scientist model reflects the reciprocal relationship between research and practice, and that the ongoing evolution of ideas requires revolutionary thinking that takes scientific advances to the next level so that the lens through which we view human behavior becomes increasingly refined.

Today's Family Psychology

Today's family psychology is a unique, stable, and mature specialized field of applied psychology founded on the core principles of psychology (cognitive, developmental, psychopathology, etc.). Family psychology is a comprehensive knowledge base that comprises research and theories explaining the processes and functioning of couples, families, and individuals within these relational contexts in various ways. It is a set of specific practices and approaches with a supporting research base. It is also a unique professional specialization with an identity and an organized network of professional organizations that guide the development and practice of family psychology.

Today, family psychologists are *systems psychologists* who inhabit all the roles of a psychologist and perform all the functions of a psychologist from a unique systemic perspective. For example, family psychology–oriented assessment evaluates intrapersonal factors such as biology and personality, interpersonal factors organized around significant relationships, and contextual factors that are environmental in nature and scope. Diagnosis is organized around intrapersonal and relational variables, recognizing their reciprocal interaction and mutual influence. Research explores and drills down in depth for questions that are best understood through qualitative analysis and also examines a broad range of factors through quantitative exploration. Family psychology utilizes evidence-based approaches that are ecosystemic in nature through understanding the reciprocity between individual, relational, and environmental variables in order to treat individual, couple, and family symptoms. A systems orientation provides a unique counterpoint to the traditional unitary focus on the Big Five personality traits in consultation and program evaluation for organizations and businesses. Family psychologists teach in clinical, counseling, school, and medical programs offering a systems psychology perspective that provides a dynamic three-dimensional perspective to other specialties. A systems orientation with its holistic orientation provides a unique collegiality for healthcare providers, enabling them to work particularly well in healthcare treatment teams.

Family psychologists practice in a wide range of settings with diverse clients utilizing unique systemically oriented approaches (Weeks & Nixon, 1991). For example, family psychologists:

- Often work collaboratively with school districts and their constituent families addressing issues such as bullying, substance abuse, oppositional issues, teacher–student conflict, and academic or social and psychological problems (Carlson, Kubiszyn, & Guli, 2004; Fine, 2005; Gorman-Smith et al., 2007).
- Are central parts of treatment teams operating within the healthcare system providing consultation and treatment for acute and chronic illness, including interventions with the patient, patient's family system, and patient's healthcare team (McDaniel, Campbell, Hepworth, & Lorenz, 2005; Weston, 2005).
- Work with family service centers and agencies providing diagnosis, assessment, treatment, and consultation around family systems and family dynamics.
- Work in forensic settings providing psychological expertise to family, criminal, and dependency courts in matters that fall within their scope of competence and in mediation centers applying the family systems lens to couple dynamics in mediation.
- Work in university counseling centers providing interventions regarding college students' adjustment to college life and the impact of that young adult's departure on the family's adjustment.
- Work in child guidance clinics and consult with school counseling services around interventions regarding the influence of the family system and dynamics on the child as triggering, maintaining, or contributing to child-centered problems, including school behavior, and in independent private practice and group practices providing treatment regarding the influence of the family system and dynamics as triggering, maintaining, or contributing to problems in the family as a whole or to individual members.
- Work in community settings such as rape counseling and spouse abuse programs providing interventions regarding the influence of the family system and dynamics on family violence and, in turn, the impact of family violence on the family's functioning and organization.

Family psychology also plays an important role in medical settings. For example, family psychologists work in OB-GYN/fertility clinics providing consultation regarding the influence of the family system and the couple's dynamics on issues of infertility (Mikesell & Stohner, 2005) and on interdisciplinary healthcare teams as an interphase with psychiatry providing interventions where the family system impacts the psychiatric issues of individuals. (e.g., impact of the father's multiple sclerosis and neurological impairment on family dynamics). Family psychologists work in internal medicine and provide consultation services to rehabilitation medicine and neurology regarding the impact of chronic illness or attempts at recovery of function on the stability of the family system (e.g., impact of the father's multiple sclerosis and neurological impairment and the subsequent impact on family dynamics).

Family psychologists work with a wide range of client populations who present with a variety of clinical issues:

- Individuals who have relationship issues (or whose individual issues affect their relational functioning), but whose intimate others are unavailable (e.g., a student whose parents are out of town) or whose intimate partner refuses conjoint therapy. Individuals experiencing relationship problems stemming from transgenerational processes.
- Couples and families who struggle with daily functioning, substance abuse, mental health, and youth behavior problems. A family psychologist is able to "enrich or improve the functioning of non-clinical or normal couples . . . to treat dysfunctional couples" (Weeks & Nixon, 1991, p. 13) (or to help couples adjust to problems of living).
- Family psychologists treat individuals and couples from all socioeconomic status backgrounds as well as traditional and nontraditional couples at various stages of life (e.g., dating, premarital, marital, gay, lesbian, separated, divorced, interracial, interethnic, and interreligious).
- The family psychologist works with larger systems such as communities and organizations to help with problems in functioning and communication (e.g., family-owned businesses, school consultation, consultation with agency personnel, church consultation).

Family Psychology or Family Therapy?

Family psychology and family therapy are commonly confused because the terms are often used interchangeably, but there are differing foci between the two disciplines that constitute significant differences in research and practice. Both family psychology and family therapy adhere to a systems paradigm, but the emphasis of family therapy tends to be on population rather than epistemology. That is, marriage and family therapy exists to treat couples and families, while family psychology treats any constellation of the family, including individuals, from a systems paradigm. The two professions share a consideration for both intrapersonal and biological processes, but family therapy's focus, vision, and energy are given to interventions at the level of interpersonal relationships and environmental context as juxtaposed against family psychology's equal focus on the intrapersonal as well as the interpersonal and contextual (Shields, Wynne, McDaniel, & Gawinski, 1994; Thoburn, Cecchet, Oliver, Jones, & Sanchez, 2011).

These differences in emphasis between family therapy and family psychology reflect other differences as well. Family therapy has traditionally focused on conceptual thinking about family systems and clinical treatment, while family psychology, in keeping with the overall tenor of psychology, has engaged in basic and applied research and diagnostic testing as part of the course of family treatment (Kaslow, 1987; Thoburn et al., 2011). Family therapy for the most part eschews diagnosis because it is seen as a way to maintain individuals in the role of identified patient or family scapegoat rather than focusing on family dynamics as a whole. Most of the theories on which family therapy is based, such as structural family therapy, strategic family therapy, or narrative therapy, have received scant attention in the empirical literature, though they have received considerable clinical validation. Family psychology on the other hand utilizes a combination of objective and clinical assessments at multiple ecological levels to achieve individual, couple, and family diagnoses that are the core for effective treatment planning. An informed and accurate diagnosis is seen as vital to the integrity of the treatment plan whether individual or relational. Furthermore, family psychology advocates for and has spent considerable research establishing evidence-based treatments. Research is viewed as a necessary complement to practice, each informing and providing validation for the other.

Family psychology views its mandate as broader than that of marriage and family therapy, advancing an ecological approach that encompasses the biopsychosocial perspective of the discipline of psychology as a whole. Thus, family psychology is as interested in biological bases of behavior and issues of personality development as it is in social factors affecting human behavior. It is a broad specialty area of psychology that is a systems-based discipline offering assessment, diagnosis, treatment, and doctoral-level research (Sexton & Stanton, 2015). Its orientation is biopsychosocial and proceeds from a variety of evidence-based theoretical modalities for individuals, couples, and families (Sexton & Stanton, 2015; Stanton, 2009).

Family psychology is not so much about doing psychotherapy with families as it is a unique way of thinking about psychology, one that requires psychologists to focus on the relational and contextual variables influencing individual function and how development interacts with individual, interpersonal, and environmental factors. Family psychology is founded on the principles and applications of systems theory, including explicit awareness of the importance of context and developmental perspectives, to understand and treat the comprehensive issues of psychological health and pathology, including affective, cognitive, and behavioral factors across individuals, couples, families, groups, organizations, and larger social systems (Stanton, 2009).

THE "PRAXIS" OF FAMILY PSYCHOLOGY

Praxis is the "practical application of a theory" and the "exercise or practice of an art, science, or skill" (dictionary.reference.com, 2015). The practical application of these domains for a family psychologist include conducting research, engaging in clinical practice, teaching, training and supervising, and engaging in theory building and program development.

Like any profession, present-day family psychology is a combination of the clinical wisdom of hardworking practitioners, the research aimed at understanding systems and clinical interventions, and the theory base that forms the conceptual foundation for understanding clients, their issues, and the change process. The intersection of these domains constitutes the "praxis of family psychology."

- *Research* is the systematic study of the profession. The core methods of scientific discovery and verification of the science of family psychology bring a nomothetic and broad view of how and in what way variables work and change within and between people. Research is objective and reliable through replication, and usually passed along through journals with peer review and outside evaluation and judgment. Research is also ideographic, drilling down into unique aspects of human being and relating.
- *Theories* are sets of organized constructs that explain certain phenomena. Theories help bring certain elements to the foreground while moving other features to the background and out of consideration. Theories can be named approaches to clinical work (e.g., structural family therapy) as well as conceptual theories that describe phenomena (such as theories about relationships).
- *Practice* is the application of the knowledge of family psychology. As with any specialty in psychology, practice and treatment in family

psychology are rooted and grounded in generating and testing hypotheses derived from assessment and diagnosis. We define practice as the cumulative wisdom (knowledge, understanding, experience) of how to proceed with the clinical application of family psychology. This knowledge base is typically passed along through training and supervision.

While important, the domains of research, theory, and practice are not the sum of the profession. Each of these domains has a particular set of core principles that bring very different and unique perspectives to the same phenomena. Researchers look at the group levels trying to identify replicable trends that predict, to some degree of accuracy, how and why

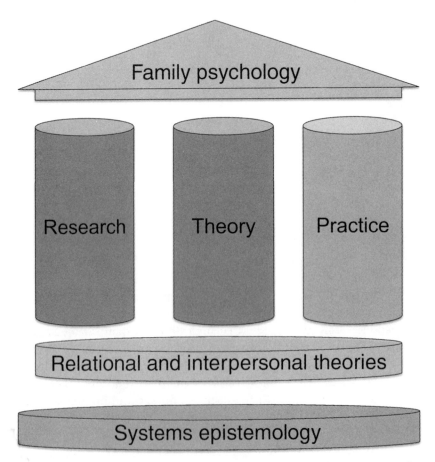

Figure 1.1 Core domains of family psychology (research, practice, and theory)

things occur between people. Those that build theories take the clinical and core ideas of the field and try to describe explanations that have internal consistency and logic. A clinician takes a very different perspective considering more of a unique or idiosyncratic focus on the individual system's characteristics, translating evidence-based research into evidence-based practice, that is, what will work for a particular client at a particular time in the developmental life of the client system.

The cumulative knowledge from these three domains guides how family psychology looks at clinical problems, formulates research projects, evaluates programs, and works with individuals, couples, and families. The praxis of family psychology is the central lens of the profession. It is a lens that is systematic and comprehensive with organized principles and practices that help systematize how a psychologist thinks and works. Good family psychology practice brings the best of tested theory to the work in a way that is implemented in a manner that matters to the therapist and the client and impacts the context in which they are in relationship. As such, family psychology as a field has a comprehensive set of tools to help clinicians think systematically, work relationally and contextually, and evaluate their work from start to finish.

BECOMING A FAMILY PSYCHOLOGIST

Family psychology has designated training pathways at the graduate and postgraduate levels. At the graduate level, family psychology is typically a minor attached to a major in clinical, counseling, or school psychology. Postdoctoral training takes place at institutes, in medical centers, in veteran's administration centers, and in community mental health settings. Comprehensive training includes knowledge of the research foundations and the development of competent practice in clinical work through actual internship/practicum experiences implementing family psychology practices. Most important are the core competencies—the functional and foundational skills and abilities that provide a family psychologist his or her professional identity. Core competencies are often defined as attitudes, skills, and knowledge (Sexton, Kinser, & Hanes, 2008; Stanton, 2012).

Attitudes represent the manner in which either the researcher or the practitioner approaches his or her subject and the general assumptions with which they approach their task. We suggest five primary attitudes for successful research or practice: (1) bringing an intentional and purposeful approach to both research and practice, (2) an essential curiosity about how things work and about what works, (3) an openness to new explanations and theories, (4) an acceptance of the inherent ambiguity and evolutionary nature of what we know about practice and research, and (5) cultivating a local clinical scientist mind-set (Sexton, Kinser, & Hanes, 2009; Sexton & Stanton, 2015; Stanton & Sexton, 2015).

1. *Purpose and intention in decisions.* An intentional and purposeful approach to research, clinical, and theoretical decisions based on the best available information is the core of being a family psychologist. The systematic and purposeful psychologist approaches clinical practice by accessing and applying current scientific knowledge appropriately, consistently, and even habitually. The purposeful and intentional practitioner becomes a local clinical scientist (Stricker & Trierweiler, 1995) desiring to know the outcomes of his or her work and subject the work to scrutiny from colleagues, stakeholders, and the public.

A purposeful and systematic practitioner approaches clinical work in a systematic and intentional manner, and at the same time, remains client centered and clinically responsive. Purposefulness in clinical practice involves habitually questioning assumptions, developing potential hypotheses, and accessing necessary information. When psychologists are systematic, it means that with each clinical question the practitioner asks (1) what is the main issue(s); (2) what are the different theories or perspectives that pertain; (3) what factors has empirical research found to be involved with this issue(s); and (4) what is the most reliable and valid information available? To perform systematically, the psychologist must set aside biases and preconceptions, avoid the temptation of superficial answers, and consider what theory and research has to say on the pertinent issues. In summary, the clinician reasons his or her way to a clinical decision based on clinical experience and existing scientific knowledge that considers unique client variables, context, and the situation at hand.

2. An attitude characterized by the qualities of being *systematic, open, complex, curious,* and *objective.* Science acquires its knowledge through systematic observation, inquiry, and experimentation. The assumption is that objective research leads to theoretical hypotheses, which then lead to further observations and experimentation. In making these observations or engaging in inquiry, it is important to control for all other factors that may influence research findings and mislead us in drawing invalid conclusions. Openness is important because results may not always support the practitioner or researcher's belief about cause. Thus, the most accurate scientific knowledge and the most useful practice information is produced through systematic and thoughtful questioning and inquiry where the results are considered in an open way, even if the outcomes challenge the core beliefs of either the researcher or the practitioner. In this way, the translation between these domains is built on the attitudes of questioning, critical thinking, and open-minded skepticism based in a fundamental

curiosity to understand. All assertions, speculations, and theories must be empirically tested, and the scientific evidence about them must be evaluated by objective and knowledgeable researchers before being accepted as valid.

The attitude of systematic inquiry is a central one in research, practice, and theory. In the research domain, being systematic means that the psychologist follows the methods of scientific inquiry in order to produce reliable and valid results. In practice, being systematic means that the psychologist approaches the task of working with clients in a thoughtful and planned manner, moving from comprehensive assessment to purposeful intervention. A systematic attitude is an attitude shared by good practitioners and researchers in that both must develop hypotheses about their tasks (how to facilitate client change or study clinical phenomena) and constantly question and reevaluate hypotheses as the process of clinical or research work unfolds.

The attitude of openness described here is inherently a personal, cultural, and theoretical consideration. Each cultural and theoretical orientation brings a set of biases that shape observations and affect findings and the degree and specificity with which evidence may be integrated into practice. Researchers and practitioners have particular perspectives on their culture, class, and gender, shaped by their culture's sociocultural, historical, philosophical, religious, gender, and class experiences, and beliefs. They have particular beliefs about clients, clinical change, and the definition of successful outcome. Such beliefs are not inherently problematic, but they do limit the awareness of other perspectives, beliefs, and explanatory alternatives for clinical or research questions. Without openness, researcher assumptions and practitioner biases will negatively taint both research and the application of research through practice. So, as well as being skeptical of common sense and personal experience, a family psychologist must also be open minded. Researchers must strive to set aside their personal beliefs and attitudes, and the limitations of their culture and gender, as well as their theoretical perspective, to carry out objective, unbiased research. In addition to monitoring and setting aside one's own biases, the open-minded researcher should, when possible, be transparent about the potential biases that may impact his or her work. This entails introspectively understanding and articulating one's own biases in addition to attempting to set them aside. The regulation and articulation of one's own biases allows for more objective and open exploration in both research and practice contexts.

3. The ability for *acceptance of ambiguity*. Ambiguity is an inherent part of psychological practice and research (Sexton & Stanton, 2015; Stanton & Welsh, 2012). The work of clinical practice is complex, and the process of

knowledge development through science is evolutionary. Thus, there are limitations on the degree to which science can translate into clinical practice depending on the questions and the areas of interest. The current knowledge of the profession is not complete, and it constantly changes as new data is discovered, theories are confirmed, and principles are overturned. Any knowledge base inherently in motion will change over time. In addition, there is much that science has yet to discover or may never discover about the complexities of practice. In some areas, there is clear evidence that can guide practice, and in other areas, there is no treatment model that fits common clinical needs. This would suggest the need for being a lifelong learner, constantly developing and adding new information based in systemic inquiry to make increasingly competent clinical decisions.

Furthermore, it is important to know that even in the best of circumstances, knowing what is deemed effective in the practice of family psychology is complex. Determining the best treatment requires consideration of the empirical evidence that exists and also the extent, utility, and clinical significance of that evidence. Unfortunately, no degree of clarity or specificity can overcome the inherent ambiguity and difficulty in creating and applying clinical practice guidelines. Consequently, no set of practice guidelines can ever produce a clear and inarguable list that makes for easy decisions, and there can never be a system that is simple to use and produces clear-cut policy, service delivery, and clinical guidance across all needs. In the end, even with systematic practice guidelines, the process of determining what works will be difficult, complex, and seem at times amorphous.

We suggest that this represents the complex and dynamic nature of clinical practice, rather than anything inherently flawed in clinical practice guidelines. It is however important to note that the inherent ambiguity of the knowledge base of science is sometimes difficult to accept and for many undermines their faith in the scientific process. It is not uncommon to hear, "science just can't study real things," or, "one study tells this while another one says something different." The attitude of accepting this ambiguity helps both the practitioner and the researcher respect the current limits of scientific knowledge while at the same time knowing that with more study, innovative research, practice advances, and continual knowledge development, many of the holes in the research knowledge base will eventually be filled. Approaching the task of practice in a research-based way requires a kind of scientific humility, accepting ambiguity as a natural and hopeful part of good practice and one of the exciting elements of the profession that keeps us always facing forward to the future.

Accepting ambiguity means being able to manage the dialectic tensions within the profession. A dialectical approach means that both researchers and practitioners are able to inherently understand that the tension is not whether the enterprises of research/science and practice go together, but in how each informs the others with regard to the specific issue(s) at hand. This approach also means that the competent family psychologist stands above many of the either/or struggles that often occur between researchers and practitioners and instead looks to see what and how existing, relevant, and available scientific knowledge can be applied in the most utilitarian and efficient way. What often gets lost in the traditional discussion of research versus practice, specific models versus common factors in practice, evidence-based practice versus practice-based evidence is that the goal of both science and practice in psychology is the same: providing the best available treatment with the highest probability of success to a client system experiencing a particular clinical issue. Considered in this way, science and practice are two sides of the same coin. Each brings a different facet to the same ultimate goal. Each produces a different type of knowledge essential to helping a client system. The core element of embracing dialectic is to roll with the tension in order to create the harmony necessary to bring knowledge and skills together to help clients and improve practice (Alexander, Robbins, & Sexton, 2000).

5. *Thinking like a local scientist.* Stricker and Trierweiler (1995) coined the term "local clinical scientist" to describe an approach encouraging clinicians to move research into their practices. In this model, practitioners use their own practice to study profiles of service delivery, types of interventions, outcomes, and even process measures, which, over time, accumulate to produce a local set of evidence for a particular practitioner in a particular setting. The local clinical scientist will systematically gather information as he or she practices. For example, the practitioner may adopt an outcome measure to determine pre (prior to therapy) and post (after therapy) levels of mental health, behavioral disorder, or healthy attitudes, behaviors, or interactions. There are many accessible measures of outcome that are easily integrated into practice. The service delivered to clients can also be tracked noting the number of times, the type of service, and the response of clients. Process measures, such as therapeutic alliance, can also be measured during the course of treatment. An exemplar of this type of practice is that of Lambert and colleagues (1996), who use a simple, reliable, low-cost instrument to measure client systems in therapy with the aim to provide therapists with ongoing process information and outcomes. Percevic, Lambert, and Kordy (2004) have also developed a unique computer system to easily enter and track client assessments in such a way as to provide a number of critical therapeutic indicators to the therapist. In such a fashion, the clinician is able to demonstrate outcomes, be more accountable, and bring an attitude of scientific mindedness to an individual practice. This is the true example of a scientist practitioner.

Lens, Maps, and Art

So how is a clinician, researcher, supervisor, or teacher to balance the various components in his or her practice and struggle with not only the complexity of each of the domains of research, practice, and theory, but at the same time make good clinical decisions as well? We suggest, and you have already seen us use, a simple set of pneumonic symbols as aids; lens, maps, and art are ways in which we have come to think about the profession of family psychology. This way of thinking is helpful because of the pragmatic and functional way in which it organizes information. We will use this pneumonic throughout the following chapters to help guide your thinking.

The *lens* of a profession is just like those found in glasses—they focus the world in a particular way to improve clarity of vision. Yet, how you see through the lens is dependent on both what you are looking at and how the lens is ground and cut. The lens of all professions is ground by the specifications, principles, and concepts of its epistemological perspective. Thus, what comes into focus through the lens of a profession is as much about the grinding as the image upon which it is focused. In family psychology, the lens is grounded in the specifications of systemic thinking along with the unique theories and models that are built upon it. The profession has a number of somewhat different lenses that emphasize and highlight either research, theory, or the lore of clinical wisdom conveyed through supervision and training. Traditional theories, integrated models, and evidence-based treatment programs are also lenses through which clients, issues, and mechanisms of change are viewed. Whatever the source, these various lenses result in bringing the different elements of the individual, couple, or family client system into sharper focus.

Maps provide guidance and direction by describing the surrounding territory in order to help provide the direction and orientation that is often beyond the immediate view of the traveler. Maps also describe what is over the horizon, the major events to come and the important attractions to look for, while providing an efficient and reliable pathway through uncharted territory. In a profession, there are a number of maps that guide the enterprise of research, theory development, and clinical practice. In research, the scientific method is adapted to the systemic principles of family psychology and guides the process of systematic inquiry. Theory-driven practice is more effective than eclectic practice; therefore, the development of models is a means to acquaint clinicians with what lies beyond the horizon (Duncan, Hubble, & Miller, 2010). In clinical practice, various practice models show the ecosystemic clinical steps along the way in helping a client or client system successfully change.

Creativity and art are central to each of the primary domains of family psychology (research, theory, and practice). For example, watching or experiencing the powerful events that occur in effective individual, couple, and family therapy can almost seem magical. *How is it that the therapist knew to ask that question? How did he or she know to focus on that person? How did the therapist know how to respond in such a therapeutic manner?* In many ways, a good family psychologist is much like a musician. A piece of music is bound by music theory and by denotation, while the musician's interpretation, the inflection or emphasis of one note over another, offers a level of creativity that makes a three dimensional experience. The best and most creative family psychologist is someone who can play between the notes in ways that identify unique and individual ways of putting information together, intervening with a client, or studying a phenomenon. In the end, successful outcome is about the creative and artful translation of scientific concepts and practices that make the client/therapist encounter a therapeutic or healing experience.

CONCLUSIONS: WHAT IS NEXT?

Magnavita (2012) suggested that systems theory may, in fact, become the unifying umbrella that unites the various, often-disparate, approaches to clinical treatment across the field of psychology as a whole. As an epistemological model, it offers a cover that both guides and directs the focus of practice and research, providing a holistic way to think and ubiquitous principles to bring to the difficult process of working with diverse clients and complex research questions. Systems theory is a way of considering the processes of how behavior fits into its relational context and how the intrapersonal, interpersonal, and context in concert maintain the very issues that both therapist and clients hope to resolve. Because systems theory is process based, its ideas are meta, going beyond theoretical constructs or cherished positions in order to consider the broad and unifying ways in which behavior, cognition, affect, history, biology, and relationships interact. As such, among current epistemological approaches, systemic thinking has more of the necessary core ingredients than any other method in moving us toward a unified theory of not only family and couple therapy, but also psychotherapy in general with the potential to move the field beyond individual theories and toward integration.

However, the very nature of family psychology creates some dilemmas. *It is only normal to struggle with many of these feelings/issues:*

- Fear of "not knowing"
- Fear of ambiguity
- Fear of not being helpful
- Fear of being incompetent

- Distrust of self
- Contextualizing research and practice
- Reconciling science and art

We suggest embracing the challenge of the dialectic between structure and creativity, research and practice, science and art, and content and process. The tension between these constructs is always going to be there; it is not going away. Because Hegelian dialectic is, at its core, Aristotelian and categorical, it seeks resolution of tension through synthesis; however, an Asian approach to dialectic, expressed in yin and yang, recognizes that the overarching goal is not mere resolution of opposition, but achieving harmony between disparate elements.

What this means in terms of clinical practice is that research, theory, and practice are inextricably tied to one another, and it therefore takes a systematic approach to integrate knowledge of the profession into practice. We also know that our practice is immediate, relational, and personal like all forms of psychotherapy and that it is the therapist who acts as a translator for principles, practices, and clinical procedures offered to the client. The transformative interventions in the therapy room are creative ones in which the therapist takes all he or she knows and matches it to the client, creating an encounter that translates the ideas (lens) and procedures (map) of the profession in such a way that change is fomented in the life of the client or client system. This kind of flexibility within structure is what has enabled family psychology to be replicated across cultures, diverse client groups, and unique practice settings in ways unlike any other method of psychology.

With this foundation comes the next step: Chapter 2 presents epistemological foundations of family psychology—the core of thinking that makes it unique. In Chapter 3, we discuss the core elements of the theoretical foundations of the field. Based on the epistemology presented in Chapter 2, the theories of the profession are rendered as specific applications to clinical practice. Chapter 4 focuses on the research foundations of the field. This is particularly important given the long-standing gap between research and the practice of all applied psychological fields, including family psychology. In Section 2 the focus is on how these systemic principles guide clinical practice. In Chapter 5 we use systemic principles to map the territory of clinical change. In Chapter 6 the central issue of case planning and assessment lays the foundation for Chapter 7 (Family-focused interventions) and Chapter 8 (couple-based interventions). Finally, in Section 3 we describe particular specialty practices (Chapter 9) and in chapter 10 we discuss training, supervision and ethics in family psychology.

Chapter 2

The Systemic Epistemology
of Family Psychology

Every generation needs a new revolution.

—Thomas Jefferson

Each of us has our own personal belief system, a way of interpreting the world and our life in (or within) that world. This belief system, or epistemology, describes internalized ways of knowing that enable us to give order and predictability to our lives, providing a stable means by which the world is negotiated. Epistemology is outside of conscious awareness; ways of knowing are imbued in the culture, learned in families of origin, school, and other meaningful milieus and encounters in each of our lives. Our personal epistemology (assumptions) plays a large role in how we think about and work with patients or client systems; in similar fashion, every professional field has its own epistemology as well. Traditional psychology is based on the epistemology of empiricism, a linear, causal, and radically objective understanding of the world, emphasizing a primarily positivistic position focused on systematic inquiry and organized discovery (Damasio, 2005). Family psychology has taken a different epistemological path.

Family psychology began with a fairly straightforward epistemological description of multidimensional nested systems, from individuals to couples, families, extended family, community, and culture. Each of these systems was viewed as having structures with boundaries defining their existence connected through a hierarchy of subsystems, each with different roles and functions. Between the elements of a given system are processes that promote stability and change, growth, and development. Because our focus is on relationships, the systems we have most interest in are those built on relational patterns that are communication driven. Patterns, roles, and rules maintain stability in relationships that are both symmetrical and complementary. Thus, family psychology has a unique epistemological perspective that focuses on the interactions between the intrapersonal, interpersonal, and contextual elements of peoples' lives.

Systemic thinking represents the epistemological core of couple and family psychology—it is what makes the specialty unique. When first developed, early systems theory represented an epistemological revolution that highlighted the place of social context and relational interaction in understanding human behavior, particularly with regard to psychology's understanding of couple and family dynamics (Goldenberg & Goldenberg, 2013). Systems theory marked a shift away from intrapsychic analysis to a focus on the relational system and its impact on behavior. What is important about systemic epistemology is that it provides a framework or a blueprint to the profession that guides conceptual models, intervention programs, and core competencies. In addition to looking inside the psychological makeup of the individual, a systems epistemology impels us to explore the space between individuals, the interactions that play a central role in more fully understanding individual behavior. This contextualization of the person viewed through a wider lens has formed the foundation of an effective systems-based psychology.

Take the issue of depression as an example. Traditional psychological research indicates that depression is the result of a biological predisposition interacting with environmental stressors that outweigh available individual resources (Barnett & Gotlib, 1988). Depression research has focused attention on areas such as (1) a potentiated predisposition (Belsky & Beaver, 2011; Belsky & Pluess, 2009; Monroe & Simons, 1991), (2) personality factors (Abramson et al., 1978; Kendler et al., 1993), and (3) negative schemata (Beck, Rush, Shaw, & Emery, 1987). An individualistically oriented treatment approach focuses on change interventions directed at individual cognition, affect, and behavior. A family psychology approach, informed by a systems epistemology, views depression differently. Family psychology research indicates that there is significance between "relationship discord and the severity and course of depression" (Rehman, Gollan, & Mortimer, 2008; Whisman, Johnson, Be, & Li, 2012, p. 185). A family psychology treatment approach targets not only the intrapersonal aspects of depression, such as personality, negative sche-mata, and rumination, but also the interpersonal aspects of depression including relationship attributions, relationship demand/withdrawal, issues around acceptance and commitment, and issues having to do with relational comfort and security (Christensen, 1987; Cunha et al., 2012; Epstein & Baucom, 2002; Jacobson & Christensen, 1996). A systems per-spective also takes into account the impact of the environment and, how culture impacts the etiology, and progression of depression (Gotlib & Hammen, 2014). The World Health Organization has referred to a social breakdown syndrome in the West, described as "a rising incidence and prevalence of psychosomatic diseases, mental disorders, anxiety and neu-rosis, prostitution, crimes, political corruption, and a variety of sexual diseases, including AIDS" (Lambo, 2000, p. 114). If traditional psychol-ogy considers the intrapersonal, interpersonal, and contextual variables of depression, it generally does so from a biopsychosocial perspective, treating the various factors modally, as discrete categories to be targeted for treatment individualistically. Systems-driven psychology, on the other hand, operates from a mind-set that considers the intrapersonal, interper-sonal, and environment as nested factors, each affecting and being affected by the others in reciprocal fashion, pressing the family psychologist to a holistic approach to treatment.

Our focus in this chapter is on the core principles of the systemic epis-temology of family psychology and the implications of that perspective on an understanding of individuals, couples, families, and the problems they struggle with and the therapeutic change process. Understanding these principles is central to having a comprehensive understanding of the research, theory, and clinical practice that comprise the daily activities of a family psychologist. While every profession has similar core domains (research, practice, and theory), the defining feature of family psychology is its unique epistemology that unites and links these domains in ways that are distinct from any other specialty.

Organizing the discussion about family psychology around these prin-ciples offers a flexible and functional way of understanding clients (or as change agents, it may be students, supervisees, or organizations), their problems, issues and challenges, and the context around those interactions that help organize and inform the art of the encounter that is the heart of the change process. A systems paradigm provides a complex, parsimo-nious, reliable, and clinically significant description of how individuals, couples, and families function and change. Systems theory apart from application is difficult to apprehend, because it tends to be an alien way of thinking for Westerners; however, when systems principles are applied to research, theory building, and treatment, a three-dimensional view of individual, couple, and family behavior begins to emerge. Once we begin to view psychology as a relational organic science, it is very difficult to go back to an individualistic and static paradigm.

REVOLUTION AND EVOLUTION: FROM THE INDIVIDUAL TO THE SYSTEM

It is easy to forget that theories, ideas, and even our most cherished beliefs are likely to form, develop, change, and evolve over time as we experience, grow, and change ourselves. The evolution of ideas is remarkably like ancient cities, the new built on top of the old, which serves as its foundation. Western civilization overturned the parochial superstitions of the Greek city-states with the advent of Platonic and Aristotelian philosophies, both grounded in knowing based on observation and reasoning. Plato suggested that to understand a thing requires gathering as much information as possible on its attributes, while Aristotle asserted that to know a thing is to drill down to its very essence, peeling away the individual uniqueness in order to reach a common core. These Western philosophies would give birth to the scientific method, an empirical approach to understanding based on objective observation, linear reasoning, categorization, a reliance on causation, and the reduction and reification of data for the purpose of theory building, testing, and codification.

During the Middle Ages, Judeo/Christian theology, which understood the universe to be organized around the mind of God, represented a kind of throwback to pre-Western forms, yet when the ideas of Plato and Aristotle were used as apologetic, set the stage for the Renaissance and the rationalism of the Enlightenment. While the Middle Ages maintained stability of thought through an adherence to theological certainties, the Enlightenment gave birth to a new paradigm for certainty in the immutability of physical laws. The contours of psychology were shaped by the Enlightenment's rapprochement with Aristotelian and Platonic epistemologies merged with Newtonian physics and Darwinian theory. Spinoza's applied Aristotelian epistemology, psychophysical parallelism, presented the idea that every physical event has a parallel mental event and vice versa, and became a precursor to a physiologically oriented psychology.

Modern psychology emerged out of the belief that the human psyche adheres to fundamental truths based not on faith, but on physical laws forged in the furnace of biological adaptation that can be reached through objective observation. Wundt would take this philosophical approach to develop a structurally based psychology. In America, James's Platonic approach led to the psychology of functionalism with an emphasis on understanding the whole through a focus on causation and observation of the environment. Meanwhile, psychoanalysis was seen as almost a separate science from the experimentally based behavioral and cognitive psychologies, which themselves were viewed by humanistic psychology as capturing only a partial understanding of human nature.

Where Freud's psychology was rooted and grounded in individualism, those who came after him were increasingly drawn to interpersonal dynamics as an explanation for both healthy development and pathological adaptation. Adler called for a more holistic ego-based psychology not merely organized around sexuality (he called his psychology Individuum or holistic psychology), and he introduced subjectivity into psychological models (i.e., that persons give their lives meaning). Harry Stack Sullivan's interpersonal theory was highly influenced by Adler as was the psychology of Karen Horney, both of whom put less emphasis on internalized fantasy and more emphasis on human development through primary relationships. In fact, the schools of object relations sought to understand personality development and psychopathology in relation to social and cultural forces, as opposed to drive/structures, culminating in Fairbairn's radical assertion that psychopathology is the result of broken relationship (Greenberg & Mitchell, 1983).

Interpersonal theory asserts that personality emerges and is best understood within the context of relations with real or personified others (Carson, 1969; Sullivan 1954). The primary dynamic principle of interpersonal theory is that behavior serves the goal of self-definition, derived through interpersonal relations with others and that the reactions of others tend to reinforce one's view of self (Carson 1991; Leary, 1957). The interpersonal models of Sullivan, Leary, and the object relations schools, combined with Erickson's developmental model and Bowlby's attachment theory, created an increasingly dynamic interpersonal approach to psychology. This interpersonal focus was complemented by the development of group psychology that developed from a predominantly analytic approach in the mid-twentieth century to an interpersonal one through the work of Bion and later Rogers. Group psychotherapy's principles of interaction were to have a profound influence on the development of family therapy.

The family therapy movement grew out of the observation that there was something more than the individual involved in the initiation and maintenance of any behavior. Freud discovered that the child's early experience with the family forms the foundation from which neurosis springs. Alfred Adler encouraged family treatment, though he did so by having a therapist see the child and the parents in separate sessions. Carl Obern-dorf gave the first paper on marital and family therapy in 1931 to the American Psychiatric Association, and Nathan Ackerman reported the first instance of a family treatment where the family was seen all together on a consistent basis in 1954. Nathan Ackerman and Murray Bowen, who are both MDs, started seeing families at Menninger's in Topeka, Kansas. Lyman Wynne was heavily influenced by Talcott Parsons, while Don Jackson and Gregory Bateson greatly influenced the early movement. The early movement generally was conducting research on schizophrenia (a topic that was a ready source of federal grant money at the time). David Levy (1943) studied pathogenic effects of certain kinds of mothering (i.e., over-protectiveness, indulgence, dominance, and child behavior disturbances), and Frieda Fromm-Reichmann coined the term "schizophrenogenic mother" to describe mothers who were cold aggressive, domineering, and rejecting.

The family systems movement had its origins in the work of von Bertalanffy's general systems theory (GST), which posited the interactive, self-regulating, and openness of living systems (von Bertalanffy, 1969). The movement grew as a reaction to a psychology that was deemed to be too individualistic in focus and found adherents from such diverse disciplines as sociology, psychology, anthropology, philosophy, and psychiatry. The movement culminated in the development of a new mental health discipline, marriage, and family therapy, which focused primarily on interventions for interpersonal relationships (Sexton & Lebow, 2015; Shields, Wynne, McDaniel, & Gawinski, 1994).

The ongoing evolution of a family systems epistemology was also fueled by the research of family-oriented psychologists (Sexton & Datchi, 2014). In fact, the earliest family-based clinical research was conducted by psychologists (Kaslow, 1987). As the field has matured into evidence-based research and practices, the work of psychologists has been front and center: functional family therapy (Alexander & Parson, 1973; Alexander et al., 2000; Sexton, 2006; 2011, in press), multisystemic family therapy (Schoenwald, Henggeler, & Rowland, in press), emotion-focused therapy (Greenberg & Johnson, 1988), psychodynamic family therapy (Wanlass, & Scarff, in press), Bowen family systems therapy (Nichols, 2003; Skowron, 2015), cognitive behavioral couples therapy (Christensen, Jacobson, & Babcock, 1995; Epstein, Dattilio, Baucom, in press; Gottman, 1999; Jacobson & Margolin, 1979), and medical family therapy (Ruddy & McDaniel, in press) all derived from psychological research, have growing bodies of research supporting their efficacy (Sexton, Alexander, & Mease, 2003; Sexton, Datachi-Phillips, Evans, LaFollette, J., & Wright, 2012; Sexton & LaFollette, in press).

SYSTEMS EPISTEMOLOGY: THE CORE OF FAMILY PSYCHOLOGY

Systems epistemology refers to a distinctive mode of thinking that has evolved since the late 1940s and early 1950s. Von Bertalanffy defined a system as "a set of elements standing in interrelation among themselves and with the environment" and indicated that "dynamical system theory is concerned with the changes of systems in time," referencing the intersection of the theory of stability with control theory, parallel to cybernetics (von Bertalanffy, 1972, p. 417). It is important to remember that systems theory is not a single theoretical approach but rather an epistemological umbrella including a wide breadth of applications in engineering, physical and biological systems, and larger social systems (Sexton & Stanton, 2015; Stanton & Welsh, 2012). In its broadest terms, systems are defined as a complex set of interacting and interrelated components together with the relationship among them that permit identification of a boundary-making entity or process (Laszlo & Krippner, 1998). While frequently seen as synonymous with marriage and family therapy, family systems theories are best defined by their systems epistemological approach rather than by the population to which they are applied. According to Sexton and Stanton (2015), systemic thinking suggests that

- Behavior is determined by a continuous process of interaction between the individual and the situation he or she encounters (feedback).
- The individual is an intentional active agent in this interaction process.
- Cognitive factors are important in the interactions.
- The psychological meaning of the situation to the individual is an essential determinate of behavior.

Systems theories view the characteristics of individuals as the result of complex dynamic interactions of individual, cognitive, and relational systems in which one develops the beliefs and narratives that explain one's context and the current couple, family, and community relationships in which one currently functions. At a very simple level, Bowers (1973) suggested that behavior was jointly influenced by the person (or trait) and the situation (or environment). Accordingly, behavior is simultaneously influenced by the person's view of the world, the interpretations, expectations, and choices the person has and makes, and by the way the person views the behavior of others in relation to self.

Systems theory ushered in a way to explain the forces that keep patterns cohesive (entropy) and other forces that tend to break down patterns resulting in change (Sexton & Stanton, 2015). Human relationships became viewed as cybernetic units, driven by information contained in the analog and digital components of human communication, in which each part interacts with reciprocal systems of influences. Instead of only peering inside the psychological makeup of the individual, systemic clinical interventions looked to the "space between" individuals and the interactions between them as a way for understanding behavior.

Because of the focus on relational systemic process (rather than content), systems thinking principles have crossed international boundaries with applications in diverse cultures around the world (Lebow & Sexton, 2015). Today, systems theories are represented by a set of comprehensive, systematic, and evidence-based clinical intervention models that have become the treatment of choice for a wide variety of relational and individual clinical problems (Sexton et al., 2013). These more current systemic clinical models have empirical support for their successful application with diverse clients across different cultures and countries.

Some versions of family systems theory suggest that the self is also made up of various internal systems that impact behavior and influence personality (Schwartz, 2013). Thus, personality of the individual is inexorably tied to the characteristics of the relational patterns, shared belief systems, and other contextual factors in and around that individual. Motivation for behavior and the personality of the individual is shaped, maintained, and driven by the relational contexts around him or her and the internal systems within. From a systemic perspective, it is the relational structures and processes within the multisystemic system of the person that best describe the development and maintenance of personality characteristics and behavior.

STRUCTURES AND PROCESSES OF RELATIONAL SYSTEMS

The primary systems of interest to family psychologists are relational systems. Relational systems have structures and processes that both define who they are and explain how they function to both maintain and identify purpose and coherence and yet at the same time change, adapt, and adjust with the contexts around them. Much like family psychology itself, relational systems that comprise family psychology are thus marked by a number of dialectic tensions: stability versus change, adaptation within consistency, individuality and patterned similarity among others. Within these tensions are two central dimensions that organize a relational system's structures and processes. The *structures* are represented by an ecology of nested sets of environments (e.g., culture, community, extended family, and family) similar to a Russian doll that unpacks to reveal smaller dolls within.

Bronfenbrenner (1979) coined the terms microsystem (the immediate setting of development), mesosystem (the interrelationships between microsystems), macrosystem (higher-level systems), exosystem (settings beyond the immediate experience of the individual that influences development), and chronosystem (the evolving interconnected nature of the person, environment, and proximal processes over time) to identify various levels and types of systemic contexts in which human life occurs.

(Bronfenbrenner, 1979; Stanton, 2009, p. 10)

He suggested that there is an evolving interaction between a person and her or his environment, so he defined human development as "a lasting change in the way in which a person perceives and deals with his environment" (Bronfenbrenner, 1979, p. 3) or worded differently as "the person's growing capacity to discover, sustain, or alter its properties" (p. 9).

The *processes* are the mechanisms or pathways through which these structured arrangements of relational systems function. General System Theory provided an early framework for looking at seemingly unrelated phenomena and understanding how they actually represent a unified system. General System Theory addresses the question: How is it that the whole is more than the sum of its parts? General System Theory has a number of basic assumptions:

- Component parts relate in mutual interaction.
- The best explanation for how various components function is the function of the system as a whole.
- Understanding a system requires an examination of systemic interactions at multiple layers (social, family, individual, organs, cells, atoms, etc.).

General System Theory was proposed in reaction to reductionism, which assumes that complex phenomena can be understood exclusively in terms of the properties of their constituent parts. In general system theory, von Bertalanffy argued that systems, such as the human body, interact with their environments and that in doing so, they acquire qualitatively new properties through the interaction of constituent parts. Systems take in information and energy to allow them to achieve their goals. Systems use feedback to regulate themselves and guide this process. What is in a system is the combination of the systemic elements, the process, and the context. It is these variables and patterns of relational organization that determines a system. As such, a system is a set of related parts that work together in a particular environment to perform whatever functions are required to achieve the system's objectives.

Norbert Wiener (1948) coined the term "cybernetics," derived from the Greek word (*kubernetes*, for pilot or rudder) to refer to the investigation of self-regulating feedback processes in complex systems. Cybernetics was unique in its focus on organization, pattern, and process rather than on matter, material, and content. It was concerned with feedback mechanisms, information processing, and patterns of communication through the study of inanimate machines, comparing them with living organisms in an effort to understand and control complex systems. From a cybernetics perspective, the most important aspects of a system to focus on are not its elements, but how those elements function together in regard to organization, pattern, and process. One characteristic of viable systems is their capacity to use feedback about past performance to influence future performance. Cybernetics suggests that systems are controlled by information, relationships, feedback mechanisms, information processing, and communication patterns. First-order cybernetics assumes that systems are passive phenomena that can be observed and manipulated, while second-order cybernetics recognizes that social systems are conscious and capable of interacting intentionally with the observer. A common example is that of light, which seems to change from particle to beam based on whether or not it is being observed (Rovelli, 1996).

Hermeneutics, semantics, and narrative add another dimension to systems meaning, by viewing "language as a creative social process" (Anderson, 2009, p. 302). The idea of inherited knowledge or understanding is not abandoned; rather, the use of language in the creation of knowledge is a living organic activity (i.e., dialogue with oneself or another) and cannot remain unchanged (Anderson, 2009, p. 303).

A major focus of postmodernism has to do with discourse and the role of language. Wittgenstein (1965) proposed that language acquires meaning as a function of social practice rather than as a referential base. Foucault (1979) explored the power that culturally embedded languages have to expand or compress with a caution against reifying the language of a community as true for any other than the members of that community and a focus on the limitations of local languages relative to what they exclude. What this means is that when working with or studying a couple, family, or individual, you have to remember that the meaning of the events you see depends on the context, limitations, and values that are part of the narrative. Language thus has come to be understood as the means by which the world is both known and constructed by each individual. As a result, it is a description of reality as a function of one's beliefs and that all we can know are our interpretations of other people and things. Descriptions are as much about the describer as the thing being described. These notions have significant implications for both research and clinical practice. Psychotherapy then becomes a collaborative approach in which the therapist is "with people, including ways of thinking with, talking with, acting with, and responding with them" in ways that are "more participatory and mutual and less hierarchical and dualistic" (Anderson, 2009, p. 304).

EVERY SYSTEM IS MORE THAN THE SUM OF THE PARTS

Whether you think of systems as cybernetic, multigenerational, or meaning based, the distinguishing feature is that the whole is greater than the sum of its parts. In trying to understand a couple, a family, an organization, a profession, or a culture, all the systems with which the family psychologist works have the following characteristics (Sexton & Stanton, 2015; Stanton & Welsh, 2012):

- *Stability—change.* In a system, there are two general tensions—the tendency to stay the same and the equal tendency to change. Processes that maintain the stability and consistency of the system are referred to as homeostasis (or morphostasis), while those that foment change to help the system adapt, adjust, and change are described by the term "morphogenesis." For families, it is essential to have stability and consistency. This is what gives s family shared meaning and a collective identity. The stability in a family system comes from the recursive behavior patterns that involve relatively stable rules, roles, routines, rituals, and mechanisms. At the same time, it is essential that families have the capacity to evolve over the course of the life cycle and meet changing demands necessary for healthy development, adaptation, and survival. Often families that lack such morphogenetic forces come to the attention of clinical services because of role rigidity or maladaptivity. We focus more specifically on the ways in which family relational patterns provide both stability and, under certain conditions, the morphogenetic push to change:
- *Circular and causal.* In systems epistemology, the best explanation for a thing is a description of its processes, rather than a simple causal statement. In families, process refers to the relational patterns that form the family core. Simple cause-and-effect patterns are indicated as "A leads to B," but descriptions and explanations of families that involve linear (or lineal) causality, from a systems theory perspective, are considered incomplete and inaccurate. Recursive patterns of family interaction, on the other hand, are of the form "A leads to B leads to

C leads to A," and it is the idea of circular causality that is used when describing or explaining family interaction. Neither cause nor effect resides in one family member or another; rather, the idea of circular causality is used to remove the concept of individual blame from family therapy discourse and place cause at the level of family interaction.

- *Constant and changing.* Bateson conceptualized that families develop "self-regulating feedback mechanisms to maintain balance and constancy" (Goldenberg & Goldenberg, 2013, p. 21). All messages have a report and command function (Ruesch and Bateson, 1951; Watzlawick, Beavin-Bavelas, & Jackson, 1967) including digital and analog communication in machines and verbal and nonverbal communication in humans. Thus, the actual words in a message (e.g., it's time for dinner) are a verbal report, similar to a digital message. However, each message also entails a meta-communication about the relationship between speakers, which is usually conveyed at a nonverbal and emotional level (e.g., "It's time for dinner!").

In the double bind theory, Bateson's group proposed that schizophrenic behavior occurs in families characterized by particular rigid and repetitive patterns referred to as double binds (Bateson, Jackson, Haley, & Weakland, 1956). In such families, double binds involve the following: (1) parents issuing to a child a primary injunction, which is typically verbal (e.g., come here and hug me); (2) concurrently, the parents issue a secondary injunction that contradicts the primary injunction, which is typically conveyed nonverbally (e.g., If you hug me, I will not hug you back); (3) there is also a tertiary injunction prohibiting the child from escaping from the conflictual situation or commenting upon it, and this is often conveyed nonverbally (e.g., if you comment on these conflicting messages or try to escape from this relationship, you will be punished).

Once children have been repeatedly exposed to double bind family processes, they come to experience much of their interactions with their parents as double binds even if all of the conditions for a double bind are not met. This theory was extremely important because it offered a sophisticated and coherent explanation for the links between family process and abnormal behavior, and it pointed to the necessity of considering communication in an entirely new way, as occurring simultaneously and at multiple levels.

- *Regulated through feedback.* Families are self-governing systems that correct themselves when aberrations occur and seek to restore stability; this became a primary tenet of early systems thinking,

Feedback refers to the process of monitoring the transformation processes and assessing outputs to see if they are within acceptable standards... When a part of a family system starts to deviate from the previously established patterns in the system, those responsible for the welfare of the system pay attention to that feedback, and try to determine if they need to intervene.

(Burr, Day, & Bahr, 1993, pp. 42–43)

There are two types of feedback in systems. Negative feedback or deviation-reducing feedback maintains homeostasis and acts in the service of morphostasis. Positive feedback or deviation-amplifying feedback serves morphogenesis. If too much deviation-amplifying feedback occurs in the absence of deviation-reducing feedback, then a runaway effect occurs, which may have positive or negative consequences for the system (Nichols, 2013). For example, a snowball effect may result in the achievement of small goals leading to the attainment of larger goals.

*   *Pattern-based relationships.* Bateson (1972, 1979) referred to the pattern of relationships between people as the pattern that connects, and it is his most acclaimed insight. Everybody in a family and the wider system of which it is part is connected to everybody else, and a change in one person's behavior inevitably leads to a change in all family members. That is, the behavior of family members is interdependent. Bateson (1972) described a process called schizmogenesis in which pairs of individuals or pairs of factions within a social system develop recursive patterns of behavior over time through repeated interaction. Within these recursive behavior patterns, the role of each member becomes quite distinct and predictable.

Batson noted two types of schizmogenesis, which he termed symmetrical and complementary patterns. With symmetrical behavior patterns, the behavior of one member (or faction) of a system invariably elicits a similar type of behavior from another member (or faction), and over time, the intensity of symmetrical behavior patterns escalates until the members (or factions) separate. For example, a marital couple may become involved in a symmetrical pattern of blaming each other for their marital dissatisfaction and ultimately separate. With complementary behavior patterns, the increasingly dominant behavior of one member (or faction) of a system invariably elicits increasingly submissive behavior from another member (or faction), and over time, the intensity of the complementary behavior pattern increases until the members (or factions) separate.

- *Meaning among the patterns.* The idea that relational patterns, even when similar, carry very different meaning to different people is born from the philosophical tradition of constructivism, that is, people themselves make meaning out of their lives. There are two traditions that tend to represent the constructive perspective. A radical constructivist perspective (von Glasersfeld, 1988) suggests that while a real reality may exist, there is no way we may know it or represent it in any absolute sense. A social constructivist focus gives greater consideration to the context within which language is created and context becomes the defining framework in relating. The notion of an internal mind bounded by the skin is replaced by the concept of a nonlocal mind that is universal and empowering of all creatures and things. Knowing is experienced and expressed through a system of language considered to have a separate existence (Gergen, 1985). Social constructivism also emphasizes the importance of context, of the way individuals and problems are created in a relationship (Gergen, 1991). As facts are deconstructed by delineating the assumptions (values and ideologies on which they are based), professionals are encouraged to take themselves and their constructions less seriously. Emphasis on differing individual perspectives of reality has led to models of therapy that have underscored the importance of conversation, of co-construction of problems and proposed solutions, and of respect for individual differences (Steinglass, 1991, p. 268).
- *Different types of change—first- and second-order change.* Systems have different types of change that they go through. First-order change suggests that the rules governing an interaction within the system remain the same, but there may be some alteration in the way in which they are applied. First-order change is continuous or graded. Second-order change occurs when the rules governing relationships within the system change; therefore, there is a discontinuous stepwise change to the system itself.
- *Equifinality* is a systemic concept that is captured by the saying "many roads to the same end." This means that things may move and resolve in ways that are unanticipated. The focus of interaction is on leverage points of functionality in a family, rather than on cause or understanding reasons behind dysfunctionality. Equifinality suggests that it is not particularly important how or what caused a family or couple to get to their current state, but only to understand how they function and where they might go next.
- *Pragmatism.* Systemic principles focus on relational processes rather than content rightness and are therefore able to explain behavior and clinical change in various cultures and with a wide range of clinical problems.

IMPORTANCE OF CONTEXT: THE PLACE OF CULTURE AND DIVERSITY IN SYSTEMIC THINKING

One of the early criticisms of systems theory came from the arena of diversity: issues of diversity, difference, and uniqueness within organized, functional, and homeostatic systems. In fact, one of the areas in which systemic epistemology needs to adapt and develop is in the area of understanding how diversity plays a central role in relational systems (Patterson & Sexton, 2014). There are really two issues in this area. The first suggests that culture is a "set of shared meanings that make social life possible" (Fenel & Richardson, 1996, p. 610). Culture shapes self-identity as individuals construct a worldview and sense of meaning and a sense of status and rank from the context in which they grow and live. The second issue, diversity, speaks to valuing the uniquess of those of different backgrounds (whether race, religion, ethnicity, sexual orientation, etc.) within the major culture.

This is particularly important given that in the United States, racial and ethnic minorities are closing in on the majority Caucasian population, comprising 22% of the overall population (United States Census Bureau, 2014). Traditional approaches to multicultural understanding and practice in psychology have focused on characteristics of awareness and attitudes in researchers, theorists, and clinicians. The consensus is that (1) multicultural awareness makes a meaningful difference in praxis, (2) particular therapist attitudes significantly impact therapy with multicultural clients, and (3) therapist/client match according to ethnicity and culture is preferable for positive outcome. However, the consensus is being challenged by a recognition of the growing complexity of multicultural factors over simplistic, dualistic categorical models (e.g., etic or emic), by dichotomous or outright oppositional factors such as client *vs.* therapist attitudes toward diversity in therapy, and by a proliferation of diversity categories. A traditional individualistic, dualistic, reductionistic, and radically objective epistemology that has been the prevailing way of thinking and performing research about multiculturalism makes it difficult to incorporate more functional perspectives on diversity and makes it more difficult to contain the growing number of identifiable subcultures in American life and reconcile factors when there are disparities.

The primary way in which these issues have been addressed in recent years is through approaches to cultural competence that focus on attitudes, counselor assumptions, biases and values, and therapist skills—, that is, having a skill set that matches the needs of a given racial or ethnic group. Understanding oneself and potential racist attitudes, modifying attitudes to maximize empathy, and developing tolerance reflect cultural competence (Constantine, 2001; Constantine & Gushue, 2003). Sue et al.

(1992) describe 34 competencies for multicultural counseling that when taken together are descriptors for cultural sensitivity (Sue, Arredondo, & McDavis, 1992; Sue et al., 1998). Attitudes and beliefs along with skills and knowledge comprise a universal diverse orientation, "an awareness and potential acceptance of both similarities and differences in others that is characterized by interrelated cognitive, behavioral, and affective components" (Fuertes, Miville, Mohr, Sedlacek, & Gretchen, 2000, p. 158), which effectively delineates an understanding and appreciation for oneself, the diversity of others, and a connectivity with a larger diverse society.

While therapist self-exploration of attitudes, beliefs, and values is essential to competent training in diversity, there is a way to think about these complex issues from a more systemic perspective (Patterson & Sexton, 2014). Family psychology offers a complementary perspective, where diversity is seen as simply one aspect of the whole system. Where traditional psychology creates a modal approach to diversity as one subject area among many, family psychology promotes integration and synthesis of a diversity ecology that has intrapersonal, interpersonal, and contextual elements. The next evolution needs to look at the dialectic of self and other, and wrestle with the dissonance of these concepts in order to find a common language and way of understanding how people work and function. We don't want to take away from everything that has been accomplished over the decades, but diversity must not be solely about characteristics, but about the threads that connect diversity to research, theory, and practice.

A systems epistemology provides a framework for complex descriptions of multicultural process and function, where focus on common systemic processes that occur in families may enhance the important work on racial, cultural, gender, and ethnic identities. This framework does not seek to reconcile dichotomous views or homogenize differing cultural perspectives, rather, relational processes, as well as group and family functioning, are viewed through the lens of the five threads that connect the domains of theory, research, and practice: ecology, dimensionality, development, context, and dialectic (see Chapter 1). Each of these five areas acts as connectors that promote functionality and process in multicultural work, making family psychology a dynamic container for the variety of factors in multicultural psychology.

Movement to a systemic epistemology requires a kind of epistemological transformation (Bateson, 1972), including the adoption of new conceptual structures that radically change the way a thinker views and interprets life. How do we capture both the common features and unique characteristics of emerging and diverse groups? The application of systems thinking provides a language that crosses the silos of unique characteristics and structures to capture the common processes in groups and families.

A systemic approach is one that recognizes the contextual aspects of diversity—that is, the individual cannot be understood except within the milieu in which he or she has grown up and is a part. Dent-Read and Zukow-Goldring (1997) have suggested that the environment shapes the person and as the latest neuroscience has discovered, the environment actually does facilitate switching on or off hox genes that promote or inhibit gene expression (Ridley, 2003). Diversity is best understood from an ecosystemic perspective where systems are seen as nested networks of relationships with reciprocal interactive influence (Stanton, 2009). The application of systems thinking provides a language within which to look across the silos of unique characteristics and structures to the processes inherent in a multicultural world.

Multiculturalism adheres to the basic tenet that everyone has an ethnicity, therefore every human encounter is a cross cultural encounter (Peterson, 1994). One of the unique advantages of using systems thinking is that it provides a specific focus on process (how systems function) and crosses the boundaries of type, providing a more effective and client-centered match to research, theory development, and intervention than the traditional focus on group characteristics. Process gets at an examination of relational patterns to divine core dynamics of families in order to create a culture of meaning that binds diverse groups together. The key is to describe the common processes in which groups and families function to understand the spaces between persons and between groups. It is the way groups and families function that is most important and that maintains their basic equilibrium. The values and unique characteristics of groups and families are incorporated with common processes across groups and families, and both elements then become a guide for matching to treatment. Family form is important because the relational patterns that follow set the climate and foundation of the psychosocial center for all family members across multiple generations. The new heuristic we are proposing provides a linkage between the broad areas of diverse family cultures and systemic descriptions of the mechanisms, methods, and the nature of the processes that connect them.

Taking a systemic process-oriented view is a *functional* approach where one focuses on the structures and processes of families with a common language. Alexander & Sexton (2003) posited a "functional" model of understanding individual behavior (particularly that of delinquent youth) within a family relational context. Basic to this notion is that families all function in a particular way, and it is the way in which they function that is most important and that maintains their basic equilibrium (homeostasis—see Watzlawick et al., 1974). Rather than the traditional diagnostic perspective (e.g., good *vs.* bad), we advocate a descriptive or functional perspective.

The values and unique characteristics of a particular family are incorporated with common processes across families, and both elements become a guide to matching them to treatment. A systems conceptualization of family processes provides the needed matrix for matching successful treatment programs to the diverse families they are intended to help. For example, we are beginning to understand the relational and interactional patterns that are central to families in conflict (Sexton et al., 2012), which promotes individual welfare and relational health.

A categorical approach to multiculturalism walks a narrow path with the problematic possibility of falling off into a ditch on one of two sides. The first is the "ditch of duality" where categories are dualistic. It has become unwieldy to view concepts such as etic and emic, acculturation and enculturation, dominant and nondominant cultures, and gender in categorical terms; therefore, they are now viewed as more complex, continuous, or fluid variables, but there are still problems. A conceptualization of diversity variables as continuous or fluid runs the risk of a proliferation of categories, something we are seeing in sexual orientation. An alternative conceptualization recognizes the dynamic tension between dualistic concepts and their dialectic nature. Dialectic engages the conflicts, tensions, contradictions, and synthetic changes that are consequences of dynamic interactions and transactions between cultures, statuses, worldviews, identities, and other human variations rather than uniquely derived from, or inherent characteristics of, any specific reference group. A dialectic perspective on assessment focuses on behavioral phenomena that arise from synthetic or discordant interactions between salient elements of human differences. For example, while etic and emic categories have begun to be viewed as more continuous variables than as categorical, a different conceptualization recognizes the dynamic tension between the two concepts, how one concept subsumes the other and how new understanding may arise in place of both.

Plato defined dialectic as discourse between two or more people who hold differing views on a subject and who seek to reach the truth through reasoned discussion (Plato, 2013). The goal is a qualitative improvement in dialogue through uncovering increasing layers of truth (Ayer & O'Grady, 1992). Dialectic is predicated on the basic premise of formal logic, that contradictory propositions are unacceptable and therefore one proposition must be incorrect (Peng & Nisbett, 1999). Dialectic has philosophical roots in Hegelian philosophy, which advanced the theory and became part of the broader system of the Enlightenment (Ingram, 1990). Hegel's theory and the broader philosophy of critical theory contemplated modern social and political life and focused on historical and social science concerns about reason, freedom, justice, and democracy. Critical theory, of which Hegel was a part, has been described as an interdisciplinary synthesis of social science and social philosophy (Ingram, 1990, p. 23).

The idea of tension between two opposing forces leading to synthesis is much older than Western philosophy, present for example, in ancient Hindu thought. The dialectical method of truth-seeking pervades the traditions of Madhyamaka, Yogacara, and Tantric Buddhism. The dialectical approach of Buddhism is extant in an account of the truth of the Cosmos known as the Perfection of Wisdom (Ernest, Greer, & Sriraman, 2009).

Ancient Chinese thought has wrestled with opposing perspectives by seeking a middle way or way of compromise. The Confucianism principles suggest that the world is a place constantly in change characterized by contradiction and must ultimately be viewed holistically. Because change is constant, contradiction is constant and nothing is isolated and independent, but everything is connected. Everything exists in the integration of yin and yang, aspects that are in opposition and yet are also connected as a whole (Peng & Nisbett, 2002, p. 743).

Dialectic as a pervasive way of thinking across cultures lends credence to Riegel's (1973) contention that human thought, particularly, scientific thinking is, "dominated by . . . manipulations of contradictions and by conceiving issues integratively which have been torn apart by formal operational thinking" (p. 363). Culture generates and transmits meaning for societies; socially constructed by its members, it compels a way of life for them as well (Kral, Burkhardt, & Kidd, 2002). Culture influences worldview and sense of identity. It assigns status by virtue of diversity, through social class, levels of education, and occupational status. Culture itself is shaped through geography, history, and other variables that are meaningful (Kuper, 1999).

The science of cultural psychology is in describing the landscape of the in-group and out-group, those who comprise one's in-group by virtue of shared ethnic makeup and cultural meanings and those who do not. The mission of psychological science is to find shared meanings between groups to enhance dialogue, understanding, and tolerance. Achieving a sense of shared meanings, understanding and tolerance requires dialectical confrontation of the opposing elements, referred to as the "five enemies of human development" (Anderson, 2005): (a) stereotypes, (b) prejudice, (c) discrimination, (d) oppression, and (e) hate. Shared meanings are found by first confronting stereotypes and prejudice within one's self. Understanding can come only when a person has confronted discrimination and tolerance finds himself or herself stepping outside the shadows of oppression. The ultimate goal of multicultural interventions is to reconcile the dialectic of human and cultural diversity through directing forces of interpersonal conflict, contradictions, and tensions to promote higher levels of unity in one's experience of self, and self in relation to others. When participants in a multicultural discourse internalize their experiences in such a way that those experiences are critically analyzed, thoughtfully interpreted, and meaningfully unified, the result is higher order relating (Ingram, 1990, p. 11).

Where the tensions between universal human characteristics and the particulars of cultural context might seem unsolvable, dialectic offers an alternative through transformational discourse (Fowers & Davidov, 2006; Islam, 2007). Dialectical discourse offers not only openness to new thoughts, but it also encourages the process of finding new meanings, connections, and ultimately, healthier ways of relating. In much the same way that three-dimensional chess is one game and not three, so too do the elements of cure and care, research and practice, theory and process, science and art, positivism and constructivism act in concert. We cannot really speak about or understand one dimension without considering the relationship with the elements in other dimensions—they are all of one cloth. The in-between spaces within dimensions are dynamic interphases where tensions between oppositional and appositional elements may be engaged. These tensions are not resolved by the convenient artifice of conceptual overlap, nor are they resolved thoroughly through concepts of embeddedness, though embeddedness does occur. The tensions between elements offer a way of relating that is holistic by embracing the dialectic and in doing so creating a different kind of knowing in relationship. Thus, praxis, which consists of the oppositional and appositional forces of research, theory and practice, comes to be seen as a wild stallion that must be tamed by breaking its will, but not its spirit.

Dialectic as a pervasive way of thinking across cultures lends credence to Riegel's (1973) contention that adult thought, particularly, scientific thinking is, "dominated by ... manipulations of contradictions and by conceiving issues integratively which have been torn apart by formal operational thinking" (p. 363). Culture generates and transmits meaning for societies; socially constructed by its members, it compels a way of life for them as well (Kral, Burkhardt, and Kidd,2002). Culture influences worldview and sense of identity. It assigns status by virtue of diversity, through social class, levels of education, and occupational status. Culture itself is shaped through geography, history and other variables that are meaningful (Kuper, 1999). As you can see, there are no easy answers. There is, however, a systemic lens that empowers and advances the goals of the diversity movement and provides a broader way to consider the whole.

UNIFYING THREADS OF FAMILY PSYCHOLOGY

Bateson (1972) noted that movement to a systemic epistemology requires a kind of epistemological transformation, including the adoption of new conceptual structures that radically change the way the thinker views and interprets life. He called this "deutero-learning" or "learning to learn" (p. 277), since it necessitates putting aside former frames of reference to see new patterns of thought. The early ideas of cybernetics and General System Theory and the more current constructivist ideas and the context of diversity have kept systems epistemology alive and well in family psychology. Epistemology is complex, philosophical, and can be abstract, so adoption of this perspective requires a process of assimilating and accommodating relevant research, practice, and theory in family psychology.

We suggest that there are five threads that unite the complexity of systems theory as it applies to family psychology and that offer a practical platform for understanding the research, practice, and theories of family psychology described in this book and in the field. These threads link and unite three primary domains of the profession: research, practice, and theory. As such, each of the domains of family psychology can be evaluated based on its attention to and application of these threads. You will find these as common elements in the best and most explanatory research inquiries, the most systemic and effective relational clinical interventions,

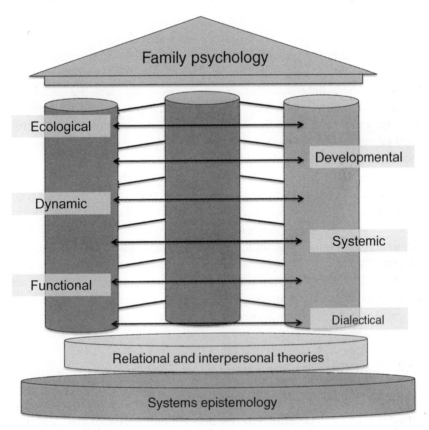

Figure 2.1 Unifying threads of family psychology

and the most comprehensive yet pragmatic of theoretical perspectives. In a sense, always asking about the role of these five principles is a way to keep centered on systemic thinking. As you move through the remainder of the book, we will focus on these unifying threads.

1. *Ecology* provides the context in which to understand family psychology research, practice, and theory. Whether it is in developing and conducting a research study or in the assessment and intervention with a couple or family, whether evaluating behaviors, data, and information—all are always embedded in an ecological matrix of nested relationships. As you will see in Chapters 3 and 4, this thread provides an important dimension to the wide range of theoretical perspectives that comprise family psychology.

2. *Dynamism* refers to the fact that all elements of a system change over time—they are *dynamic*. In the same way that families and couples go through developmental stages over time, the field of family psychology is also dynamic and changing. The meaning we place on various aspects of theory is influenced by research and changes how we practice as we discover and gain new knowledge. Our wisdom about how best to practice family psychology grows with each generation. The theories that are central to us today may change or even be discarded in the future.

3. *Development* is a dimension that pervades every aspect of family psychology. To understand individuals, couples, and families is to know that they are not static but organic, evolving, growing, and developing over time. From a systemic perspective, development or change can be understood only as the multiple, mutual, and continuous interaction of all the levels of a system over time, from the molecular to the cultural. The chronos system, which is part of the ecosystem, recognizes change as a process that unfolds over many timescales from milliseconds to years to aeons.

4. *Systems* and family psychology are synonymous. Relational systems define the couples and families with whom family psychology works and the domains of research, practice, and theory in family psychology are equally *systemic*. As you will see, understanding a client or answering research questions must be done by considering the "whole," which includes the patterns, meaning, and processes inherent in each discrete activity. There is a *systemic* focus to theories in our field in that each shares the common epistemological perspective that emphasizes the "space between" variables (whether data or persons), as well as the elements themselves.

5. *Functionality* refers to a focus on how and what works for s system at any given time, utilizing a descriptive rather than causal approach.

Early family therapy models suggested that the primary focus of inquiry and treatment should be on the "function" of the behavior within a relational system rather than its rightness. This does not mean to suggest that just because a behavior might "fit" with a couple or family, it is necessarily acceptable. Instead, the principle means that each behavior fits within a pattern of meaning and interaction that work to maintain it and that these functions must be understood before change can occur. The focus on functionality—how the client system works—is what makes family psychology effective across cultures (Sexton, 2010).

6. *Dialectic* suggests that the nature of the world outside the realm of perception is interconnected, contradictory, and dynamic. This is very much in line with systems psychology and in fact dialectic reinforces systemic thinking. For example, there is a real tension in family psychology between the traditional positivist position represented by a nomothetic approach to science and postmodern constructivism with its ideographic approach to reason. Dialectic offers a bridge between quantitative and qualitative methodologies, by negating each as individualistic approaches and affirming each through a more transcendent systems approach that incorporates aspects of both to provide a research foundation that is ultimately more holistic and therefore hews more closely to truth. Dialectic is the means by which we connect modal elements into interconnected networks.

We don't usually think of the questions we ask in therapy as dialectical, but that is exactly what they are, moving the therapeutic dialogue to the emergence of new levels of ecosystemic understanding. For example, we might ask the question, "What are Johnny's symptoms?" We prime the discussion at the Individual micro systemic level (I consider the individual a system, so I begin there). The question, "When did the symptoms begin" actually negates the former, absorbs it (sublates) and moves the discussion to the chronos system. The next question, "did anything happen in the past that might have precipitated the symptoms," negates the former questions and moves the discussion to the meso interpersonal system when perhaps the answer is, "yes, Johnny's parents divorced 18 months ago." The next question, "what were the ramifications of the divorce," moves the discussion further along to the societal exo systemic level when it is reported that Johnny's mother had to apply for welfare. The discussion moves to a cultural macro systemic level when she reports that as an East Indian American, she was rebuffed by her family for instigating the divorce, with its subsequent impact on Johnny's lifestyle and mood. Each question in a sense negates the previous underlying assumptions, subsumes them, and creates a new context of understanding. The dialogical progression leads to the dialectical method moving therapy's focus from one system to the next, while incorporating all previous systems, creating a greater holistic understanding for patient treatment and care.

CONCLUSIONS: WHAT IS NEXT?

There is something unique at the core of what it means to be a family psychologist. Interestingly, the core is not something you can really touch or directly see, but systemic thinking, while invisible, is the epistemological core of couple and family psychology—it is what makes it unique. Systemic epistemology is the conceptual scaffold that supports the activities of family psychology researchers, teachers, trainers, supervisors, and practitioners. What is important about systemic epistemology is that it provides a framework or a blueprint to the profession that guides conceptual models, intervention programs, and core competencies. This contextualization of the person viewed through a wider lens has formed the foundation of effective clinical practice.

At the same time, this grand and all-encompassing epistemology of systems thinking is very difficult to apply. In the next chapter, we take this core and apply it directly to an understanding of people and problems, how relationships function, and the origin and sources of clinical issues. Bringing a unique systemic perspective to these issues opens up a whole new way of looking at human behavior. Seeing through a systems epistemological lens is akin to being able to see the shape embedded in a hologram. At first, all one sees are various images and designs that have complexity but very little shape. The paradoxical task is to defocus your eyes and allow the image to emerge—in fact, it seems to magically appear. And interestingly, when the image finally emerges, avoid seeing it. When systemic epistemology is applied to the structures and process of human behavior and relational systems, a whole new picture emerges of how to view individuals, couples, and families. Once you apprehend the whole, there's no going back to the part.

Chapter 3

Through the Systemic Lens: Families, Problems, and Change

We must look at the lens through which we see the world, as well as the world we see, and that the lens itself shapes how we interpret the world.
                                                            —Stephen R. Covey

Praxis, in its simplest construal, means "theory plus action."

The idea of working with entire families was a transformation in thinking and theorizing for the field of psychology. This way of working with more than individuals and their psyches was presaged by Fairbairn's assertion that psychopathology is the result of broken relationships (Fairbairn, 1958). In fact, when relationship systems and the contexts in which people live are taken into account, new and innovative solutions to individuals' problems may be found. These relational systems include the complex set of interacting and interrelated components together with the relationships among them that permit the identification of a boundary-making entity or process. Relational systems seem to have structures with boundaries that define their existence along with hierarchy, and subsystems each with different roles and functions.

While intriguing, systems epistemology was necessary, but not sufficient, for praxis; what was needed were theories that could build upon the systems principles to create epistemologically congruent ways of thinking about clients, their problems, change, and development. Theories and clinical models built on the foundations of systems theory create a lens for viewing families, problems, and change in light of the new paradigm.

Theories provide a basis for understanding and bringing meaning to our experiences and observations of individuals, couples, and families. Theories are essentially applied epistemology; they are like lenses that are ground for clarity; specific theories highlight and bring into focus psychological information in a particular way. What is important about these different specific ways of knowing is that they comprise the core assumptions and beliefs upon which clinical decision making is based. These theoretical principles are the basis for the clinical change models and approaches described in Section II.

In this chapter, we take another step through the looking glass into family psychology by examining the nature of the theoretical lens. In Section II, we focus extensively on the change process through the eyes of various theoretical lenses. However, in this chapter, we back up a bit and consider how systemic constructs explain the mechanisms by which families work and change. In particular, we will focus on the role of relational patterns, attributions and beliefs, evolution and development, and race, culture, and ethnicity as we consider how families function.

THE ROLE OF THEORIES

Theories inform us that certain facts among vast arrays of accumulated knowledge are important while others are less so, and they can provide old data with new interpretations and consequentially new meaning. Theories identify important new issues and prescribe the most critical research questions that need to be answered to maximize understanding of psychological issues. As Campbell (1990, p. 650) noted, "While there are many ideas in any given field, a theory is, by nature a comprehensive and systematic way to organize ideas into useable constructs." Theories provide a means by which new research data can be interpreted and coded for future use.

- Theories provide a means for practical identification of problems.
- Theories provide a means for prescribing or evaluating solutions to applied problems.
- Theories provide a means for responding to new problems that have no previously identified solutions.

It is clear that not all ideas about individuals, couples, or families will meet these criteria. In many ways, psychological theories are much harder to generalize than those about physical phenomena explained by physics.

In psychology, theories are frankly built on more conjecture and guess-work. In part, this is because the phenomenon of understanding individ-uals, couples, and families is much harder than rocket science. In rocket science, the equations and variables are well understood, and the task is to use that understanding to overcome particular engineering problems. Family psychology is much more complex because while we know many of the variables, there are many we don't know. While we know to look for the connections between persons, it is difficult to measure and catego-rize those connections. Thus, the theories of family psychology are not all equal; some describe the landscape of individuals, couples, and families better than others.

Theories can arise from clinical work, through model development, and by way of research. Whether a theoretical explanation is based on research findings or exploration and integration of psychological princi-ples, each must be judged on its ability to successfully and reliably explain the phenomena under study. No single perspective will ever capture all aspects of phenomena; thus, it is theory that provides the unifying con-cept for the sometimes diverse perspectives between research and prac-tice. Because research and practice are different avenues of knowing, the diversity of ideas in these different perspectives helps us better capture an accurate understanding of complex phenomena. As noted in Chapter 1, as a science-based profession, family psychology relies more on scien-tific findings, clinical wisdom, and theoretical perspective over personal opinion and our most cherished personal beliefs. There may be tensions between the domains of research, theory, and practice, but when taken together, they comprise the primary lens or way in which family psycholo-gists describe the psychological world and prescribe clinical treatment for psychological issues found in that world.

THE PIONEERING THEORIES OF FAMILY PSYCHOLOGY

The theoretical framework of family psychology has evolved in very dis-tinct ways since its beginnings in the late 1940s and early 1950s in very dis-tinct ways. A traditional focus on systemic constructs has, in many ways, been challenged by the emerging era of postmodern epistemological per-spectives. This emergence has shifted attention from relationships them-selves to the meaning of events and situations for individuals in an attempt to recognize the role of self-reference in the systemic process. Postmodern epistemology has, like prior philosophical approaches, spawned a number of theories and schools of practice, the most prominent being narrative therapy. More recently, there has been an emerging interest in integrative approaches that focus on dovetailing older models with emerging newer approaches. Finally, we are only now experiencing the emergence of what some have labeled mature clinical models, or those approaches that are by definition integrative, clinically responsive, meaning focused, and possess attention directed to multiple systems (individual, family, and environment).

The revolution in the field of psychology was instigated by larger-than-life personalities who founded models based on particular tenets or aspects of systems functioning. These revolutionaries developed intervention techniques and shared clinical expertise at workshops and professional meetings, while gathering followers and generating a sense of excitement around their discoveries (Goldenberg & Goldenberg, 2009). Some of the key models are described as follows:

Structural Family Therapy. Salvador Minuchin (1974) was working with low-income families in Philadelphia, where he developed a theoretical orientation intentionally targeted to that population. The model was designed to (1) be a systems-oriented therapy, (2) be useful with those moderately educated, and (3) be cost effective for a low-SES clientele. His theoretical framework was oriented around the idea that family structure is integral to effective family functioning. Minuchin suggested that family structure dictates interaction between family members and that the contours of structure are dictated by the boundaries between family subsystems (Nichols, 2013). The structure of a family is shaped by the cultural context, establishing family member roles over time through repetitive patterns of behavior. These patterns of behavior ultimately limit interactional options and inhibit the family's adaptation to novel and developmental scenarios (Minuchin, 1974, p. 89). The fundamental property of structure is the hierarchical organization inherent in generational boundaries. Positive family functioning requires that generational subsystems play out their respective role boundaries without being too rigid (limited interaction) or too diffuse (undifferentiated boundaries leading to chaotic relating). By avoiding the extreme poles of relating, subsystems offer emotional connection, mutual support, and room for personal responsibility. For example, positive functioning occurs when the parent–child boundary promotes emotional connection and support while maintaining parental authority and spousal privacy (Nichols, 2013).

Strategic Family Therapy. Strategic family therapy focuses on the communication patterns of family members. The modality evolved from Bateson's cybernetic model, which emphasized circular feedback loops and the subsequent models organized around concepts of communication.

The primary thinkers, Bateson, Jackson, Haley, Weakland, and Watzlawick, represented diverse disciplines such as philosophy, anthropology, and the social sciences. All were revolutionaries in their own right, banding together at the Palo Alto Mental Research Institute to develop novel approaches to therapy outside the bounds of traditional psychology. The development of the strategic model progressed through the work of Jay Haley and Cloé Madanes as well as the Milan group in Italy led by Mara Selvini-Palazzoli (Goldenberg & Goldenberg, 2013). Bateson's *Steps to an Ecology of Mind* (Bateson, 1972) and the *Pragmatics of Human Communication* (Watzlawick, Beavin-Bavelas, & Jackson, 1967) promulgated key ideas such as the impossibility of non-communication (you cannot not communicate; even silence is a form of communication), meta-communication (i.e., communication about communication), content and report components of communication, complementary and symmetrical relationships, and family homeostasis (based on the cybernetic idea of feedback loops).

Experiential Family Therapy. Carl Whitaker came from a psychoanalytic background, and Virginia Satir was a protégé of Carl Rogers, and both found themselves rebelling against rote individualistically oriented theory in favor of dynamic positive therapeutic experiences for couples and families (Goldenberg & Goldenberg, 2009). While the two claimed to eschew theory, in fact, their experiential therapies were rooted and grounded in phenomenological and existential-humanistic concepts, united with a systemic approach to influence treatment (Goldenberg & Goldenberg, 2013). Whitaker often worked with a co-therapist, used idiosyncratic interventions to take the spotlight off an identified patient, and purposefully broke social taboos in order to enable a couple or family to experience more positive emotions toward each other, thus drawing them closer together. Whitaker originally saw the work of therapy as re-parenting—in fact, his early work involved taking a patient back to early life and feeding him or her with a bottle in a rocking chair. Over time, Whitaker adopted a more systems-oriented approach, insisting that all family members be present, while using what were considered outlandish interventions to stimulate new emotional experiences and behaviors in the family system (Becvar, 2003; Goldenberg & Goldenberg, 2013; Napier & Whitaker, 1978).

Satir used the strength of her personality to elicit and expand human positive interactions and growth between family members. She sought to help families caught in the hopelessness and loneliness of everyday life to break out of despair by having each member report feelings and experiences completely and honestly to one another. She sought to create a family environment that would level the playing field for all members, foster an atmosphere of negotiation instead of power dynamics, and demonstrate respect for each person's uniqueness (Satir, 1972). Devoted to connecting with families herself in a real way, she focused on identifying problematic communication practices that blocked authentic communication in order to free families up to live out their more genuine and loving intentions (Goldenberg & Goldenberg, 2013). She identified five styles of communication: the placater, the blamer, the super-reasonable, the irrelevant, and the congruent to help individuals identify their own and others' styles (Satir, 1972).

Interpersonal and Object Relations Family Therapy. Many of the early pioneers in family therapy were trained in psychoanalysis. Adler's ego-based psychology and the child guidance movement it spawned in the United States and the British object relations schools focused less on the inner fantasy life of the child as the impetus for personality development and became increasingly oriented to the impact of a child's relationships on personality formation and maintenance. Horney, Sullivan, and Leary were highly influenced by Adler's holistic approach to psychology, leading to their development of interpersonal theories. Klein, Winnicott, and Masterson increasingly focused on the actual mother–child relationship in personality formation culminating in the idea that psychopathology is the result of a broken relationship and the relational aspects of psychotherapy are its cure.

Ackerman would have a profound impact on psychodynamic family theory, though his approach did not continue much beyond his death (Goldenberg & Goldenberg, 2013). The successor to the early attempts to extend psychoanalytic theory to the family was object relations family therapy popularized by Scharf and Scharf (1987). Object relations theory is concerned with the cognitive, affective, and emotional processes that mediate interpersonal functioning in close relationships (Stricker & Healey, 1990). Greenberg and Mitchell (1983) define object relations as an "individual's interactions with external and internal (real and imagined) other people, and to the relationship between their internal and external object worlds" (p. 13). The goal of object relations is individuation, separation, and the development of self. The concept of individuation/separation has sometimes been confused in family therapy with the Bowenian concept of differentiation, but the two, while not dissimilar, bear distinct differences. From an object relations perspective, individuation is the process of achieving independence and a sense of self-identity (Blos, 1975; Mahler, Pine, & Bergman, 1975; Skowron & Friedlander, 1998). The quality of the first human relationship becomes the prototype for all other intimate relationships (Horner, 1984, p. 3). These patterns, or mental pictures, are organized into patterns of patterns, then schemas, which become consolidated and stabilized through repetition.

The primary critique of the early pioneers in family therapy was that therapy relied heavily on their formidable personalities, making it difficult or impossible for others to learn their approaches or have the same degree of therapeutic success (Goldenberg & Goldenberg, 2013). In addition, the approaches used by these pioneers relied on little, if any, research. What was available tended to be mostly anecdotal. The third critique was that family systems therapies often did not seem completely systemic, often giving short shrift to intrapersonal elements (e.g., biology, heritability, and personality), while viewing any focus on the individual as reinforcing an emphasis on the identified patient (someone who metaphorically embodies the pain of the entire family) in lieu of couple, family, and other contextual elements. Finally, family therapy has an antipathy toward diagnosis as negatively labeling persons; its critics point to the lack of diagnosis as significantly hampering assessment and effective evidence-based treatment. Despite the critiques, family therapy has forced the mental health field to address the biopsychosocial aspects of psychopathology in systemic rather than individualistic fashion. The revolutionaries of the 1950s and 1960s created a climate where today we much more clearly see the connections and mutuality between the brain and its parts, between the brain and body, and in the relationships between brains (self and others) (Siegel, 2001). Current models in family psychology rely heavily on research outcomes, are systematized for ease of education and training, and follow a systems paradigm without eschewing the values of psychology, research, assessment, diagnosis, and treatment.

RELATIONAL FAMILY SYSTEMS: SYSTEMIC PERSPECTIVES ON FAMILIES' RELATIONAL SYSTEMS

A family/couple is *defined* as a group of individuals who live together with shared beliefs, purposes, and emotional attachments. These relational groups are more than a collection of individuals who share space and time. The family is a social system, which supports the survival and welfare of its members. The family system is a *unique social system* (unlike any others) with entry only through birth, adoption, or marriage. It is not voluntary (for most) so exit only comes by way of death or divorce. The relationships of couples and families are cocreated with a shared history, shared internalized perceptions and assumptions, a cocreated map of the world, a shared identity, shared sense of purpose, and strong, powerful, and durable reciprocal emotional attachments that last a lifetime (even beyond).

From a family psychology perspective, this means that individuals are part of families, couples, and extended family systems that span generations as well as broader communities and cultures. The idea is that individuals are nested within family systems, and families are nested within broader social and cultural systems, which include the extended family, parents' work organizations, children's schools, children's peer groups, involved helping professionals, the wider community, the family's ethnic group, the prevailing culture, and the family's religious or spiritual community. For example, Bowers (1973) suggested behavior was jointly influenced by the person (or trait) and the situation (environment). This means that personality or individual characteristics are, in part, the result of complex dynamic interactions between our biological predispositions and the relational systems in which we develop, with our beliefs and personal narratives developing out of the context in which we are embedded.

Some versions of family theory, including integrative family systems theory and Ackerman's psychoanalytic family therapy theory, suggest that the self is also made up of internal systems that impact behavior and influence personality (Schwartz, 2013). Thus, the personality of the individual is inexorably tied to the characteristics of the relational patterns, the shared belief systems, and other contextual factors in and around that individual. Motivation for behavior and the personality of the individual is shaped, maintained, and driven by the relational context around him or her as well as the internal systems within. From a systemic perspective, it is the relational structures and processes within the multisystemic nature of the person that best describe personality characteristics.

The early theoretical ideas of the founders of the field share a set of common core ideas that translate systems epistemology into a way of understanding how families work, what they are, how they approach problems, and how change occurs (Sexton & Stanton, 2015). In this systemic view, families comprise the following:

- *Family roles, routines, and rituals.* Family rituals are stylized routines with special significance to mark transitional events in the individual and family life cycle such as birth, adoption, illness, death, marriage, separation, starting and concluding relationships, and commencing or completing educational courses or work experiences (Imber-Black et al., 2003).
- *Process* describes how a system functions, including ideas such as flexibility, cohesion, and communication. Also, process describes problematic family processes such as triangulation or demand–withdraw couple interaction.

- *Ever evolving over time through various developmental phases.* The evolution of families over time is best represented by the family life cycle. Family life cycle models emphasize the interaction between time and change (White & Klein, 2007) to understand the changes required as a family transitions over time in response to potential disturbances to the family system that may result in discontinuous change or symptom development (e.g., as the first child in a family emerges into adolescence, this may challenge the parental hierarchy and impact decision making, boundaries, family rules, and other existing system dynamics; the family that struggles with this transition may evidence tension, conflict, or other symptoms). Early family life cycle models emphasized somewhat rigid stages, often based on a construct of child aging and child development (e.g., birth of the first child, entrance of the first child into kindergarten), and the models varied from a few stages to dozens depending on the number of transition events deemed important by the model originator and/or the number of children referenced in the model (Cusinato, 1994; Falicov, 1988; Gerson, 1995; Kapinus & Johnson, 2003), although couples without children could also be conceptualized as having a family life cycle model (Pelton & Hertlein, 2011). Death, divorce, and other family life changes were incorporated into the models (Ahrons, 2011; Brunhofer, 2011).

Carter and McGoldrick (2004) have provided the most widely accepted model of the family life cycle. They believe that the individual grows and develops within the family developmental process through a culturally determined set of phases: launching the single young adult, joining of families through marriage, families with young children, families with adolescents, launching children, and moving on to become families in later life. As families move dynamically through time, there are stresses and anxieties produced as the family moves forward, coping with the changes and transitions of life some of which are predictable developmental stresses, while others are unpredictable and random (winning the lottery, death, war).

- *Race, ethnicity, and culture are a central part of the context* of couples and families. System theories have evolved to think about culture, diversity, race, and ethnicity as being significant features that have an impact on the behaviors, personality, and functioning of individuals, couples, and families. Diversity in general, and family diversity more specifically, is typically described around the structural characteristics of race, ethnicity, and sexual orientation (e.g., Sue & Sue, 2012). This approach results in focusing on the unique characteristics of each group. However, a systemic approach to diversity, gender, race, and ethnicity avoids social and cultural reductionism, whereby a client's gender, race, or social class automatically explains that person's beliefs, attitudes, and behavior. As Falicov (2003) suggested, "Although inter-laced with historical moments, cultural discourses, and sociopolitical forces, the client's biography is always unique" (p. 40). Falicov (2003) argued that family therapy's current focus on multiculturalism encom-passes both cultural diversity that respects cultural preferences among clients and social justice practice that focuses on the effects of power differential inequities on individual, family, and couple well-being.

One of the ways in which systemic theories are culturally sensitive is in their focus on functional *process*. Rather than observing behavior and functioning from the outside, functional process is an approach based on curiosity, individuality, and respect for the unique ways that cultural diversity functions within the system of the individual, family, or couple. The multidimensional-ecosystemic-comparative approach (Falicov, 2015) focuses on four basic aspects of relational life and the relational processes used to respond and adjust to relational life when trying to understand a presenting problem: (1) migration, (2) ecological context, (3) family organization, and (4) family life cycle. It is the unique interaction of these factors in concert with relational patterns, beliefs, and narratives that define individuals in a cultural milieu.

A SYSTEMIC VIEW OF CLINICAL PROBLEMS

From a systemic view, the targets of clinical work go beyond the spe-cific changes requested by the client. Understanding clinical problems takes us far beyond a clinical diagnosis and requires an understanding of how the behaviors of individuals function within the relational context in which they are embedded. Relational patterns illustrated by repetitive and escalating attempts to solve problems that are based on rigid roles, communication that is confused or contains inconsistent relational state-ments, triangulation that creates overinvolved relationships, or distant dis-engaged relationships, make solutions difficult. Carr (2012) developed a multidimensional approach for understanding clinical problems from a systemic perspective.

A systemic perspective asserts that the same principles that describe healthy behavior describe the emergence and maintenance of clinical problems. Relational problems are most likely to occur when outside events force a relational system to adapt and change. There are a num-ber of normal (e.g., family life cycle changes) and abnormal (e.g., trauma, abuse) events in life that require couples, families, and individual systems to cope through adaptation and adjustment. Early systemic models suggested that flexible family and individual systems were able to adjust to the changing context, while those that experienced difficulties adjusted by adopting more rigid roles, rules, and relational patterns (Carr, 2013). Over time, the very solutions used to remedy the situation become part of problematic behavior that, despite all attempts to help, ultimately and ironically serve to maintain the problem. Thus, clinical problems are those events for which the individual or family has unsuccessfully adapted, resulting in ongoing patterns of problem-maintaining behaviors and beliefs that reinforce the problem and serve to create family stuckness, or the inability to adapt and successfully resolve pressing issues at hand.

Five specific areas of relational systems that impact the development and maintenance of clinical problems include (1) family relational patterns; (2) shared attributions, beliefs, and individual expectations; (3) contextual and historical factors; (4) race, ethnicity, and culture; and (5) structural elements within systems (boundaries, hierarchy, subsystems).

1. *Family Relational Patterns* are those common behavioral sequences between family members that, over time, become a common way of interacting. Core relational patterns become the typical way in which relational systems respond to events that occur around them. Relational patterns contribute to the development and maintenance of problem behaviors in a number of ways. For example, Minuchin (1974) suggested that family relational patterns impact the individual via the structural relationship between the individual and subgroups within the family. Each subsystem has different roles and differing degrees of permeability. Accordingly, clinical problems can be the result of coalitions among family members that make it difficult to successfully adapt to the daily needs of the family. Similarly, Watzlawick, Weakland, and Fisch (1974) suggested that individuals are a collection of behavior patterns that gain meaning in the system through relational information and communication, and that problems become clinical problems only because of the solutions that are applied by both individuals and member coalitions of the system.

It is the reinforcing nature of recursive relational patterns that result in problems becoming an ongoing part of family and individual functioning. For example, the attempt to solve a small problem or disagreement may become an entrenched maladaptive pattern of interaction such that the problem for the family becomes the way they try to solve their problems. Similarly, communication that is confused or contains inconsistent relational statements makes solution even more difficult to attain (Carr, 2013).

Bowen and others (Hargrove, 2009) have proposed that problematic relational patterns can span generations. Families choose particular coping strategies that they pass on to the next generation, but those strategies they chose not to use do not get passed on. Therefore, each new generation has, in effect, fewer coping strategies at its disposal and is less adaptive in how it attacks problems or issues in the family. Bowen suggested that healthy individuals are those who maintain a degree of psychological interdependence and independence from their family of origin. Differentiation allows for transgenerational independence and individual decision making that better meets the adaptational needs for current family situations.

Relational coalitions and alliances are forms of what are often called relational triads where groups of three members form a relationship centered around certain interactional patterns. Triads are quite natural in families because they form a stable relationship much like the three legs of a stool. With only two legs (or, in this case, members) the relationship becomes unstable when problems occur beyond the members' coping capacities. Minuchin suggested that such coalitions form rigid patterns in the family, endure over time, and prevent the family from moving forward in its development. An example of triangulation would be when parents seek to enlist a child's support against the other (covert/overt), or through parent–child coalitions, in which one parent sides with the child against the other parent. Haley described how triangles are illustrative of:

- Cross-generational coalitions
- Two persons of the same generational level or status enlist a family member from a different level
- Coalitions of two family members at different levels arise against a third family member
- Coalitions can be covert and hidden from conscious awareness

There is also an emotional intensity factor to relational patterns. *Rigid* or chaotic patterns of family organization typify families with extremely high or low levels of flexibility, while *enmeshed* or disengaged patterns of family organization typify families with extremely high or low levels of cohesion. It is the loss of flexibility and cohesion that makes it more difficult to attend to and successfully resolve the daily problems that families face, creating greater vulnerability and risk for successful adaptation and development.

2. *Problem attributions, beliefs, and individual expectations* that develop around relational patterns also contribute to the development and maintenance of clinical problems (Carr, 2013). Attributions play a role in defining the intentions of the person exhibiting problem behavior. When family members attribute negative characteristics or intentions to each other, these attributions may lead them to persist in problem-maintaining behavior and elicit problem-maintaining behavior in others (Sexton, 2010). For

example, in defining a family member *as bad, sad, sick,* or *mad,* a belief system is created that shapes how one approaches that individual and, thus, contributes to the maintenance of the problematic behavior. Claiborn and Lichtenberg (1989) suggested that the belief systems that form faulty cognitive constructions also support and maintain problem behaviors, which involve the ways in which the individual interprets interpersonal situations, such as attribution of intent to other behavior and beliefs about the relationship, which ultimately support behaviors that fulfill those constructions. In each case, the beliefs, narratives, and attributions about others and the source of problem behavior, as well as the belief in the capacity of the self or other to change, play an important role in understanding clinical problems systemically (Claiborn & Lichtenberg, 1989).

Taking an interactional perspective, Claiborn and Lichtenberg (1989) suggested that problems are, at their core, interactional sequences that promote trait like individual characteristics that form the common ways individuals interact with the people and systems around them. From this perspective, maladaptive interpersonal behavior can be categorized in two ways:

- Individuals who tend to use the same interpersonal strategies across varied situations that demand more diverse responses. This behavior represents rigid interpersonal strategies. In addition, a characteristic of rigidity is the lack of sensitivity to feedback from the situation, which makes adaptation unlikely.
- Similarly, self-fulfilling styles can result from a person's own initial behavior shaping the interpersonal situation prompting others to respond with complementary behaviors that then become the reason and justification for behaviors to continue.

3. *Contextual and historical influences* can be assessed via genograms and other tools that provide a way to have an *overall* view on one's self within the context of multiple generations of relationships to which a person is connected (Carter & McGoldrick, 2004). Understanding any intergenerational influences and learning how those influences impact current relationship is a way to help family members overcome the barriers inhibiting them from making adaptive decisions in the here and now.

4. *Risk and protective factors of the context.* According to Sexton and Stanton (2015), another specific way to consider the impact that systems have on families and individuals is to think about the risk and protective factors that contribute to both healthy behavior and clinical problems. Within a systemic approach, it is the unique combination of risk and protective factors that result in a probability, predisposition, or propensity

for pathology, rather than a causal link to behavior. For example, in the area of childhood behavior problems, Webster-Stratton (1996) categorized risk factors into three groups: (1) child risk variables, including a diffi-cult temperament or high rate of disruptive, impulsive, inattentive, and aggressive behaviors (Campbell & Ewing, 1990); (2) parenting variables, including ineffective parenting strategies and negative attitudes (Patter-son & Stouthamer-Loeber, 1984); and (3) family variables, apart from the parent–child relationship, which include parental psychopathology, mar-ital factors, socioeconomic factors, and other stressors (Webster-Stratton, 1990).

Risk and protective factors are particularly suited to family psychology because they describe ways to alter behavior, rather than labeling the indi-vidual with characteristics that are considered static and enduring. This approach helps organize the complex information from multiple systems (individual, family, and social) into useful categories for conceptualiz-ing problems through a probability lens (determining the likelihood of problems), rather than in terms of causality. The risk and protective factor model can be helpful in organizing critical information, such as how mul-tiple systems function with regard to difficulties as well as strengths. Risk and protective factors are most often considered in two categories: *dynamic* factors, or those features of individual and context that are changeable, and *static* factors that are unlikely to change. This approach also helps deter-mine the factors to target in clinical work and the factors that are unlikely to change and therefore require a different set of interventions to facilitate successful coping (such as Gottman's (1999) admonition that sometimes couples have to agree to disagree to move forward).

5. *Structural and relational factors.* Families also have *structural elements* that organize their ecosystem. In fact, the family is a system with bound-aries organized into subsystems, and around each system is a boundary that sets it apart from the wider social and cultural systems of which it is one subsystem. To facilitate adaptation and survival, the boundary around the family must be semipermeable to allow information and resources to enter and leave the family. From a systemic perspective, relationship system boundaries are not intended to be closed. Instead, relational sys-tems are open systems that exchange information and resources with the larger system of which they are part. To do so, the family's boundary must be permeable enough for the family to survive as a coherent system and permit the intake of information and resources required for continued survival (e.g., allowing kids to go school to get an education, having con-tact with the community, to work, to have friends and social support). Where boundaries are too impermeable, family members may develop constricted lifestyles and become socially isolated.

CONCLUSIONS: WHAT IS NEXT?

Systemic thinking is challenging. It requires consideration of how multiple systems may impact the current problems of a client. Understanding the behavior of an individual, couple, family, or organization means looking beyond the simple, beyond the obvious, and beyond the casual to the patterns, meaning, and processes through which these relational systems operate. Applying the lens of family psychology in this way ensures that relational patterns become central to theory building. Understanding a client requires attention to the same interdependent ties that mutually influence both change mechanisms and outcomes. Whether in research or practice, the focus from a systemic perspective is not on individual variables, the isolated events in a client's past, or the isolated problems to be solved in life, but on the patterns, trends, and themes central to the functioning of the system under consideration.

If you are to successfully understand and work with individuals, couples, and families, you must see the system. That means you have to look beyond the individual problem and what is presented. In each issue and struggle, there is likely to be more to the story. In each couple and family, you can also expect complexity in which there are few quick, simple solutions (first- *vs.* second-order change), and all things are complex, maybe even too complex to totally understand. In fact, in every system, everything is in relationship. The *connections* between people are in the communication and behavioral sequences/patterns that connect each space between. You also have to readjust how and what you look for when thinking about relational systems. Instead of the elements (the different behaviors or individual variables), you have to learn to pull the patterns and trends into your foreground view. Your targets of assessment and intervention are the patterns that connect.

In the next chapter, we focus on the final core *leg* of the family psychology stool-research, which is the scientific *lens* of family psychology. We will discuss research methodology, research findings of more than 50 years of systemic study of couples and families, and the most effective interventions for change.

Chapter 4

The Scientific Foundations of Family Psychology

Discovery consists of seeing what everybody has seen, and thinking what nobody has thought.

—Albert Szent-Gyorgyi

Family psychology research has progressed significantly and has contributed to a strong scientific foundation for the profession. Like the other two core domains of family psychology (theory and practice), family psychology research has evolved into a complex, systematic, and diverse set of unique and creative strategies to study the complex processes associated with couple and family life. Current clinical intervention research now investigates complex and highly specific clinical change models (e.g., multisystemic therapy [MST], functional family therapy [FFT], multidimensional family therapy [MDFT]). We now have research and statistical methods that allow us to describe the trajectories of therapeutic change and understand the degree to which therapist activities, the timing of interventions, the therapeutic alliance, and other specific processes influence these trajectories. Research is now able to capture multidimensional relational processes from multiple perspectives and thus explain the complexity of family and couple treatment. Treatment specificity has made it possible to develop systematic research programs of treatment models and of core therapeutic change mechanisms. We also know an increasing amount about the process of couple and family treatment. For example,

Knobloch-Fedders, Pinsof, and Mann (2007) and Friedlander et al. (2011) have advanced our understanding of the therapeutic alliance in family therapy and its relation to outcomes, which has also informed the development of change models and treatment interventions.

Families are complex multidimensional relational units comprising multiple individuals who come together through invisible, yet powerful, relational bonds that take on their own characteristics and nature. To gain a sense of the whole, family research must examine the ways in which the family functions as a relational unit, how individuals interact as family, and the common problems and unique collective relational bonds that unite each member to the others. To be clinically useful, research with families encompasses a range of areas, which include describing how they function, explaining the problems they experience, and exploring intervention research aimed at identifying how best to effectively intervene in the family's relational context.

To accomplish this difficult task, family psychology research has also become diverse in its current methodology, which allows for the study of more complex and detailed outcome and process questions. This diversity is in response to the complexity of studying family interactions and change processes. Driven by necessity, the diversity of approaches also improves the potential to generate clinically useful findings. Family psychology research has become so significant that Liddle, Bray, Levant, and Santisteban (2002) suggest that the current research in the area of family intervention science represents a significant knowledge base of clinical expertise and a growing body of outcome and process studies that meet the highest standards of research methodology.

Our focus in this chapter is on providing an introduction to the scientific foundation that is the result of more than 50 years of family psychology research. We will illustrate how the research upon which family psychology is built is systematic, significant, and has much to offer to the domains of clinical practice and theory. Being a good consumer of research requires an understanding of how research is developed in order to understand its strengths and limitations when it is applied in clinical settings. In this chapter, we focus on the role of science, methods of studying families and couples, and what the research currently tells us about effective practice of family psychology.

SCIENCE AND THE SCIENTIFIC METHOD

The scientific method is one way of knowing, with potential to inform psychologists in ways that other methods do not. Rather than authority (ways of knowing based on expert opinion), personal experience (it must be true because it worked for me), or a priori beliefs (everyone believes this), science is a way of knowing that uses systematic methods to establish reliable and verifiable knowledge through methods that can be replicated over time. More specifically, it is systematic inquiry, organized discovery, and the verification process that is aimed at developing knowledge over time (Sexton & Alexander, 2002). Research and its accompanying methods are the process by which scientific knowledge is developed. While appearing very complex with complex statistical analysis and multiphasic multilevel research designs, research is really nothing more than a set of rules or procedures to systematically gather information in a manner that is reliable (it can be replicated) and valid (it represents what is intended to be studied). Methods vary from controlled laboratory experiments, to systematic observation, to cognitive testing, to surveys and case studies—each with its own advantages and disadvantages that must be understood in order to evaluate the accuracy of the research findings. Rather than a specific type (empirical/quantitative *vs.* naturalistic/qualitative), the research process is actually just a systematic, inquiry-based, and knowledge producing set of methods and skills.

A *systemic* approach to scientific inquiry is particularly difficult because traditional rules often don't fit the three-dimensional view of systemic epistemology. Yet, science is more than just the traditional medically based studies in which a single small variable is studied with a tightly controlled linear process of discovery. Family psychology uses diverse methods, with multiple perspectives, in real settings to map complex relational systems as discussed in Chapters 2 and 3. Family psychology science employs methodological diversity in response to the complexity of studying family interactions and change processes. For example, researchers now collect data from multiple participants (e.g., parental figures and children) and combine them strategically to answer process questions such as, does the discrepancy in individual alliance scores for parents and children predict dropout in family therapy (Heatherington, Friedlander, & Greenberg, 2005)? Family psychology researchers also use mixed methods to study contextual influences and the role of meaning in shaping family interactions (Weisner & Fiese, 2011). In this situation, valuable studies consider multiple perspectives over multiple time points in regard to multiple constructs. Driven by necessity, the diversity of approaches also improves the potential to generate clinically useful findings.

Family psychology research is also a *dynamic* process in terms of what we know and the methods we use to build knowledge as it evolves over time. In fact, this is one of the major difficulties in bridging the research/practice gap. Some researchers look at research evidence and say, "it constantly changes." In fact, it does and it should. The aim of research is to expand and refine our understanding of the complex phenomena we study. As empirical knowledge accrues over time, it takes new shape and meaning. New research methods, including techniques for data analysis, have made it possible to investigate areas we could not previously study and to model family processes in relation to mental health outcomes. New findings shed new light on what we believed to be true two decades ago and compel us to look at family relationships, psychopathology, and therapeutic change in more complex ways today.

DOMAINS OF FAMILY PSYCHOLOGY RESEARCH

There are two domains of research in family psychology. First, are those studies that seek to explain and *describe* clients, their problems, their context, and the interactions between them. These are the types of studies that help us understand the relational patterns in couples or families, the etiology of clinical problems, or the characteristics of clients and communities that may signify risk or protective factors. This type of research helps us understand how client systems function both intrapersonally and interpersonally and explore risk and protective factors as well as mechanisms of relational functioning that might lead to successful clinical treatments. Studying clinical problems not only helps us determine successful treatment for problematic symptoms, but it can also help us understand broader cultural, community, and family contexts that may be part of clinical problems or primary features in family functioning. The same methods described later are used to understand families, etiology, and risk and protective factors.

The second type of research studies the efficacy and effectiveness of clinical interventions of family psychology. While seemingly simple, determining what works is actually quite complex. The successful study of clinical interventions requires a high quality of research in clinically relevant settings, with actual clients, in which each of the core elements of a clinical intervention is clearly specified including the intervention, technique or treatment program, outcomes that are clinically relevant, mechanisms of change that are proposed to produce the change, and the moderating client and therapist factors that may alter the relationship between outcome and intervention. Clinical intervention research provides the foundation for the effective clinical practice of family psychology. What is unique about clinical intervention research in family psychology is that there are a range of methods and approaches for capturing the unique interplay among presenting problems, therapeutic factors, demographic variables, and model-specific change mechanisms (Seedall, 2009; Sexton & Datchi,

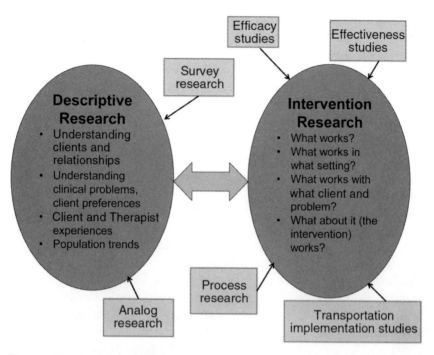

Figure 4.1 Research domains

2014; Sexton, Kinser, & Hanes, 2009; Sprenkle, Davis, & Lebow, 2009). Each of these types of research produces different information for different clinical questions.

TYPES OF FAMILY PSYCHOLOGY RESEARCH

There is a wide range of family psychology research approaches. Each approach fits a particular type of question, has strengths and weaknesses, and is a vital tool in gaining a systemic, three-dimensional view of families and successful treatment.

Outcome studies investigate the absolute (as compared with no-treatment) and relative efficacy (as compared with a clinically legitimate alternative intervention) of an intervention or treatment program. Clinical trial studies (often referred to as randomized clinical trials, RCT) are the result of randomized studies in which the emphasis is on high levels of internal validity, with some expense paid to ecological or external validity. RCTs are the traditional gold standard of clinical research and follow the same logic as similar studies used in medical research (Wampold & Bhati, 2004).

Comparison trial studies evaluate interventions/treatments in relation to a systematically developed and relevant comparison intervention or treatment and are most helpful in answering questions about whether a program or intervention works, with whom it might work, and in which settings it might work. Comparison trials may not include randomization or many of the other strict methodological controls of traditional clinical trials.

Traditionally, outcome studies (whether clinical trial or comparison) are used in three ways. *Efficacy studies* answer questions about which treatments work under the most stringently controlled conditions. Efficacy studies have high methodological control, but are limited because they differ from actual clinical conditions. *Effectiveness studies* answer questions regarding the power of therapeutic interventions in actual clinical settings with conditions that replicate those that clinicians genuinely face. Although there may be decreased methodological control (in the traditional sense) in these types of studies, they do have high clinical relevance. Effectiveness studies are often conducted in community settings, where it is not possible to match the high degree of experimental control of traditional efficacy studies. Finally, *moderator studies* address questions about which particular client, problem, or contextual features moderate or affect the strength of the relationship between treatment and treatment outcomes.

Process-to-outcome studies link the conditions of therapy (preexisting and specific within-session processes) with the outcomes of clinical interventions. These studies help identify the mechanisms of action in evidence-based interventions/programs. Studies of complex phenomena like couples and families must consider complex questions. That is done through the study of moderators and mediators of treatment outcome. *Moderators* are factors of the client system, the context, or the clinical problems that may change the relationship among the major variables of interest. For example, the gender or age of adolescents is a crucial variable to consider when testing treatments designed to change the involvement of youth in the mental health system. *Mediators* are variables that provide a bridge between the variables of interest. In a sense, the mediators create the relationship of importance. For example, in a study similar to the one noted earlier, treatment programs for adolescents have an impact when the therapeutic relationship is considered. Without a measure of therapeutic alliance, many treatment programs are not related to any outcome. Thus, it is the alliance (mediator) that provides the link in the complex formula between treatment and outcome measure.

Clinical intervention research is currently at the point where consideration of moderators and mediators is the standard because it allows the complexities of clients and of the therapeutic process to be studied, thus, increasing the potential utility of the investigation. As studies become more specific, they study increasingly specific interventions and focus on a growing number of relevant moderators and mediators. *Change mechanisms* research is among the most specific research in that it is theory driven and specific to a treatment model.

Systematic case studies provide an ideographic view of the clinical process and are particularly useful in identifying the individual experiences in the change process that might lead to a better understanding of clinical mechanisms or outcomes. These qualitative studies consider the therapeutic change process from the perspective of an individual client/therapist/setting or in naturalistic settings of clinical practice. While limited in generalizability, these studies might provide evidence needed to understand processes within models or application sites.

Transportability and implementation studies consider various issues related to the transportation of couple and family therapy interventions/treatments to the community settings where they might be practiced. Such studies consider the *contextual variables* (e.g., therapist variables, client variables, organizational service delivery systems) that may either enhance or limit successful community implementation. While using similar methodologies as effectiveness studies, the focus of these studies is on the variables that potentially explain the contextual impact that may mediate the outcomes of established studies in community-based clinical studies.

Meta-analytic research reviews contribute to understanding and identifying common elements, new treatment mechanisms, or differential results across studies. Meta-analysis is a technique that uses a collection of studies to determine a mathematical effect size that can then be summarized systematically across many settings, thereby increasing the power and relevance of research findings. This methodology is particularly important in

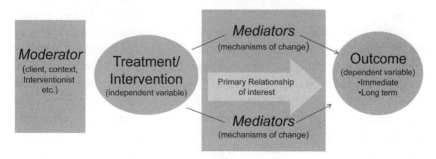

Figure 4.2 Intervention research components

distilling the specific studies into clinically meaningful trends that can be applied and used in practice.

WHAT IS GOOD FAMILY PSYCHOLOGY RESEARCH?

Relational systems and clinical interventions are complex with no single method or approach capturing and representing the domain adequately. While no single standard of research excellence is currently extant, at a minimum, high-quality studies of clinical treatments should include the following: (1) clear specifications of the contents of the treatment model (e.g., treatment manual), (2) measures of model fidelity (therapist adherence or competence), (3) clear identification of client problems, (4) substantial descriptions of service delivery contexts in which the treatment is tested, and (5) the use of specific and well-accepted measures of clinical outcomes.

While there is no best research type, there are criteria to use in order to be a good consumer of research. Clearly, one study does not make a successful intervention, and the most clinically useful research is based on the interaction among client factors, therapeutic influence, and specific change mechanisms that lead to measurable outcomes in couple and family research. Despite the inherent ambiguity and complexity in studying relationship interactions, it is possible to identify both the important domains to consider when evaluating the research evidence and how to summarize that research into levels that have clinical utility. The guidelines for evaluating research in couple and family psychology (Sexton et al., 2011) suggest that clinically reliable research should have the following minimal criteria:

1. *Replicable and Identifiable Clinical Interventions.* Interventions are the mindful intentional actions of therapists engaged in a clinical context with the express purpose of improving the client's functioning across domains. *Treatment interventions* range from singular discrete actions to comprehensive treatment programs and models that represent increasing levels of complexity and specificity. Techniques are discrete, single, relational, or structured activities with a narrow range of desired outcomes. By contrast, *treatment programs/models* are comprehensive treatment paradigms with theoretical principles, clinical change processes, change mechanisms, and adherence measures (Chambless & Hollon, 1998). Wampold (1997) delineates bona fide treatments as those with clearly articulated mechanisms for clinical change that are therapeutic, systematic, and individualized

to the client. Clearly, interventions that are highly specific have the advantage of being replicable, open to study, and amenable to measures of adherence that ensure quality control. Without a specific and replicable intervention, it is difficult to be confident in an intervention's clinical utility.

2. *Comprehensive and Research Evidence.* A single study does not explain complex phenomena. Similarly, all studies with typical ways of evaluating evidence rely exclusively on the statistical strength and methodological rigor of the studies testing an intervention. Traditional approaches to determining strong evidence rely on ratings of the quality of the research methodology alone. Determining what is comprehensive evidence for a clinical intervention is a balance between internal and external validity. This balance can also be conceptualized as efficacy versus effectiveness research. Efficacy research typically emphasizes internal validity, whereas effectiveness research is typically seen as emphasizing external validity. More specifically, absolute efficacy or effectiveness determines whether a treatment works compared with no-treatment. By contrast, studies of relative efficacy provide evidence that a treatment is efficacious compared with viable alternatives (e.g., treatment of different modality, alternative treatment model). Relative efficacy provides critical information about which treatments are the best choices in a specific clinical situation (Wampold, 2003). Interventions that produce results that exceed viable treatment alternatives certainly demonstrate a stronger effect than those tested against no-treatment control groups.

3. *High-Quality yet Diverse Research Methodologies.* Different research methodologies offer unique perspectives from which to judge the evidence of an intervention or treatment program. With different questions and in different developmental contexts, the most appropriate research method is likely to change as more specific clinical questions are asked. Thus, there can be no single standard of methodological excellence. Instead, studies of family psychology interventions/treatments should include clear specifications regarding the contents of the intervention/treatment model (e.g., manual) and measures of intervention/model fidelity (e.g., therapist adherence or competence). They should also clearly identify client problems and provide a complete description of service delivery contexts in which the intervention/treatment is tested along with the use of specific and accepted measures of clinical outcome (Sexton & Gordon, 2009).

From a systematic perspective, this also means that the traditional gold standard method for clinical research, the RCT, might not always be the best or the most effective approach to take when asking questions about clinical change in relational systems. In family psychology, RCTs are a necessary but not sufficient approach to understanding, evaluating, and promoting effective practices. Psychological treatments can be thought of as having various levels of evidence from the broad (does it work compared with no-treatment) to the specific and clinically nuanced (why does this work in this situation with this person). Determining what are good treatments would be based on these different methods matched to the level of evidence most appropriate (Sexton & Gordon, 2011; Sexton et al., 2013). For example, in determining what works, RCTs provide a valuable tool for validating absolute and relative efficacy (Kazdin, 2006). However, once established, alternative approaches are necessary to answer the more fine-tuned and clinically rich questions. These methods may include qualitative studies, case studies, matched control designs, and meta-analyses. To do so, each method would need to be used when it fits the question at issue rather than used for its exclusive value, while at the same time meeting established methodological quality.

4. *Diversity of Clients and Clinical Problems.* Evidence that has been systematically gathered across diverse clinical populations and utilizes specific replicable interventions and change mechanisms provides potentially relevant information to clinicians. Clients bring their unique worldviews to the therapy interaction; consequently, studies that apply treatments to typically underrepresented populations with a diverse range of problems help clinicians know if a treatment is valid for a variety of clients, not just white, middle-to-upper-class students. Thus, it is critical that studies identify relevant demographic characteristics of the sample under investigation (e.g., race, ethnicity, sexual identity, social class). In this way, clinicians are able to determine the applicability of specific treatments to their particular clinical population.

5. *Attention to Mechanisms of Clinical Action.* Clinical intervention programs are frequently composed of a variety of specific clinical change mechanisms, which make up the active ingredients that contribute to client change. Some interventions have clear and well-articulated change mechanisms while others do not. Programs in which the proposed change mechanisms have been empirically validated are stronger programs because they provide support for the whole of the intervention. In addition, knowledge of these common or specific change mechanisms gives clinicians insight into the specific elements of intervention programs. When there is not only outcome research but also the necessary process research to demonstrate that the theoretically

proposed methods of action for a particular intervention are reliable and valid pathways for change, our confidence in the practice is
greater. Clinicians find utility in the mechanisms that they need to use
in addressing the unique features of a particular case.

6. *Comprehensive Clinical Outcomes.* Studies of family psychology must
attend to individual change and relationship change from multiple
perspectives over time. In fact, in couple and family research, it is the
relational changes that are of primary outcome interest. A comprehensive view of outcomes would involve changes in individual functioning, couple/family functioning, reduction of clinical symptoms, global
measures of client well-being, or cost–benefit analyses of the community implementation of an intervention/treatment. This means that
we cannot assume that symptom reduction corresponds to changes in
a client's daily functioning. Additionally, in couple therapy research,
relationship satisfaction is often measured as an outcome even if relationship dissatisfaction is not the focus of treatment. Knowing these
types of demonstrable outcomes available for an intervention/treat-
ment may determine applicable use in clinical settings.

WHAT DO WE KNOW ABOUT WHAT WE DO?

The research of family psychology has produced a significant knowledge base of systemic evidence to support both the epistemology of family systems and the clinical interventions that result. Similarly, we know
increasingly more about how families and relationships function due to
the systemic application of the ideas presented in the previous sections.
Let's take a look at the outcomes of these methods and consider what we
know about what we do. It is beyond the scope of this chapter to describe
all that we know about the two major categories of family psychology
research: (1) describing and understanding clients and problems and (2)
clinical intervention research. However, it is important to represent the
significant breadth of knowledge to the degree possible. In the following
sections, we provide an overview of the research foundations.

SUPPORT FOR THE EPISTEMOLOGICAL PERSPECTIVE

It is impossible to prove the validity of an epistemology. Some of the
core ways of knowing are just that—complex ways of thinking based on
cultural assumptions that are not specific enough, quantifiable enough, or
measurable enough to ever study. As a result, it is important to look at the
implications of an epistemology or theory and see whether or not expected

relationships occur. To study the epistemology of family psychology, we have to look, for example, at whether or not there are identifiable connections between the ecological, systemic, and developmental aspects of systems theory and the behavior of individuals.

Sexton and Stanton (2015) provided a recent comprehensive review of the research describing clients and clinical problems from a systemic perspective. For example, we do know that characteristics of the family environment contribute to individuals' increased vulnerability to mental illness (Beach, Wamboldt, Kaslow, Heyman, & Reiss, 2006). The degree to which family members show hostility and criticism and are emotionally preoccupied with the mentally ill is a factor in depressive, manic, and psychotic episodes of individuals (Hooley, Phil, Miklowitz, & Beach, 2006). It seems that the expressed emotion of the family acts as an environmental stressor that interacts with individual genetic vulnerability and increases the likelihood of potentiation or relapse for depression, mania, and psychosis. Conversely, there are findings that also suggest that the psychiatric symptoms of an individual force changes in family relationships that may result in interpersonal difficulties; in turn, relational conflict influences the course of mental disorders. This work has led to the identification of similar family-expressed emotion and communication factors as reliable risk factors for the onset of schizophrenia (McFarlane, 2006).

We also know that certain couple and family relational processes such as conflict and rejection, low family emotional support, ineffective communication, poor expression of affect, abuse, and insecure attachment bonds are related to individual symptoms of depression (Beach & Whisman, 2012; Bernal, Cumba-Avilés, & Sáez-Santiago, 2006). For example, depressed adults are more likely to use ineffective parenting strategies and to experience parent–child conflict. In turn, these relational difficulties increase parents' and adolescents' predisposition toward depressive episodes. Two major reviews of treatments for schizophrenia concluded that there is consistent and robust evidence demonstrating the positive impact of family interventions in delaying and possibly preventing relapse (Dixon & Lehman, 1995; Hahlweg, 1987).

The research findings that symptoms impact relational systems, which reciprocally impact individual behaviors and symptoms are important and strong support for the core systemic principles of family psychology. Furthermore, the findings have led the way for successful treatments that focus on intervening with families to help prevent relapse of psychosis and/or the treatment of depression. In the future, it is likely that we will also see effective prevention programs that are able to target the ecological and relational systems around a person to help in the prevention of psychological disorders.

Support has also been provided for the notion that families and parents are very important in youth development. As a child's primary social context, both family relationships and parents have a significant impact on a child's mastery of social competence and interpersonal and self-regulatory skills. Families with high conflict (anger and aggression), poor parenting, and cold, unsupportive, or neglectful family interactions contribute to childhood psychopathology (Knutson, DeGarmo, & Reid, 2004). Family dynamics that are unresponsive or rejecting of children contribute to the development of conduct disorders and aggression (Repetti, Taylor, & Seeman, 2002), while protective parenting factors (quality of parental instructions, frequent joint activities, monitoring, structuring the child's time, and constructive discipline strategies) are all directly linked to positive youth development (Hutchings & Lane, 2005). Because the quality of parenting has been recognized as one of the most influential moderating variables (Dishion & McMahon, 1998; Repetti et al., 2002), it is often utilized as a point of entry in the treatment of children with conduct behavior problems. While clinicians legitimately may feel unable to effect change on a number of social and community factors (e.g., socioeconomic status, stability of residential community), they can promote parenting strategies that take into account the influence of contributing environmental factors.

Finally, we know with high certainty that larger community and social systems can provide both risk and protective factors in youth development and risk factors may initiate and promote problematic behaviors and mental health problems. Adverse social and community factors impact children and families in a variety of ways. The premise of resilience or protective factors is based on the individual variation of response to similar experiences. In a unique study seeking to identify the multiple systemic complements to drug use, Sale et al. (2003) found that it is the interrelationship between internal and external factors, particularly connectedness of youth to their families and school, that is most critical in predicting drug use in youth. In attempting to identify the systemic pathways of influence, three internal factors were identified: school connectedness, family connectedness, and self-control. In the external risk and protective factors domain, family supervision, school prevention environment, community protection environment, and neighborhood risk were included in the model. Their model shows that family connectedness is a key to the substantial path of influence on substance use. It clearly supports the interactive nature of protective influence—internal, external, and normative—against substance use.

While there is no way to validate an epistemological perspective, we can test for interactions between the parts of the system to ascertain whether they work in the way that systemic epistemology might predict. The extensive history of developmental, family relationship, and risk and protective factors research demonstrates that individuals are largely impacted by their relational and ecological systems, and it also seems that individual problems change systems. Thus, it does appear that the structures and processes of family systems (see Chapters 3 and 4) are supported by the cumulative research found in family psychology.

DO FAMILY PSYCHOLOGY CLINICAL INTERVENTIONS WORK?

The study of the effectiveness of couple- and family-based psychological interventions has existed for more than 50 years. Clinical intervention research focuses on what have been called the fundamental questions of psychology practice that were raised more than 50 years ago by Eysenck (1952):

a. Does this intervention/technique/practice work?
b. Where, with what, and for whom does it work: In which setting? With what problems? And with what type of client?
c. What about it works? What are the clinical mechanisms that produce change?

Early studies sought to research whether family psychology (as a broad modality) was effective, what about it works, and with whom it might be successful. Reviews produced strong evidence to conclude that couple and family interventions are efficacious for a range of clinical problems (Gurman, 1971; Gurman & Kniskern, 1991, 1986). Family therapy produced positive results for a wide variety of specific clinical problems, concluding that some interventions were more effective than individual or standard treatments for a number of disorders. Gurman and Kniskern (1991) identified more than 200 relevant studies of couple and family treatments. The authors found that broad systemic practices were efficacious and that family therapy was often as effective, and potentially more effective, than many individual treatments for problems attributed to family conflict. In a later review, Gurman, Kniskern, and Pinsoff (1986) used the results of 47 overlapping reviews of the couple and family literature published between 1970 and 1984. Sexton, Alexander, and Mease (2003) and Sexton et al. (2013) found strong support for systemic family and couple therapy as a broad intervention and the current evidence-based models as specific effective approaches for a large group of clinical problems. Finally, Sexton and colleagues (2013) conducted the most systematic review of the research to date and analyzed couple and family psychology research in regard to the various levels of evidence supporting various models. The findings suggest that a number of widely used and available clinical intervention programs meet the highest levels of research evidence. Given these results, Sexton et al. (2013) concluded that the literature supporting couple and family psychology is at least as strong as it is for other forms of psychotherapy and for some clinical problems significantly better.

The qualitative reviews also suggest that family psychology treatment is an efficacious form of treatment, particularly for the broad areas of relationship dissatisfaction and to a lesser extent for specific individual's presenting problems. Successful outcomes are most apparent when family psychology treatments are compared with no-treatment groups and to a lesser extent to other comparison groups. For example, Sexton et al. (2013) found that improvements in marital satisfaction are experienced by about 40% of couples in treatment. Although several types of family psychology treatments have not yet provided evidence of their effectiveness, those varieties that are researched tend to demonstrate similar degrees of client improvement to other types of treatment modalities.

A number of meta-analyses support both the broad and specific interventions of family psychology. For example, Shadish and colleagues (Shadish, Ragsdale, Glaser, & Montgomery, 1995) found a weighted mean effect size ($d = .47$) for systemic family therapy that is lower than reported findings for group and individual therapies, but it still suggests that those receiving family-based interventions fared better than those receiving no treatment at all. Dunn and Schwebel (1995) found that couple therapy was more effective than no-treatment in fostering changes in various areas of couple relationships at posttreatment ($d = .79$) and follow-up ($d = .52$). These results were apparent for a variety of outcomes, including cognition, affect, and general attitudes toward relationship quality. Shadish et al. (1993, 1995) found couple therapy to be moderately more effective than no-treatment ($d = .60$). More specifically, these authors identified two outcome domains in which the effect of marital therapy was significant: global marital satisfaction ($n = 16, d = .71$) and communication/problem solving ($n = 7, d = .52$).

Does family psychology work with specific clinical problems? In a number of clinical problems areas, family psychology clinical interventions are particularly effective. Most often, it is the highly specific and well-designed treatment programs that produce the strongest outcomes with specific problems. It is also worth noting that many of the clinical problems for which family psychology is most effective are some of the most difficult problems faced by psychologists in practice (e.g., depression, severe mental illness, conduct and oppositional defiant disorders (ODD) and substance abuse problems in youth and adults).

For example, the treatment of schizophrenia, through family psychoeducation (FPE) targets how family members respond to patients' progress such as medication adherence and recovery (McFarlane, Dixon, Lukens, & Lucksted, 2003). Prior reviews indicated that FPE was successful in postponing the recurrence of psychotic episodes and in reducing relapse rates by more than 50% compared with routine care (Sexton et al., 2003; McFarlane et al., 2003). Recent reports confirm the effectiveness of psychoeducational interventions as an adjunct to pharmacology in diverse cultural contexts and define FPE as an evidence-based practice in the treatment of adult schizophrenia (Bird et al., 2010). Though further research is needed, these authors concluded that couple therapy might be effective in treating depression in women. In addition, couple therapy may improve the outcomes for substance-using adults when supplementing other forms of treatment.

There is also evidence that family systems therapy models produce significant positive outcome as the treatment of choice for childhood and adolescent behavior problems. Farrington and Welsh (2003) conducted a meta-analysis of controlled outcome studies regarding the efficacy of differing types of family-based programs designed to prevent delinquency and antisocial child behavior and they found significance in treatment. There is also support for the success of family therapy and parenting programs in the treatment of youth and parental depression (Beach & Whisman, 2012; Paz Pruitt, 2007). In particular, research findings suggest that *attachment-based family therapy* and *systems integrative family therapy* are effective approaches (Diamond & Josephson, 2005; Paz Pruitt, 2007; Trowell et al., 2007). Empirical evidence has accumulated to confirm that behavioral parent training has positive effects on childhood behavior problems associated with attention deficit hyperactivity disorder and ODD(Diamond & Josephson, 2005; Kaslow et al., 2012; Roberts, Mazzucchelli, Taylor, & Reid, 2003). Contemporary research has established the success of three family-focused programs: *Parent–Child Interaction Therapy*, *Triple-P*, and *Incredible Years*, which are evidence-based manualized interventions for preadolescent children (Sexton et al., 2013).

Family therapy is effective for a proportion of children and adolescents with anorexia, bulimia, and obesity (Carr, 2013). In a systematic narrative review of six uncontrolled and five randomized treatment trials of family therapy for adolescent anorexia, Eisler (2005) concluded that after treatment, between one half and two-thirds of cases achieved a healthy weight. At 6 months to 6 years of follow-up, 60–90% of adolescents were fully recovered, and no more than 10–15% were classified as seriously ill. Two trials of family therapy for bulimia in adolescents indicate that it is more effective than supportive therapy (Le Grange et al., 2007), and as effective as cognitive behavior therapy (Schmidt et al., 2007), which is considered to be the treatment of choice for bulimia in adults, due to its strong empirical support (Wilson & Fairburn, 2007).

A meta-analysis by Waldron and Turner (2008) analyzed findings from 17 studies of outpatient treatments for adolescent substance use disorders. The sample included seven individual cognitive behavioral therapy (CBT), 13 group CBT, 17 family therapy, and nine minimal treatment control conditions. The mean effect size of all treatment conditions was 0.45, a small to moderate effect. Only three models fulfilled criteria as well-established models for substance abuse treatment—two systemic treatment approaches (MDFT, FFT) and one behavioral approach (group CBT). Three additional family-focused models were classified as probably efficacious: two systemic approaches (brief strategic family therapy, MST) and behavioral family therapy. None of the treatment approaches appeared to be clearly superior to any other in terms of treatment effectiveness for adolescent substance abuse.

What about family psychology works? We know much less about the change mechanisms of effective family therapy than we do about the outcomes of broad and specific intervention programs. While there is considerable interest in identifying the ingredients of change, process research is complex and usually embedded in the study of specific treatment interventions situated in specific contexts of service delivery. The multiple variables in and outside of the treatment program that influence client outcomes are hard to isolate and test in relational and most often conjoint interactions between therapist and family. It is often challenging to separate discrete interventions from relationship factors in order to determine their respective effects on the outcomes of couple and family therapy. Change mechanisms are part of a complex set of purposeful interventions in therapy, and understanding them outside the context in which they occur may neither be practical nor be sensible.

To date, much of the process research that has been conducted falls within three domains: (1) establishing a therapeutic alliance with family members, (2) managing conflicted family interactions, and (3) changing family interactions. While not an exhaustive list, it is intended to illustrate the major findings of this work.

Therapeutic alliance. As early as 1978, Gurman and Kniskern concluded that "the ability of the therapist to establish a positive relationship . . . receives the most consistent support as an important outcome-related therapist factor in marital and family therapy" (p. 875). As it is studied today, the alliance is "a multilevel and systemic construct that describes the interactions of individual and group processes and their influence on the development of the therapeutic relationship in family therapy" (Sexton & Datchi, 2014, p. 20). Process research has investigated the link between the alliance and client outcomes in family therapy and identified several family and treatment variables that moderate the strength of the relation.

Reducing within family and couple negativity and blame. A comprehensive review of the process of family therapy concluded that, in general, negativity may be predictive of premature termination (Friedlander, Wildman, Heatherington, & Skowron, 1994). Yet, research findings also suggest that conflict/negativity is malleable in treatment. For example, Melidonis and Bry (1995) demonstrated that therapists could reduce family members' blaming statements and increase their positive statements by asking questions about exceptions and by selectively attending to positive statements. Similarly, reframing interventions have been shown to reduce the likelihood of family members' defensive communications in family therapy (Robbins, Alexander, Newell, & Turner, 1996; Robbins, Alexander, & Turner, 2000). Diamond and Liddle (1996) demonstrated that in successful resolutions of therapy impasses, therapists were able to create an emotional treaty among family members by blocking and working through negative affect and by amplifying thoughts and feelings that promoted constructive dialogue.

Does family psychology work with diverse clients? Questions about the effectiveness of family therapy with diverse populations continue to be an underrepresented focus of family therapy research (Sexton et al., 2013). For the most part, study samples include primarily white and non-Hispanic races with the exception of family therapy research on conduct disorder, youth drug abuse, psychoeducation for major mental illness, and child/adolescent internalizing problems (Sprenkle, 2012). Both MST and FFT have been tested in ethnically and culturally diverse communities in the United States and Europe (Flicker, Waldron, Turner, Brody, & Hops, 2008; Harpell & Andrews, 2006). The most current research suggests that MST enhanced youth behavioral outcomes compared with alternative treatments for racially diverse adolescents in the United Kingdom, and that juvenile offenders with severe mental health problems were on average less likely to re-offend when they had participated in MST in Washington State, and further, that the positive effects of MST on behavior problems persisted over time in a non-English-speaking Norwegian community (Butler, Baruch, Hickey, & Fonagy, 2011). Likewise, when implemented with high levels of model adherence, FFT was found to reduce recidivism among juvenile offenders in community-based settings in the United States and Ireland (Graham, Carr, Rooney, Sexton, & Satterfield, 2014; Sexton & Turner, 2010).

BEING A SCIENTIST-PRACTITIONER-BASED FAMILY PSYCHOLOGIST

The embodiment of science in clinical practice is the scientist-practitioner model, a central core of training and practice of psychology since its inception (Hilgard et al., 1947; Raimy, 1950). This model espouses and aspires to the integration of science and practice, and is relevant to both new professionals entering the field and seasoned practitioners. According to Belar and Perry (1992), the goals of the scientist-practitioner model are critical thinking and bridging the gap between scientific foundations and professional practice. Jones and Mehr (2007) identified three vital assumptions at the core of the scientist-practitioner model. The first is the expectation that psychologists will develop the requisite knowledge and skills to create and consume scientific knowledge and develop through the methods of clinical research proficiency in facilitating effective psychological services. The second assumption is that research is necessary in order to develop a knowledge base of what constitutes successful practice. The third assumption is that direct involvement in both clinical practice and research activities creates an interaction effect for the study of important social issues. In short, the ideal realization of the scientist-practitioner model is a professional who is directed by systematic scientific methods for the development and enhancement of practice, with the best interest of the client as the primary focus (Jones & Mehr, 2007).

In reality, being a scientist-practitioner is not an easy role to take on. It assumes that the findings, from various types of process and outcome studies and wide-ranging types of studies of clients, therapists, and the clinical change process, can be integrated into the clinical decision-making processes of a practitioner. The successful scientist-practitioner must be a practitioner who can consume the broad and vast knowledge of science to find guidance in the clinical treatment process. Thus, translating science into practice assumes a very complex set of research and clinical knowledge and skills put to use in clinical decision making. Furthermore, with the growth in research findings, a practitioner is no longer able to stay informed on current research by reading a few journals each month. In fact, estimates are that it would take 627.5 hours each month to stay up to date with all relevant research (Walker & London, 2007). To be successful, the scientist-practitioner must be able to translate the language of research into a way that answers and informs questions about his or her particular practice. To do so, he or she must have an understanding of what research is helpful, how to consume it well, and how to understand its limitations. We approach this later by suggesting levels of intervention and levels of evidence as the knowledge base for the successful translation of science into practice.

We suggest that the practical difficulties translating science to clinical practice have more to do with the manner in which the two domains are linked together or the space between science and practice. Considered in this way, it is the process of translating between these domains that has

Table 4.1 Levels of Evidence for Family Interventions

Levels of Evidence	Level 1	Level 2	Level 3
	Evidence-Informed Treatment/Interventions	*Promising Techniques, Interventions, Programs*	*Evidence-Based Treatment Programs*
Programs and interventions	Adjunctive family psychoeducation	Adolescent Transition Program (ATP)	Cognitive behavioral therapy (CBT)
	Behavioral family-based intervention	Chicago Parent Program COACHES	Multidimensional family therapy
	Fast Track Group Based Family Therapy	Coaching our acting our children	Multisystemic therapy (MST)
	Group individual family treatment (GIFT)	CONNECT— Parent Groups	Parent-Child Interaction Therapy
	Group-intensive family training (GIFT)	COPE Family Strengthening Program	Families in Transition—FIT Family Check-Up (FCU)
	Medical family therapy parents who care	General Family Therapy	Parent-Focused Intervention
	supportive expressive therapy	Intensive Family Therapy	Parent Management Training
	Systems-integrated family therapy (SIFT)	Mediation Training	Attachment-Based Family Therapy
		Solution-Focused STEPP	Functional Family Therapy
		Strengthening Families Program	Incredible Years
		General "Family Focused" Treatment	Triple-P Positive Parenting
		General Parent Training	KEEP
			Oregon Social Learning Center—PMTO

not been well defined by conceptual models or realized in the competencies that may accompany models. It is unlikely that a new model (e.g., scientist-educator) is needed, but instead, we will discuss a more comprehensive definition of the scientist-practitioner model and identify and describe the basic and expert competencies of translating science into practice. We approach this problem by highlighting two primary aspects of conceptual model levels of evidence and levels of practice that link and help move information between these domains in a way that results in better overall treatment.

Table 4.1 illustrates what can be learned when a level of evidence approach is used within the scientist-practitioner model. In Table 4.1, Sexton and Gordon (2009) took the guidelines for evaluating evidence for family psychology (Sexton et al., 2011) and applied them to current practice programs in family psychology. Those with the strongest evidence produce the most reliable programs suggesting that if done correctly, they will result in outcomes similar to those in the foundational research. Those with the weakest evidence have less reliability and validity for use as clinical intervention programs.

THE RESEARCH-PRACTICE DIALECTIC

There is probably no place in family psychology that more clearly demonstrates dialectic than the tensions found between research and practice. The long-standing research-practice gap that includes the current debates and controversies surrounding the use of evidence-based treatment and scientifically based clinical treatment protocols suggests that, while a noble aspiration, the true realization of the scientist-practitioner model has been elusive and largely unrealized as a central construct in psychology. Instead, many professionals have come to identify themselves as *either* scientists or practitioners. This split is actually quite understandable. Scientists generally focus on the nomothetic (group and similarities) level of information, while practitioners have a more ideographic (individual and unique) focus. Over time, these different areas of primary focus have increased the difference between the scientist and practitioner roles. The increasing research-practice gap has even given rise to calls to redefine the central scientist-practitioner model of training in psychology established at the Boulder Conference on Graduate Education in Clinical Psychology in 1949 to be more focused on scholar-practitioner or educator-practitioner models (Committee on Training in Clinical Psychology, 1947; Raimy, 1950).

The nature of the gap between research and practice can be summed up by the tension found between science and art. We want to suggest that

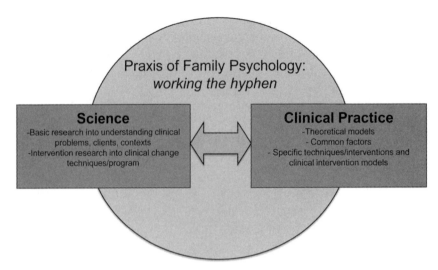

Figure 4.3 "Working the hyphen"

family psychology is both an art and a science and that the gap is a dialectic tension. In previous chapters, we have described dialectic as the tension found between oppositional constructs. The common approach to resolving that tension has been to take an either/or stance, choosing one construct or the other, such as science or practice. A second very Western approach is to embrace the Hegelian notion of dialectic, which is to seek resolution of tension through the sublation of one construct by the other, absorbing aspects of the negated construct, and creating a synthesized construct that more closely hews to a both/and stance. Conceptualizing science as an evidence-based activity and practice as an evidence-based treatment activity has largely pursued this kind of reconciliation of tension in science and practice. That is, the domain of science is to research verifiable generalized treatment options (nomothetic), and the domain of practice is to implement those treatment options in a way that upholds the unique aspects of the client system being seen (ideographic).

Hegelian dialectic is still bound by categorization, however; that is, the resolution of tension is to be found in synthesizing thesis and antithesis. We want to suggest a more Eastern approach, which does not require resolution at all between science and practice, rather simple harmony between the domains. In this way, there is no need to reconcile the scientist-practitioner model into, say, a local clinical scientist model, nor do we have to write off the clinician programmer model as unscientific. What we realize in emphasizing harmony is that, in the same way that music and algebra are both expressions of mathematics, research and practice are both expressions of science; in fact, there is no difference between art and science except in how they are perceived and expressed.

Family psychology is uniquely constituted in its systems epistemology to embrace the science of research and practice as aspects of a whole. The family psychologist is a translator, so to speak, moving knowledge into action with a particular client at a particular time in a unique context. Attention to the translation between research and practice is the mark of a good scientist, given the central role of scientific research in the understanding and practice of the wide range of activities that fall under the umbrella of professional psychology. Furthermore, identifying the competencies that science and practice share provides a base that is far stronger than one conceptualized as linkages between the two; this requires a conceptual shift away from viewing science and practice as distinct domains toward one that considers them as aspects of the same construct. We suggest that research and practice are, in fact, different sides of the same coin, each bringing a unique perspective to understanding the same process of client change. Thus, both the accumulated knowledge of methodologically sound and systemic science and expertly conducted clinical practice are necessary, and neither is sufficient to bring the best available treatments to the clients who seek services (Sexton, Gordon, Gurman, Lebow, Holtzworth-Monroe, & Johnson, 20011). Considered in this way, research and practice in psychology are both reflections of science and art and their relationship is critical to the success of each; recognition of this fact offers the potential to overcome the largely artificial gap between them. What is interesting is that at the end of the day, like algebra and music, the underlying processes of research and clinical practice are very much alike.

CONCLUSIONS: WHAT IS NEXT?

Grappling with how to use and integrate research into your work is sometimes harder than it seems, and navigating the research practice gap is not always easy. You will meet many that struggle with research findings, particularly when they do not match their preconceived and cherished beliefs. The skepticism is warranted. It is not easy to integrate the complexity of studying increasingly comprehensive treatment interventions (from interventions to treatment programs), increasing specificity of client problem (from broad to specific), and increasing specificity of the agency or system contexts in which practice takes place. In addition, there is more than just treatment to consider. For example, the person of the therapist is an equally important feature in the delivery of any clinical intervention or treatment program. However, despite research's dynamic and ever-changing nature, complexity, and sometimes difficult fit with practice, it is still provides the guiding principles for family psychologists. As we noted in Chapter 1, it is one of the three founding pillars of the profession. The complexities do not mean that research is not a substantive and valuable source of information for you in clinical treatment and policy development. It would be nice if it were easy; but the joy of working from a systems epistemology is in learning to hold and work with multiple dimensions at one time. Some of those dimensions will lend themselves to integration, while others will need to be held and worked with while in dynamic tension.

Our assumption is that it is good to have an evidence base for what therapists do in clinical practice with clients. In some areas, there is clear evidence that should guide practice. In other areas, there is no treatment that fits; in that area, clinicians should look at how the available relevant empirical evidence can inform treatment. If there is none, practitioners should use the most well-established common factors established by the field and use practice to field test new and innovative approaches in order to promote growth in the field.

In the next section, we switch directions and focus on the maps that guide the process of the clinical practice of family psychology. The section begins with a "mapping of the territory," where we focus on the common principles of systemic family psychology practice. In the chapters that follow that foundation, we address assessment and case planning, and family-specific and couple-specific clinical interventions.

Section II

The Clinical Practice of Family Psychology

Chapter 5

Mapping the Territory of Clinical Practice

A map does not just chart, it unlocks and formulates meaning; it forms bridges between here and there, between disparate ideas that we did not know were previously connected.

—Reif Larsen

It is in the clinical practice of family psychology that theory and research come together to identify how couples develop clinical problems and the most useful and effective ways to intervene to help promote positive change. When research and theory come together to yield reliable and clinically useful models, maps are the tools needed to translate the topography of the in-between spaces of research and theory into the complex tableau of the therapeutic relationship. It is in the interactional therapist/client system that the therapist translates research models and theoretical approaches into useful interventions. In doing this kind of work, the family psychologist must not only know what to do, but also how to constantly adapt to the client system's unique terrain, the contingent and evolving needs of the therapeutic relationship as therapy moves forward.

In the clinical world of family psychology, the *map* metaphor is useful. Think of the family psychology clinical map as a pathway, which when followed and navigated well, given the complexities of who is on the journey and the variety of conditions, will result in positive and noticeable change for clients. Every historical and current evidence-based model of family psychology offers a map to follow. As students of cartography use a variety of maps such as topographical maps, thematic maps, road maps, political maps, and population maps, depending on the need, so must each theoretical map in family psychology have its unique focus and emphasis in regard to the lens through which clients, relationships, and clinical problems are viewed. Each theoretical map has a different perspective on the goals and processes of treatment, yet, there are also common core elements in every theoretical family psychology map that are based on systemic principles that govern all couple and family psychology intervention approaches. It is true that some models may focus on particular elements of what we present here, while other models choose different elements. What is common among these approaches are the relational, intervention, and process features of the clinical change process.

The very features that make family psychology unique are the same ones that make mapping the territory of therapeutic change complex. Consider the number of variables: therapy is a complex interaction of the client, the therapist, the context, and the history and nature of the issue or problem. Systems thinking/theory is a useful and functional tool to map the territory of therapeutic change because of its focus on context, process, and relational interactions in a format that is comprehensive and coherent. In fact, systems theory is what brings coherence and comprehensiveness to the territory of change in family psychology. Knowing the complexity and systemic nature of the process of change allows the family psychologist to be more specific, effective, and humble about where and how to intervene.

Just as in theory and research, systemic thinking provides an important foundation for the science of mapping the complex territory of clinical change process. The goal is to describe the core elements and the tensions inherent in a systemic view of change as well as the ecological focus of family psychology clinical treatment. Using the map metaphor, we end the chapter by taking a dynamic view of therapy, focusing on the core tasks and goals of early, middle, and late stages of the process of change in couple and family treatment.

MAPPING THE TERRITORY OF THERAPEUTIC CHANGE IN FAMILY PSYCHOLOGY

To be clinically useful, a family psychology map would need to have a number of features. It would need to be *purposeful*. That means that the map would have *goals* and *objectives* that are like checkpoints along the way to successful change. The map would also need to be *directional*.

The map must provide guidance and information in a utilitarian manner on the twists and turns along the way. A useful family psychology map is *goal oriented*; it has a starting point and ending point, providing guidance through the early to middle to final phases of treatment. Successful maps are *specific* and *relevant* and provide therapists with skills and markers along the way to ensure that the trip is going as planned and in just such a manner; family psychology theories provide an outline of the course of treatment with relevant outcome markers along the way.

Early systemic theories took a simple approach, targeting discrete actions to be dealt with in single sessions. The goal of early theory was to dislodge and disrupt the homeostatic functioning of the family, turning up the heat in an attempt to force the family's relational system to function differently. Current systemic clinical models bring a dynamic, relational, and multifaceted perspective to the common features of all treatments: assessment, alliance building, problem formulation, goal setting, intervention, and termination. These models are systemic treatment plans that consider change as an epigenetic process with each phase building on the one before (Sexton, 2010). A systemic view of therapeutic change includes four components critical for truly understanding the therapeutic territory (Sexton & Stanton, 2015):

- *Relational* factors refer to the interactions and relationships between participants.
- *Purposeful interventions* of the family psychologist theory/model, technique, or intervention. These are the active change mechanisms intended to facilitate change in the client system.
- *Change process.* Although process is the least understood and least discussed aspects of change, it is likely one of the most important. Understanding and mapping the most effective clinical change process requires implementation of theory and experience wedded with solid research. Successful clinical change is far more than a static intervention or simply establishing a strong therapeutic alliance. Rather, it is a systematic series of steps and stages through which the family psychologist and the client system progress together. The early stages of clinical treatment develop a therapeutic relationship that enhances change, the middle stages initiate timely and considered clinical interventions, and the ending stage consists of generalizing change made in the therapeutic setting and ongoing stabilization and maintenance of change.
- *Evidence*-based treatment is a map of change, guided by systematic and reliable clinical information about individual, couple, and family

behaviors, relational patterns, supporting narratives, and beliefs guiding the ongoing process of treatment from multiple perspectives.

A systemic view that emphasizes the ecological, the dialectic, the systemic, the contextual, and the functional provides a scaffolding for organizing and effecting the most efficient approach to lasting change. A systemic perspective brings a dynamic, relational, and multifaceted perspective to the common features of all treatments: assessment, alliance building, problem formulation, goal setting, intervention, and termination. In fact, in some current systemic treatments, interventions consider treatment not to be discrete circumscribed practices but unfolding systemic plans that consider change as an epigenetic phase process, with each phase building on the one before (Sexton, 2010).

We have referred to a multifaceted perspective in understanding a family psychology approach to the dynamics of change in clinical treatment. Sexton, Ridley, and Kleiner (2004) have proposed a bridging model that views the therapeutic process as a multi-layer change process that recognizes systemic complexity and the reciprocity of various factors that comprise therapy. This comprehensive model recognizes the systemic complexity and reciprocity of various factors in the therapeutic process.

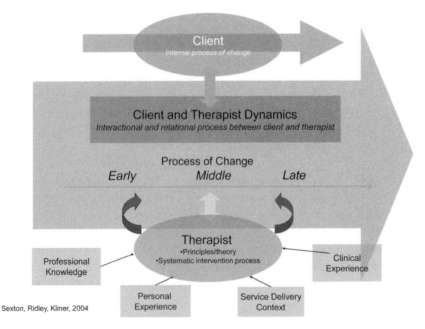

Figure 5.1 Components of clinical change

Each of the specific models of systemic treatment has a unique treatment intervention approach that is consistent with the clinical mechanisms of various treatment models. However, there are also a number of common interventions that are shared across specific approaches that illustrate the breadth and diversity of systemic clinical interventions. In the following sections, we focus on the common ways in which systemic approaches view core components of clinical treatment including the role of the therapist, the therapeutic alliance, the formulation of treatment goals, and common clinical interventions. Within the clinical treatment context, there are three primary components: the therapist, the client system, and the relationship created between them.

Role of the Therapist

Systemic intervention models consider the therapist to be a central part of a treatment *system* that also involves the client system(s), the treatment model, and the relational interactions in the room as the treatment is being implemented. The therapist plays an important role beyond the personal characteristics he or she brings to the dyad or system. Sexton (2007) suggests that the therapist functions "as both an independent factor and a key link within the therapy process" (p. 106). As such, the role of the therapist is one of purposeful facilitator of the core mechanisms and processes of change, adapting and adjusting the treatment model to the unique idiosyncratic nature of the client or family (Sexton, 2010). Alexander (1998) was one of the first to describe the role of the therapist in systemic treatments as offering a balance between structure and support. In more recent descriptions of the role of the therapist in systemic evidence-based models, Sexton and van Dam (2010) describe it as one that is a dynamic balance between clinical protocol (model structure) and creative relational matching (support) necessary to implement effective treatment.

The systemic therapist as the purveyor of structure and support provides a translation of the clinical model to the client relational system (Sexton, 2007). To do so, the therapist uses many of the common core skills currently associated with good psychotherapy (e.g., alliance, empathy, understanding, and respect) to deliver the change mechanisms of a treatment model. However, these common core skills and relational factors are complicated in systemic practice because there often are multiple clients being seen at any given time and multiple relationships being attended to in every treatment interaction. The tricky part of the therapist's role is to lead, collaborate, and support the whole of the family rather than any individual part. She or he offers *both* support and structure to the direction and purpose of clinical interactions. The singular factor in providing effective treatment is offering support and structure that is balanced in its approach to the formation and use of alliances between the various perspectives reflected by the client system. Sexton and van Dam (2010) described this role as a purposeful facilitator of the core mechanisms and process of change adapting and adjusting the treatment model to the unique structure and process of the client or family.

Client or Clients?

In individual approaches to clinical treatment, identifying the client is simple—it is the person sitting in front of you, seeking your help. In fact, most clinical interventions begin with a concern, complaint, or referral regarding specific signs, symptoms, or behaviors of an individual. One of the immediate features that family psychology brings forward is that presenting signs, symptoms, and behaviors must be considered in light of context: the relational patterns, narratives, and historical background of the individual. As a result, the family psychologist always sees the individual signs, symptoms, and behaviors that often initiate clinical treatment as systemic issues. This means that the problems of individuals are also the problems of the couples and families in which the individual is embedded. In family psychology, the client is the relational system. It is the primary entry point, the primary unit of analysis for assessment and persons in context provide the impetus for treatment. This makes treatment complex in that the family psychologist must balance the issues and agendas of each individual in the client system with the overall goal of what is good for the couple or family (which will have a concomitant positive affect on every individual in system). This is not to say that family psychologists always conduct conjoint or family treatment. It does suggest that the client concern, or the target of therapeutic change, is always put into a broader systemic and relational context.

The Therapeutic Relationship

Probably the most talked-about feature of therapy across all specialties is the therapeutic relationship. On the surface, this relationship is much like other positive and supportive human relationships. It is a relationship in which conversation and discussion promote certain conditions that help the client open up, engage in treatment, develop motivation, and acquire skills that promote change. However, a therapeutic relationship comprises more than a summative factor of the therapist at work on the client; it also includes the interactions, meanings, and influence that make up the space between client and therapist. The therapist and client system interactions are more like those of a family, bound and influenced by the same systemic principles discussed in Chapters 3 and 4. The counseling relationship is composed of relationship rules, patterns, and meanings that, when therapeutic, both set the stage for specific interventions and introduce change mechanisms. What is unique about a systemic lens on the therapeutic relationship is that the relationship itself is recognized to produce a fundamental effect that is both supportive and influential in promoting clients to think, feel, and behave differently.

Clinical Interventions—Common or Specific Factors

There is a major debate between what are called common versus specific factors that influence the course of psychotherapy (Sexton & Stanton, 2015). Duncan et al. (2003) and Sprenkle et al. (1999) were the first to suggest that the discipline of psychology and the field of family therapy were weighted down by a plethora of idiosyncratic change models and should move to consider a common factors model that is client directed and outcome informed. Interestingly, the common factors movement is not new. The idea of common factors in counseling dates back to Saul Rosenzweig's 1936 publication in which he suggested that common factors across schools of psychotherapy are responsible for facilitating change. Since that 1936 publication, we located almost thirty lists of common factors in the psychotherapy literature. For example, Frank (1971) proposed six common factors that produce change: an intensely emotionally charged relationship, a rationale that explains the nature of a client's distress, provision of new information about the sources of the client's problems, strengthening of the client's expectation of help through the therapist's personal qualities, provision of the experience of success, and facilitation of emotional arousal. In recent years, new lists of common factors have emerged that continue to build from these early conceptualizations. Orlinsky and Howard (1986) identified five categories of common factors in the counseling literature: the therapeutic contract, therapeutic interventions, therapeutic bond, client self-relatedness, and therapeutic realizations. Similarly, Grencavage and Norcross (1990) identified five superordinate categories of common factors in the literature: client characteristics, therapist qualities, change processes, treatment structure, and therapeutic relationship. Furthermore, they stated that the most consensual commonalities across all categories accounting for change included the development of a therapeutic alliance (56%), opportunity for catharsis (38%), acquisition and practice of new behaviors (32%), clients' positive expectancies (26%), beneficial therapist qualities (24%), and provision of a rationale for change (24%).

Common factors have also gained support from the conclusions of early qualitative reviews and meta-analyses of both individual psychotherapy and family therapy outcome research. In individual therapy domains, the early meta-analytic studies found individual therapy to be successful (when compared with no-treatment conditions) but were unable to identify differences among the broad theoretical approaches studied (Smith, Glass, & Miller, 1980). These early findings have been replicated in more recent meta-analyses, which also have been unable to quantitatively differentiate the treatment efficacy of traditional schools of therapy. Reviews of marriage and family therapy have resulted in similar findings. The qualitative reviews (Gurman & Kniskern, 1981; Gurman & Kniskern, 1986) and meta-analyses (Hazelrigg, Cooper, & Borduin, 1987) found strong main effects for marriage and family therapy in general; they also were unable to demonstrate or support the differential effectiveness of specific models of practice. Specific models that did have some degree of research support as particularly effective were active or highly directive in nature (Hazelrigg et al. 1987). The most recent meta-analysis of marriage and family therapy research has replicated these earlier findings (Shadish & Baldwin, 2002).

So, there appears to be little question that common factors contribute to effective psychotherapy, whether in individualistic or systemic approaches. The question is whether a common factors model can provide the guidance necessary to do an adequate job of mapping the territory of clinical treatment in a way that enables the family psychologist to navigate complex multilevel interpersonal processes (Sexton, Ridley, & Kleiner, 2004). In our view, it does not and never will as it is currently conceptualized. First, common factors do not change neurology, and people only permanently change when neurology changes. Second, common factors do not provide the directional steps that facilitate change. Common factors provide a milieu or context in which change may occur but do not explain the process of change and therefore leave the clinician at a loss for guidance in the most basic need to know what therapeutic steps to take first, then second, then third, and so on. Sexton and Alexander (2002) argued that, in the midst of facilitating change, clinicians are best served by having comprehensive principles that explain clients and their problems as the basis of a map or set of systematic procedures that describe the process of change. Having conceptual principles allows the therapist to make informed clinical decisions, and a procedural map increases the probability of achieving successful outcome. What a map does is provide direction that increases the efficiency and likelihood of success in the journey. What a map does not do is explain the events of the journey or remove the critical decision making required to overcome unexpected events along the way (e.g., explain all that will happen along the way, where there will be delays). Regardless of the events that occur in any journey, the outcome is greatly facilitated by a directional map. The uniqueness and richness of the journey remains a delightful mystery despite having the road map, for there is no way to know the detours, unique signs, sounds, or events in the process, but a map of the process does allow clinicians to be efficient and responsive to the organic and dynamic needs of the client system and increases the likelihood of successful outcome.

Relational Components of Change

We have noted that common factors influence the change process and that they are necessary but insufficient elements in clinical treatment. They are insufficient in and of themselves because (1) while they provide the milieu in which change may occur, they do not provide direction for facilitating change; and (2) they often cannot adequately address the complexity of multisystem perspectives. This seems somewhat counterintuitive because psychotherapy is, by nature, a relational and interpersonal process. Regardless of the efficacy and logic of a specific clinical intervention, it always takes places in the context of a relationship between participants. Rogers (1970) first focused on what he called the necessary conditions for clinical change embedded within the humanistic tradition in psychology. These factors have become synonymous with good therapy: empathy, positive regard, and congruence. Rogers's core set of therapist characteristics became prominent in the field of psychotherapy during the 1950s and 1960s as a by-product of the popularity of his person-centered therapy (earlier called client-centered therapy).

- *Empathy, congruency, and positive regard.* The importance of therapist empathy cuts across clinical intervention models and approaches. Empathy involves viewing the world through the client's eyes, thinking about things as the client thinks about them, feeling things as the client feels them, and sharing in the client's experiences. The process of expressing empathy relies on the client experiencing the counselor as one who is able to see the world as he or she (the client) sees it. Therapist empathy is also a significant predictor of a strong therapeutic alliance. Positive regard is a feeling in the therapist of unconditional respect, with no conditions on acceptance of the client as a person. Warmth is clearly part of this regard, as is the ability to convey respect.

Congruence refers to the therapist's ability to freely and deeply express him or herself during the course of therapy. Rogers believed that the therapist must be genuine and not deceive the client about his or her feelings. Although many models do not emphasize this quality in the therapist, few therapies are likely to be successful with an incongruent therapist.

- *Respect* is a core attitude that is the basis of any clinical engagement strategy. The dictionary definition is "a feeling of deep admiration for someone or something elicited by his or her abilities, qualities, or achievements" (*Oxford Dictionary*, 2015). *Respect* is more than merely being understood. Instead, respect is being able to acknowledge the struggle of the client system and believing that a couple or family is functioning as well as possible within the circumstances and that they have the ability and resources to make it through. *Respect* means that the therapist goes beyond understanding and empathy to also providing help that is practical, geared toward the unique needs of the couple or family.

- *Hope and expectation of positive change.* Hope is the feeling that the client system has when, after a discussion with a therapist, they believe that things can improve and that working with this therapist in this setting and in this program is worth the expenditure of resources (time, energy, and money). It might provide a way out of a difficult struggle. Hope, as described in this manner, is central to engagement and motivation. Hope comes when the therapist finds evidence of client effort and improvement and positively reinforces it, regardless of how small. Hope comes from a focus on working things out in the here and now rather than trying to find out why there are issues.

Therapeutic Alliance

Over the past 50 years, we have learned that these common factors are important but far from sufficient in producing the foundation of an effective therapeutic change process. In fact, while therapy is built on features common to any healthy relationship (honesty, respect, and strength), therapeutic relationships are also very different. The therapeutic alliance is much more than the support inherent in the common relational factors described earlier. Bordin (1994) was the first to address the possibility that the therapeutic alliance was more than the personal dimensions described by Rogers. He suggested that a successful therapeutic alliance has three components: (1) agreement between patient and therapist on the goals of therapy, (2) agreement that the tasks of therapy will address the problems the patient brings to treatment, and (3) a belief that the quality of the interpersonal bond between the patient and the therapist is sufficient to facilitate change. The creation of these features comes from the relational negotiation between the client system and the therapist.

While it seems to be quite simple, the alliance, as described earlier, is quite complex in the context of couple and family relationships (Sexton & Stanton, 2015). For example, the manner in which views are solicited and validated in family therapy must be conducted with attention to how alliance building with one family member impacts his or her alliance with other family members, and the family system as a whole (Pinsof & Catherall, 1986; Rait, 2000). The common and somewhat simple practice of validating the clients' views and experiences has the added complexity and danger of creating splits where one family member is perceived by other members as having a greater degree of agreement on the goals and tasks of therapy with the therapist than the rest (Pinsof & Catherall, 1986). For example, a therapist was seeing an individual client who discussed her father's alcoholism and wished to confront him. She indicated that the entire family was being adversely affected by the father's condition. The therapist set up a family meeting and asked each family member to indicate why he or she was there. The client began by outlining what she saw as her father's problems with alcohol and its deleterious effect on the family. Clearly, she expected other family members to back her up, but instead, every family member pointed to her as the one in the family causing problems for not accepting her dad and for making waves. Needless to say, the family's view of the therapeutic alliance between the therapist and his client created a significant wrinkle in achieving any kind of useful family intervention. Interestingly, Robbins et al. (2000) found that different alliance profiles are required for the successful application of different types of systemic treatment models. For example, the therapeutic alliance appears to be best achieved in functional family therapy through a balanced relationship with the adolescent and the parents and through a strong relationship with the parents in multidimensional family therapy (Sexton, 2010).

From a systemic perspective, therapeutic alliance requires the therapist to negotiate agreement on the goals and the tasks of therapy among the various stakeholders, form emotional bonds with multiple individuals on multiple levels, and create reciprocal relational processes (Friedlander, Lambert, Valentín, & Cragun, 2008). Friedlander et al. (2011) suggested that successful systemically based therapeutic alliances are based on engagement in the therapeutic process, an emotional connection to the therapist, and safety within the therapeutic system wherein the client system and therapist have a sense of shared purpose in the treatment. It is also important to note that the development of alliance cannot be separated from the overall clinical intervention process. In fact, collaborative alliance creation is a common clinical intervention early in treatment for a number of systemic clinical models, but is not the sine qua non of effective ongoing treatment.

Figure 5.1 illustrates the complexity of the alliance in the context of couple and family therapy. Note that the alliance is only as powerful as the client system perceives it to be. However, in couple and family work, there are multiple clients, each with an individual alliance to the therapist. This means that as one person's alliance grows with the therapist, it may be that another's wanes. In a way, the therapeutic alliance provides a kind of interpersonal alchemy to the clinical change process, because it is not only a feature of the therapeutic relationship but also an intervention in and of itself. The therapeutic alliance offers an opportunity for change, growth, and transformation that is far beyond the contours that research and theory give it. The therapeutic alliance transcends itself when it develops as a therapeutically appropriate attachment relationship. As the alliance facilitates the therapist's provision of the appropriate clinical needs of the client system it mediates, the therapist transitions from evidence-based research and theory into evidence-based practice, where therapist skills

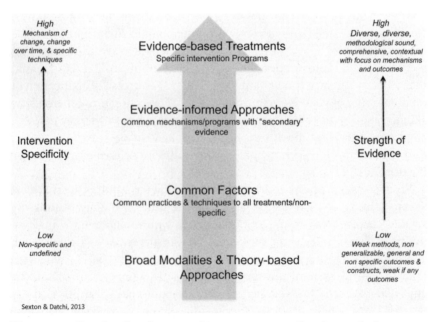

Sexton & Datchi, 2013

Figure 5.2 Levels of evidence and intervention in family psychology

integrate with the client system's individual strengths and family resources to foment change and growth.

CLINICAL INTERVENTIONS IN FAMILY PSYCHOLOGY

It is not uncommon to hear clinical interventions talked about as tools. In fact, a common metaphor is that psychologists are to pick up useful tools (akin to hammers and saws) and put them in an easily accessible tool box where they can be drawn upon when the task at hand calls for a specific tool (intervention). However, in family psychology, interventions are much more than discrete tools. Interventions range from specific purposeful behaviors of the therapist to systematic sets of complex relational steps designed to promote specific change mechanisms known to increase the likelihood for successful treatment outcome.

The treatments and interventions used by family psychologists are the activities/actions of intervention in a therapeutic context for the purpose of helping the client achieve desired goals. Treatment interventions range from singular discrete actions to comprehensive treatment programs that represent increasing levels of both comprehensiveness and specificity: (1) *a technique* (single activity with narrow range of desired outcome); (2) *intervention* (techniques that might go together to achieve a desired outcome); and (3) *treatment program/model* (comprehensive treatments governed by research-based theoretical principles, clinical change processes, change mechanisms, and adherence measures). Those techniques, interventions, or treatment models with the highest level of specificity are most likely to be replicated and therefore have a higher probability of producing clinical reliability.

Each of the specific couple and family therapy models (see Chapters 7 and 8) have their own unique set of therapeutic techniques based on theoretical assumptions, yet there are also common aspects of systemic clinical interventions that address typically seen interaction patterns, belief systems, and broader contextual factors that contribute to the maintenance of clinical problems. Some common interventions aim to disrupt problem-maintaining interaction patterns and build on interactions in which the problem does not occur. Others aim to help family members reauthor their constraining narratives to be more liberating and flexible belief systems and personal and family narratives. Still others aim to modify the negative impact of historical, contextual, or constitutional factors and build on contextual strengths (Carr, 2013). It is important to note that systemic change interventions are frequently part of larger systemic treatment models that have stages of treatment that build on one another over time.

Common Interventions

The following eight clinical interventions are common family psychology approaches to clinical change (Sexton & Datchi, 2014; Sexton & Stanton, 2015). This is not an exhaustive list, but one intended to illustrate the range of clinical interventions that are most common to the specific models under the systemic umbrella. More specific clinical interventions are presented in the chapters on couple and family treatments that follow. In each of those specific approaches, you will see aspects of each of these common factors.

1. Alliance-based relevant and obtainable treatment goals. One implication of the work on therapeutic alliance is that the agreements between the therapist and the client system are not merely administrative but are part of the central relational process. In fact, the very process of developing treatment goals is one factor of an alliance-based relationship between a therapist and a client system. Bordin's conceptualization of effective treatment included the idea that agreement on task and goals were equally as important components as personal connection (as marked by respect, empathy, etc.). Treatment goals are more than simple contracts and agreements. Rather, they represent shared beliefs about the issues or problems to be addressed in treatment and therefore influence engagement in the treatment process.

To get a better idea about this important construct, consider how treatment goals are developed. A systemic view of clinical problems (see Chapter 3) suggests that they go beyond the individual perspective of the client to the larger systemic and ecological context. As human beings, we all have the unique ability to be self-reflective. Social psychology has shown us that the self-reflective process is important to how people consider the problems they experience and the solutions that they believe to be helpful. In fact, by the time a client or client system comes to treatment, they have invested considerable energy and attention toward trying to determine the cause of the problem or issue they are facing and what to do about that problem or issue. Social psychologists attend to the attributions that people make of their problems; to whom they assign responsibility for an event. In that way, clients, like all of us, have a limited perspective in this attribution process. In other words, they are within the context that they are trying to explain. Thus, as humans, they tend to commit the fundamental attribution bias (Runions & Keating, 2007) or the tendency to assign responsibility outside of themselves as the sources of any problems they are experiencing. Using this framework, Sexton (2010) described the problems clients bring to treatment not as goals for therapy but as problem definitions that reflect nothing more than individual perspective. Problem definitions are more than cognitive and attributional processes; they must also contain emotional reactions to the attributions. He promotes subsequent relational sequences and patterns that "fit" and function for the client or client system's view of the problems or issue. Refining these problem definitions into therapeutic goals requires contextualization, reframing, and shaping the problems or issues to fit an overall family frame of reference. Such refinement places clients' individual desires into a relational context that is relationship focused, involving all members of the client system (albeit differently), and it is alliance based (non-blaming).

2. Reframing to promote meaning change. Reframing is one of the most universal therapeutic techniques across all systemic therapies. Initially made popular by the early communication theorists (Watzlawick, Weakland, & Fisch, 1974) and strategic therapies, it has become an almost household word in the realm of family psychology. Reframing is rooted in attribution and information processing constructs of cognitive psychology (Jones & Nisbett, 1971; Kelley, 1971; Taylor, Fiske, Etcoff, & Ruderman, 1978), social influence processes of social psychology (Heppner & Claiborn, 1988), and the more recent systemic (Claiborn & Lichtenberg, 1989) and social constructionist ideas regarding the meaning basis of problem definitions (Gergen, 1995; Friedlander & Heatherington, 1998; Sexton & Griffin, 1997). There are many names for the common forms of reframing, including positive connotation, finding positive intent, and therapeutic interpretation. Regardless of the label or specific method, successful reframing creates alternative cognitive and attributional perspectives that help redefine meaningful events. It thus reduces the negativity and redirects the emotionality surrounding them. The mechanism of reframing involves offering an alternative explanation for the cause of the problem behavior, providing an alternative construction of the problem, or even using humor to imply that all is not what it seems (Sexton, 2010). With reframing, clients are offered a new framework within which to conceptualize a sequence of events, and this new way of conceptualizing the sequence makes it more likely that the problem will be resolved rather than maintained (Carr, 1995). For example, a husband complains that his wife is a nag, constantly complaining about his watching the sports channel and not giving him a moment's peace. The therapist's reframe consists of, "I wonder what it's like to have someone love you so much that she'll risk the label 'nag' in the hope of spending more focused time with you?"

3. Building within system alliance to promote engagement and motivation. Developing within client alliances is a central intervention that helps build client system engagement and motivation to change. The facilitation of trust and agreement on the goals and tasks of therapy is complicated in that family members often present with differing goals, levels of invest-ment in therapy, and conflicting ideas about what exactly will lead to change. Family alliances are promoted by assisting family members in addressing differences in the formation of universal consensus about the description of the problems and the direction to pursue in treatment. In fact, the universal consensus required to set common treatment goals is a method to build and maintain family member alliances, bolstering trust, reducing negativity, and reducing negativity blame between family members and the counselor, thus facilitating a shared sense of purpose (Friedlander et al., 2008). The literature has indicated that facilitating a shared sense of purpose among family members is a useful first step in inviting family members to take risks with new roles and ideas that may eventually lead to meaningful change (Friedlander, Escudero, & Heath-erington, 2006).

4. *Changing relational structures to promote behavior change.* One of the earliest systemic clinical interventions targeted changing the struc-tural orientation of the family. As noted earlier, the structural family therapy approach focused on adjusting the naturally occurring rela-tional triangles involved in maintaining clinical problems (Minuchin, 1974). Therapy involved interrupting the typical family interaction sequence and imposing structural changes including the forming of stronger and more clear boundaries between subsystems and interrupt-ing the detouring and pathological triangles in which the symptomatic individual was caught (Haley, 1976). Although approaches differ in the specific interactions identified and therapeutic strategies recommended for changing interactions (from highly directive to nondirective), all of them provide means of helping couples and families learn to interact in new ways.

5. *Improving interpersonal competencies to maintain change.* All rela-tional interaction patterns involve the ability to communicate, problem solve, and manage conflict, among many other social competencies. As individuals improve at any one of these relational skills, they bring an enhanced ability to maintain positively functioning couple or family inter-actions while poorly developed social skills can either maintain problems or prevent their resolution (Carr, 2013). Competency and skill-building interventions often target the relevant risk and protective factors evident in the client system. Building protective behaviors involves targeting the behavioral skills of client(s) in order to increase their ability to competently perform the myriad of tasks (e.g., communication, parenting, supervision, problem solving, and conflict management) that contribute to successful family functioning. As the risk behaviors decrease, the problematic behav-iors no longer have a functional role in the family relational system. As

family protective factors increase, the client(s) become empowered and build their ability to manage the inevitable new challenges of the future (Sexton, 2010). A good example is when the therapist helps a couple recognize the negative filter that defines their communication (the tendency to only see or hear what you don't like about the other person) and help then rebuild a positive filter, focusing and commenting on the things they like or that are positive about who the other person is and what he or she does.

6. *Externalizing problems and finding exception.* Externalizing is a practice that was developed as part of narrative therapy (White, 1989). It is an intervention that creates a perspective in which the person has a relationship to the problem and in which the person *is* not the problem and the problem is not *inside* the person. Externalizing views problems as coming from outside the person (e.g., in relationships with others, with cultures, with institutions). The goal is to emphasize the problem as outside the person rather than as a characteristic or deficit of the person. Externalizing the problem functions to change the meaning of the problem and, by virtue of separation, helps exercise control over the problem (Roth & Epston, 1996). A good example is when a therapist says, "anorexia is attacking you, how can you fight it off?" The diagnosis is externalized giving the client psychic room to deal with it.

7. *Changing relational patterns through negativity and blame reduction.* Unresolved negative or conflicted family interactions during the course of therapy can lead to poor outcomes and early termination (Alexander, Barton, Schaivo and Parsons, 1976; Friedlander, Wildman, Hetherington, & Skowron, 1994). When negativity and blaming are reduced, more positive interactions occur among family members that contribute to a sense of hope. Blame and negativity have been found to decrease through the use of relational reframing (Robbins et al., 2000). In some current systemic models, the reduction of negativity and blame is a method to reduce the within-family risk factors that prevent change of relational patterns, associated beliefs, and other contextual factors. As a result, the systemic reduction of blame and negativity is an early stage goal of systemic treatment that, when successful, reduces barriers to further change (Sexton & Alexander, 2003).

8. *Relapse prevention to maintain change.* During therapy, clients build a growing sense of perceived control over situations that were previously marked by anguish, anger, negativity, and blame. With each subsequent success, individual and collective family perceptions of self-efficacy grow. This upward spiral continues until the family or family member experiences a high-risk situation that poses a threat to their perceived control and decreases self-efficacy, eventually increasing the

probability of relapse. If a slip does occur, it is not uncommon to experience a sense of cognitive dissonance that may promote the adoption of a more individual and blaming attribution, increasing the likelihood that a full-blown relapse will occur (Sexton, 2010). Relapse prevention helps make the changes accomplished in therapy part of new interactional patterns that can resist future challenges resulting in relational stability that will maintain the new behaviors. When a person copes effectively with a high-risk situation, he or she is likely to experience an increased sense of self-efficacy. As the duration of new behaviors increases, families have the experience of effectively coping with one high-risk situation after another, and the probability of relapse decreases significantly.

PROCESS OF CHANGE

Clinical tools, such as the ones summarized earlier, are useful only as they fit the particular needs of the client(s) for facilitating the change process. Accordingly, successful systemic practice involves both the structure of a theoretical map to guide the therapist and family through relational change mechanisms and therapist creativity to adroitly match the appropriate theoretical model to client needs (Sexton & van Dam, 2009).

For example, in early sessions, the primary goals are usually problem formulation and systemic, family-based, collaborative goal setting. In the early stage of treatment, it is important to intervene to interrupt relational patterns, narratives, and beliefs that get in the way of forming collaborative family-based perspectives on the problems and goals of treatment. Accomplishing these early tasks prepares clients to be motivated and ready to take on the next phase. In the middle phase of treatment, specific interventions focus on a variety of prosocial skill-building, belief, and narrative changes that interfere with the solving of the presenting concern(s). In the final stage of treatment, the foundations of a common problem formulation and an improved repertoire of relational skills marshaled in the pursuit of changing repetitive patterns serve to reinforce and maintain therapeutic change and generalize new ways of coping to new problems found in the client's broader system (Sexton, 2010). Many of the current evidence-based models of treatment have incorporated a similar temporal process that includes evidence-based change mechanisms to systematic clinical protocol (Sexton et al., 2013). For example, functional family therapy follows a three-phase approach of engagement and motivation, behavior change, and generalization (Sexton, 2010). Similarly, multidimensional family therapy employs a five-stage approach (Liddle & Diamond, 1991).

Early Phases: Formulating Problems and Treatment Goals

In the earliest stages of any FP treatment, therapist and couple/family have to form a relationship that is defined by the roles described earlier. Within the supportive and relational core conditions of any good therapeutic relationship, there is also a purpose and set of goals to accomplish. The goals are the important first steps of change regardless of the client, problem, or therapist. These early sessions of any family psychology clinical intervention have a number of specific goals:

- Engagement and motivation
- Therapeutic alliance
- Understanding of client, relationship, and context through assessment
- Goal setting that is obtainable, relevant, and functional

In systemic treatment, clear definitions of clinical problems and treatment goals are more than a negotiated contract and agreement between therapists and client. Instead, formulating problems and treatment goals are mutually constructive processes where developing treatment goals engages the client(s) making therapy relevant to them and helps begin the change process by building between family member alliances, spur rudimentary problem solving, and enable conflict management. To be therapeutic, problem formulation needs to include (1) information the family has discussed in the sessions through systemic and thematic guesses and hypotheses offered by the therapist and (2) framing of this material in ways that are motivating to the family, engaging them to reshape beliefs that may contribute to the family being stuck (Sexton, 2010). This approach opens up possibilities when each family member's wishes and needs are respected as they articulate the differences and similarities between their positions in considerable detail, while the therapist invites them to explore goals to which they can ultimately agree.

When achieved, these early phase goals set the stage for further and more specific interventions. It is important to note that the accomplishment of these goals goes beyond setting the stage for the future. Instead, when accomplished through the collaborative work of the therapist and couple or family, the outcomes are significant changes in the relational climate, an openness and investment in the treatment process, and a willingness to change and try new, albeit yet to be defined changes.

Middle Phase: Specific Interventions to Accomplish Treatment Goals

The middle phase of family psychology treatment builds and expands on the relational foundation and client changes of the early phase to specifically accomplish treatment goals. This phase is constructed around a comprehensive understanding and formulation of the clinical concerns. Specific clinical interventions purposefully target the beliefs, patterns, and organization of the relational system in which the specific problem exists. Specific change techniques are focused on helping change the relational conditions to promote changes in presenting problems. For example, a couple might be encouraged by their therapist to make changes in how they communicate with each other or in how they negotiate house rules. Family psychologists need to be conversant with specific techniques to promote improved communication, negotiation, problem-solving, and other prosocial relational skills. Successful change in this phase has as much to do with how the therapist promotes implementation as it is in what techniques and skills are implemented. What this means is that the therapist adjusts, adapts, and makes ongoing changes as he or she better understands appropriate fit of the mechanisms of change to the uniqueness of the couple or family. Successful family psychology interventions are ones that are adapted and adjusted to fit the couple or family, rather than requiring the family to adjust to something that does not fit their unique way of functioning. In this way, the middle phase of any treatment is about both using the best intervention for the problem and implementing those in ways that match the couple or family.

Ending Treatment: Consolidating and Maintaining Change

From a systemic perspective, clinical change is complex not only because it requires finding and implementing the best mechanisms to promote desired outcomes, but also because any change is always subject to the homeostatic forces of relational systems that, in promoting stability, naturally resist change. This means that the significant and important changes made in earlier phases of treatment must not only be maintained, but also be consolidated, stabilized and generalized such that they become the new stable relational system of the couple or family.

CONCLUSIONS AND WHAT IS NEXT?

These unique features of family psychology practice are connected to research and theory through the ecological, systemic, dialectical, and functional threads that weave amongst them. The *ecological* thread is represented by our approach recognizing the multiple domains of therapeutic change that impact at intrapersonal, interpersonal, and environmental levels. Clinical practice is constrained and encouraged by individual traits, family patterns of interaction, and environmental features such as therapy payment systems and organizational delivery systems (e.g., managed care). The clinical work of family psychology is also *systemic* in that it involves the very same relational patterns, meaning systems, and relational structures and organization of any relational system. Systemic change process is also *dialectic*al as a supportive, understanding, respectful relationship environment as well as a purposeful, influential, and professional environment that has little resemblance to a close personal relationship. Clients who seek the services of family psychologists receive care that goes well beyond what could be achieved through a singular focus on clinical experience or research to achieve competent clinical decision making and considered therapeutic interventions. Therapy is a *functional* process in which a family psychologist manages multiple client constellations within a client system and a complex process of interpersonal interactions that engages clients, builds alliances, and shapes obtainable and functional goals that are designed to improve problematic conditions, symptoms, or concerns.

It is important to note that despite the aspirational goal of making clinical change scientific and effective, it is far more complex and much remains unknown. Not knowing the answers to what makes change, work should not deter you. Over time, the field will know more. Yet, we are likely never to know and fully understand everything. As family psychologists, you will be best served by mapping the clinical territory by way of the core elements of science, research, theory, and clinical wisdom. In fact, the APA (2006) task force on evidence-based practice suggested that best treatments are a combination of the best available research evidence, the judgment and experience of the clinician, and the applicability of the interventions to the patient's client(s) values and goals.

The next three chapters build on these core ideas focusing on a systematic model for individual, couple, and family assessment and clinical intervention program theories that are theoretically sound and evidence based.

Chapter 6

Case Planning and Clinical Assessment

A painter told me that nobody could draw a child by studying the outlines of its form merely, but by watching for a time his motions and plays, the painter enters into his nature and can then draw him at every attitude.

—Ralph Waldo Emerson

In couple and family treatment, there are often seemingly magical moments that occur in which the therapist says just the right thing at the right time in the right way. There is a paradigm shift in the therapeutic interaction that foments healing. Similarly, there are moments when the client hears or experiences something during the therapeutic interaction that illuminates a way through barriers that have prevented a solution, opening the way to move forward. As magical and profound as the clinical interventions of family psychology may seem and as fine-tuned as the collective clinical wisdom is of the profession, all good treatment is actually based on underlying systematic and comprehensive assessment and case planning.

In family psychology, the goal of assessment is to understand current individual, family, and/or couple functioning and the systems that maintains areas of concern. Through an analysis of the client's core patterns, beliefs, and contexts of the relational and social systems assessment can point to the inner logic or rationale for symptomatic behavior. Given the complexity of the task, assessment in psychology is often a combination of clinical subjective observation and objective measurement. Interestingly, systemic theories have always been a poor fit with traditional nomothetic assessment and diagnostic models. In fact, early couple and family therapy intervention models were based on a rejection of what was perceived to be radical objectivism, linear causality, and reductionism in traditional diagnostic and assessment process. Instead, early systemic clinical models focused more on here-and-now interactions and descriptions of relational processes rather than individual clusters of behavioral characteristics or scores on standardized measures. While family therapists still maintain a reactive stance to objective assessment, leaning heavily on subjective clinical judgment, family psychology has split the difference. Research is clear that objective assessment leads to more accurate diagnosis, but clinical judgment is useful as well (Dawes, Faust, & Meehl, 1989). This point has often been seen as a feature that differentiates family psychology and marriage and family therapy. However, the ecological nature of family psychology, which requires assessment of nested systems (intrapersonal, interpersonal, and environmental), is more suited to a depth approach in the assessment process, one that is not only nomothetic (objective) but ideographic as well (subjective or unique to the particular client system). Qualitative assessment, including an in-depth analysis of a client's family of origin, can provide useful diagnostic and case formulation material not found in more generalized objective approaches.

Today's family psychology assessment measures a range of factors, from those that focus on family process (e.g., cohesion, warmth, support, supervision, and other risk factors) to those that measure family and couple relationships, individual symptoms, and even the ongoing process of therapy itself. While assessment and treatment may seem to be orthogonal to research given that research tends to emphasize the nomothetic and clinical assessment emphasizes the ideographic, the fact is, research and assessment are two sides of the same coin. Family psychologists are scientists, and the clinical scientist, like the research scientist, operates on the basis of hypothesis generation and testing. The purpose of clinical and objective assessment, drawn from the initial referral, intake and testing, is to give the clinician data from which to make relevant hypotheses that will then inform treatment (Goodheart, Kazdin, & Sternberg, 2006). Hypotheses are shaped, interpreted, and reshaped in light of new information. Hypothesis generation occurs throughout the course of therapy, making family psychology distinctly scientific in its approach to the human condition.

Our goal in this chapter is to provide an overview of the two essential aspects of clinical treatment: assessment and case planning. Assessment and case planning are important during treatment by helping to pinpoint those areas of adjustment and adaptation needed to help meet the individual needs of the client system. Comprehensive lists of assessment measures and techniques can be found in other more specific sources (Beavers,

Hampson, & Hulgus, 1990; Fischer & Corcoran, 2007; Holahan & Moos, 1983). Here we illustrate the systemic epistemological scaffolding into which current and future assessment measures fit. The chapter begins by considering the role of assessment and clinical case planning in the practice of family psychology, and then focuses specifically on a systemic approach to assessment and case planning.

THE ROLE OF CLINICAL ASSESSMENT AND CLINICAL CASE PLANNING

At first glance, it is easy to think about psychological assessment as analogous to medical tests and medical diagnosis; symptoms lead to diagnostic tests that pinpoint a problem that can be addressed with a specific treatment leading to a cure. Psychological processes, particularly in family and couple work, are actually more complex. Understanding relational systems involves an understanding of not only the internal processes of one individual but also the relational connections that link each person in the couple or family. This means that assessment must take into account information garnered from multiple perspectives that must then be shaped and interpreted by the therapist in a manner that makes the material meaningful and useful for diagnosis and treatment. To that end, there are a number of core principles that differentiate family psychology's systemic perspective on assessment from the type of assessment that might be performed by a clinician working from the medical model. Clinical assessment in family psychology is:

- *A dynamic and relational process* that begins the moment treatment commences and doesn't end until the final interaction. It involves a collaborative process between multiple stakeholders in order to accomplish therapeutic objectives.
- *Ideographic* and *nomothetic*, meaning that both individual client characteristics and the broader norms and group-based standards are important in the assessment process.
- *A multisystemic process* that must go beyond understanding intrapersonal factors inherent in individuals to include significant interpersonal relationships and relevant environmental factors that impact individuals and the client system as a whole.

While individual assessment may include psychosocial functioning, development, psychiatric, medical, and academic histories, family assessment understands these areas of assessment as components of a greater whole. That is, developing a map of the client(s) requires that the family psychologist hold up a different lens through which to view the client(s), providing different levels of information. Typically, as clients relay their story to the therapist, they focus on the need for the significant people in their lives to change how they think, feel, or behave. In individual assessment, the therapist must take the word of the client who is the only one present, However, in family assessment, the therapist actually has the data for family functioning right in front of him or her, directly observing functional and dysfunctional interpersonal exchanges, as well as thought processes, affect, and the individual and corporate behavior of the client(s). In family assessment, interpersonal dynamics increase exponentially with the multiple relationships present in the therapy office. For example, with a therapist and one client present, there are two directions for interpersonal exchange. With the addition of another person in the room, the number of potential interpersonal pathways increases to 9, and with 4 people in the room, the number increases to 16. The complexity of potential exchanges requires that the therapist be more directive than he or she normally might be in individual therapy (Patterson et al., 1998).

A systemic perspective recognizes that assessment and case planning also contribute to the clinical change process.

- A systemic perspective provides essential *feedback* to the family psychologist with regard to how to fit interventions to the unique contours of the client/family/couple, how treatment is progressing, and what the impact of treatment is having on the client. For example, at one time, substance abuse treatment was done strictly with individuals, with a common artifact of treatment being the destruction of the client's significant relationships (Goldberg, 1985). The substance abuse field began to recognize the need to consider not only the intrapersonal factors of treatment, but also the interpersonal factors; today individual, couple, and family treatment is common in substance abuse case planning.
- A systemic perspective is a central part of *treatment planning* because it helps pinpoint individual, relational, and contextual risks and protective factors that may contribute to clinical problems of clients or offer avenues for positive change.
- A systemic perspective is a method that *enhances therapeutic motivation*. The clinical interview serves as a way to both assess functioning and at the same time collaboratively formulate a treatment plan that is, in and of itself, therapeutic. The collaborative formulation of problems not only creates an accurate and multidimensional understanding of the nature of the client's concerns, but also enhances treatment by building engagement and motivation through the therapeutic alliance. Crafting a common perspective by family members on concerns

also creates within family alliances that constitute an integral part of therapeutic change.

- A systemic perspective provides *a scaffold* for entertaining multiple assessment perspectives that is both objective and subjective, as well as encouraging methods that provide information at multiple levels of the client system—the intrapersonal, interpersonal, and the environmental. For example, an individual clinician might treat a client's phobia about driving by conducting a traditional functional analysis of the client's behavior and in the end provide a case plan that utilizes traditional cognitive behavioral interventions such as relaxation, breathing, and systematic desensitization. However, a systems approach is going to include interpersonal information, and that information informs the therapist that the phobia started during an argument between the client and her husband, and when she tried to leave, he forcibly took her car keys from her and threw them up into the bushes. This places effective case planning and treatment in a different light, understanding the individual phobia stems from interpersonal dynamics, with the recognition that there will be a need for a focus on couple as well as individual issues.

Clinical Assessment

There are three primary domains of assessment in family psychology practice: (1) diagnostic focus on the client, couple, or family; (2) process focus aimed at assessing and tracking the process and impact of treatment itself; and (3) outcome assessment or the determination of whether or not the treatment was successful.

In each area, the goal of assessment is not to determine what is right or wrong, but to understand the potential risks and protective factors that may stand in the way or promote success in achieving the goals of treatment. In Chapter 3, we focused on the theoretical foundations of the risk and protective factors perspective. In family psychology, a biopsychosocial assessment approaches family psychotherapy with a "gradual linking of specific types of family communication patterns to the occurrence of specific individual psychiatric disorders" (Miklowitz & Clarkin, 2003, p. 357). Additionally, biopsychosocial assessment will uncover family members' individual strengths and family resources, which may be capitalized upon in treatment. Assessment should occur at multiple levels of the family system (Grovetant & Carlson, 1989; Snyder, Cavell, & Heffer, 1995).

1. *Diagnostic assessment* is focused on understanding the client(s) and the clinical concerns, level of functioning, and the nature and interaction

of significant relationships. Assessment also focuses on clusters of behaviors (taken early on to help better understand the client's functioning and relevant clinical issues). Frequently, this type of assessment focuses on clinical symptoms such as depression and/or relational conflict. However, to be systemic, diagnostic assessment needs to go beyond behaviors or symptoms to view concerns from ecosystemic and systemic contexts including historical/transgenerational influences, relational patterns, contextual/ecological risk and protective factors, beliefs/narratives, and attributions.

As we have noted, there are two aspects of psychotherapy assessment: formal objective assessment and subjective clinical observation. Snyder et al. (1995) suggest approaching family assessment from the perspective of levels of systems: individual, dyadic, nuclear, and extended family systems. These systems should not be treated modally, but in concert, recognizing the recursive nature of sociality, with each subsystem affected by and affecting the others.

In many ways, the goal of diagnostic assessment is to understand what each individual brings to the table, and how individual influences may shape and influence the relational patterns of the couple or family unit. Common factors that contribute in such ways are patterns of clients' previous relationships that might set the stage for their beliefs and narratives and shape the contours of their behavioral patterns. In addition, each client brings biological and physiological predispositions that influence response and processing of information.

2. *Process assessment* consists of an ongoing, consistent evaluation of therapy as it progresses through time. Process as an assessment variable is currently gaining much attention in the field (Bickman 2005; Pinsof, 2013; Sexton, Patterson, & Datachi, 2012) and while all good treatment involves gaining feedback from clients, current models of process assessment involve the use of questionnaires given as an ongoing part of treatment that measure various therapeutic factors that are necessary for longer-term outcomes. For example, therapeutic alliance is needed in any good treatment episode. Ongoing measurement of the therapeutic alliance from the perspective of client stakeholders all aid the therapist in evaluating whether client needs are being met or whether there is need for adjustment. Process assessment also involves the ongoing measurement of the client's perspective regarding therapy progress. Progress information gives the therapist the opportunity to track success and also adjust treatment if necessary.

There are a number of useful systems to gather and integrate ongoing assessment into family psychology treatment. For example, The Family Institute at Northwestern University developed a multisystemic and multidimensional measurement feedback system designed for monitoring alliance and client progress in individual, couple, and family therapy called the STIC. The creators of the Systemic Therapy Inventory of Change (STIC) view therapy as an intervention not only with an individual client, but also with a system that includes anyone involved in the presenting problem (Pinsof, Goldsmith, & Latta, 2012). The STIC system includes sets of questionnaires completed by clients before the intake (STIC INITIAL) and before each session (STIC INTERSESSION). The STIC INITIAL forms begin with demographic questions, followed by anywhere from two to six systems scales, based on a client's demographics. These systems scales address individual problems and strengths (IPS), recollections regarding family of origin (FOO), relationship with romantic partner (RWP), family and household issues (FH), parental perception of child functioning (CPS), and the quality of the parent–child relationship (RWC). As an example, a client with a romantic partner and children would fill out all six scales, while an adolescent would complete two (IPS and FH). All six take about 45 minutes to complete. Based on these initial results, primary targets of change become the first to be focused on in therapy. Before each subsequent session, clients complete the shorter STIC INTERSESSION forms, in addition to alliance measures fit to the modality of therapy (Pinsof et al., 2012).

All of the data becomes part of the clinical profile (CP), provided online. The CP provides graphs and an outcome analysis and guides the clinician in the decision-making process through highlighting the primary targets of change. These targets typically include six key factors per case (Pinsof et al., 2012). The feedback from the STIC also facilities treatment plans throughout the course of therapy in a collaborative manner (Pinsof et al., 2012). Pinsof et al. (2012) view the STIC as empowering for clients through the facilitation of collaboration with therapists and providing opportunities for the recognition of problem areas in clients' relationships. For example, the STIC is able to show a client their own and their partner's ongoing data, and gives the client a key role in how it is interpreted and used in therapy.

Functional family therapy (FFT) is an evidence-based treatment model for youth and families with behavior problems (Alexander, et al., 2000; Sexton, 2010). Like many evidence-based treatments, FFT has a number of efficacy and effectiveness trials showing its success in reducing youth behavior problems, improving family functioning, and reducing family conflict (Sexton, 2010). The most recent FFT outcome study found that in community-based settings, FFT was most successful when practiced by therapists who followed the model (Sexton, & Turner, 2010). Thus, it became clear that in order to maximize the potential outcomes when implemented in complex community settings, therapist needed help in implementing the model with fidelity and adherence (Sexton & Turner, 2010). The FFT Clinical Feedback System (CFS; Sexton, 2010, powered by Care4software) is a product of that effort and the work of Bickman, Sexton, and Kelly (NIMH: RO 1 MH087814).

The FFT–CFS uses state-of-the-art web-based computer systems to administer and collect information using brief questionnaires completed by the clinician, caregiver, youth, and teacher. Using electronic data entry, user-friendly feedback reports are immediately available to the clinicians and their supervisors. The FFT–CFS is unique in that it is a single system that provides real-time information to therapists, supervisors, administrators, evaluators, and researchers regarding model fidelity, client outcomes, and service delivery profiles. The specificity of the FFT model allows for the monitoring of treatment, training, and clinician model adherence in a systematic manner that is not possible with other, less specific treatment interventions. The FFT–CFS is, therefore, both a clinical decision making and a participant-based research tool.

The FFT–CFS has both a measurement core and a systematic feedback system. The FFT Clinical Measurement Inventory (FFT–CMI) is the measurement core and is built on the assumption that continuously measuring the major domains of clinical practice will improve the quality of FFT if it is done in a relevant way (Sexton, 2010). The FFT–CMI consists of brief and psychometrically sound measures to be completed by clients, therapists, and supervisors. These measures can be taken electronically or on paper (to be put in the system manually) and inform four central domains of clinical decision making: treatment planning (service delivery, case conceptualization, and session planning), treatment progress and process (family relational factors, alliance, phase-specific progress, general improvement, and symptom level), model fidelity (therapist model fidelity from supervisor–client perspective), and client outcomes (family and symptom changes).

There are three primary domains of clinical feedback in the FFT–CFS. The first domain measures the symptom level of youth functioning, which is central given the primary goal of youth behavior change. The second domain is phasic, evaluating the impact of session goals on all members of the system within the parameters of the treatment model. The third domain of clinical feedback measures the client's report of progress. Because FFT is a conjoint family therapy, both measurement and feedback are based on multiple individual perspectives (youth, caregiver, etc.), increasing both the complexity and utility of the system.

3. *Outcome assessment* is a domain of clinical assessment that allows therapists, individuals, couples, and families who receive treatment to determine the degree of change that has occurred. Outcome assessment is more often associated with research as a way of measuring pre- and post-change; however, contemporary approaches to assessment have moved this type of assessment into the larger domain of clinical assessment. Measuring outcomes can serve as a marker for therapists and agencies to measure how effective their services are in meeting the clinical needs of the clients whom they serve. To accurately measure outcomes, measures used need to focus on clinically important areas of individual, couple, and family functioning that were the targets of treatment. With the development of new technologies, routine outcome measurement is well within the domain of every practicing family psychologist.

Case Planning

Objective and subjective clinical assessment that is obtained from the ecological levels of the individual, the interpersonal, family, and community will generate volumes of information that must be collated, categorized, summarized, and interpreted for the purpose of generating theory-driven hypotheses. These hypotheses provide the platform for the creation of a relevant case plan.

Treatment plans typically identify the specific goals and objectives of the larger plan of treatment. Good treatment plans include specific objectives that, when accomplished, lead to the fulfillment of the larger overarching therapeutic goal. Most mental health and community-based treatment systems have models and individual requirements for the ways in which treatment goals are formulated. Treatment plans are built on a foundation of the following areas of information:

- Demographic data
- Presenting problem and symptoms
- Psychosocial history
- Relevant testing, and medical and psychiatric histories
- Theory-driven assessment of clinical and objective data
- Diagnosis
- Treatment goals
- Treatment interventions
- Prognosis

Session planning is a part of treatment planning, although not always an overt process. However, it is possible to identify specific goals that are the target of each session. Sessions plans are not to imply that the therapist does not carry out the session in collaboration with the needs of the client; rather, session plans act as an organizing agenda such that when combined with collaboration from the client system provide direction for attaining treatment goals. Thus, session goals typically focus on the activation and intervention in the process of the couple or family. Session goals are likely to change from those core early processes (alliance building, motivation enhancement) to the middle phases (systemically focused intervention within the couple and family) to those later-phase tasks (relapse prevention, maintenance, and system support).

Praxis of Clinical Assessment in Family Psychology

In family psychology, clinical assessment is described by Carr (2009) as a recursive reformulation process in which the interview itself acts as a measure to develop and check hypotheses regarding how the family functions, focusing on three common areas: problem maintaining family relational patterns, problem maintaining beliefs and narratives, and problem maintaining social ecosystemic pressures (Carr, 2009).

Assessment is primarily a relational process. Much of the data of family psychology assessment is gained through clinical interview, which allows the therapist to not only gather data, but also make direct observations of family functioning and direct the discussion to uncover and identify important information that helps formulate assessment. In real practice, clinical assessment happens as the therapist process unfolds over time. Psychologists are at heart scientists, and the clinical scientist like the research scientist operates on the basis of hypothesis generating and testing. The purpose of clinical and objective assessment, drawn from the initial referral, intake, and testing, is to give the clinician data from which to make relevant hypotheses that will then inform treatment (Goodheart et al., 2006). Hypotheses are shaped, interpreted, and reshaped in light of new information. Hypothesis generation occurs throughout the course of therapy, making family psychology distinctly scientific in its approach to the human condition. In the following sections, we follow the assessment process from the beginning to the end illustrating how the constructs of systemic thinking and the principles presented early work in a practice setting. We describe assessment from the referral, to intake, treatment, and termination of the case.

Referral. Two important aspects of referral in family psychology are obtaining and managing referrals. The initial phone contact can reveal important information about the nature of the perceived issues, the family members most involved, the perceived identified patient in the family, and what other professionals might be involved in the family's care (e.g., the legal system, medical/hospital, or school). The family psychologist must make an initial determination of (1) whether therapy is to be with an individual or family, and (2) if with a family, which family members to invite to the initial intake session. The family psychologist should ascertain from the initial phone conversation some idea regarding the services for which she or he is being retained.

Clinical intake session. The intake and initial session are designed to provide order, form, and structure to ongoing therapy. While the telephone contact is the beginning point for initial assessment of the client system, the intake session is the beginning of formal assessment. Clinical intake forms should be constructed so that information for individuals and family members can be easily gathered. Part of managing a referral includes recognizing the unique and inherent emphasis of family psychology on working with multidisciplinary teams. In addition to identifying the client and motivating the client to come in for treatment, the family psychologist should ascertain the services for which she or he is being retained. Often, the client or client system is not sure what is wanted, especially if he or she is acting on a professional's suggestion or a requirement from court. Make sure that he or she is competent to perform the necessary treatment.

The intake session is designed to provide order and structure to ongoing psychotherapy. The primary focus should be on creating a safe place where each family member can share his or her experiences in the family as transparently as possible. Because of power differentials among family members, the psychologist needs to have family members contract with one another regarding what is said in therapy, such that everyone agrees there will be no recriminations when the family leaves the therapy office and returns home. This is vital and fidelity to the contract needs to be followed up on in subsequent sessions. Clinical intake forms should be constructed so that information for individuals and family members can be easily gathered (Patterson et al., 1998).

As noted in Chapter 3, three common domains describe the systemic functioning of relational systems: relational patterns, narratives/beliefs, and the historical or multigenerational influences on current behavior. These forces impact both the relational structure (boundaries, hierarchy, alliance, etc.) and the relational process of the couple and family (alliance, blame, rigidity, differentiation, flexibility, adaptability, and boundaries). There are levels of assessment that guide the interview process. Assessment of individual family members should first entail an assessment of the safety of each family member, taking appropriate action where necessary to ensure the safety of any member who might be in imminent danger of harm to self or others. Assessment of individual family members should also include the assessment of possible neurosis, personality disorder, or psychosis that might affect the functioning of the family as a whole. Research indicates that individual family members manifesting neurosis can pass on the neurosis to other family members (Katz, Beach, & Joiner, 1999). Additionally, the psychologist should assess for relational conflicts between family members that affect the psychological well-being of individual family members.

Dyadic relational processes involve dysfunctional patterns of communication, such as high expressed emotion or skewed emotion; alliance dyads in the family; emotional, verbal, and/or physical aggression; amount of anxiety and avoidance in dyad attachment and negative filters in dyad relating. Dyads should also be assessed for their ability to tolerate what is unlikely to change (the ability to agree to disagree) (Gottman, 1999; Gurman & Jacobson, 2002). Objective measures used at the level of the dyad include the Marital Satisfaction Inventory (Snyder, 1981), Parenting Stress Index (Abidin, 1995), Sexual Functioning Inventory (Derogatis & Melisaratos, 1979), Child's Report of Parental Behavior Inventory (Schaefer, 1965), and Dyadic Adjustment Scale (Spanier, 1976).

Family relational systems assessment is focused on those areas of family functioning described in Chapter 3: family alliances, boundaries, parenting styles, boundaries between generations, family hierarchy, roles in the family, and decision making in the family. The family's social network also needs to be assessed. A dense, supportive social network can serve as a prophylactic against individual, dyadic, and family pathology, and a strong social network can be a repository for coping resources (Han, Kim, Lee, Pistulka, & Kim, 2007; Perry, 2006). Equally, a family's social network can draw resources away from the family, creating heightened stress and conflict. For example, church or school activities may be perceived as sources of strength for the family, but they may require responsibilities and commitments that take members away from family life, becoming a greater source of family stress and burden and thus creating a net loss of resources to the family. The extended system may be the source of coalitions and alliances that work for or against a family's life (Hartman, 1995).

Becky often spent an hour or more on the phone with her mother every night, which was a source of irritation to Mark, who characterized his mother-in-law as a parasite on their family. While Becky did spend a lot of time listening to her mother's complaints (mostly about her father), she was also able to complain about Mark to her mother, who would often wistfully commiserate, "Why don't we just dump these two fellas, take the kids, and move to California?"

As can be seen from the example, while Becky and her mother may have thought that their commiseration was helping (the belief that it's good to vent), it was, in fact, proving toxic for both their marital relationships.

Extended systems may be analyzed through the eco map and genogram, offered as pictorial representations, providing measures of family and community factors that may be construed as assets or liabilities to family life. Using the eco map or genogram, the psychologist should assess the impact on the family life of multigenerational family dynamics, the school system, religious obligations, outside programs, such as sports, and the legal and medical systems where pertinent (McGoldrick, Gerson, & Petry, 2008).

A part of the intake interview for some treatments is a guided *psychosocial history of the family*. The psychosocial history provides the family psychologist with an overview of family patterns of interaction and functioning over three generations. The family psychologist looks for the major players in the family over the course of three generations: where the family lived with concomitant moves, what family members do or did for a living, any religious heritage, any major physical or psychological illnesses, any history of alcohol or substance abuse (or other compulsive behavioral patterns), any history of physical or sexual abuse, how family members died, and, most importantly, how family members get or got along with each other. The psychologist gleans information on family patterns of communication, family alliances, and specific family conflicts. Information becomes more detailed as the history moves to the present generation's relationships. The psychologist should obtain information on current members of the family: who is living at or away from home, current and previous marriages, and divorces and blended family issues if applicable. It may also be useful to have family members share specific stories about their lives, providing diagnostic value through the identification of personal life or corporate family themes. For example, having a couple describe how they met and became committed can have diagnostic value in determining the likelihood for success in couple's therapy (Gottman, 1999; Mosak & Pietro, 2006; Stone & Hoffman, 2005).

Psychiatric, developmental, and medical history of the family helps identify developmental issues, medical conditions, or psychiatric history that might be pertinent to treatment. For example, if the case involves behavior problems, the psychologist will want to know if there were any pertinent developmental issues such as an abnormal birth and childhood head trauma. Collateral information (e.g., report cards, medical records, and/ or custody reports) can be useful in fleshing out the assessment picture. Additionally, notation of previous outpatient or inpatient mental health services in the past or current use of any psychotropic medications will be helpful. Finally, as stated earlier, it is crucial to assess for suicidal or homicidal ideation. This includes information about major symptoms, issues, and events that brought the client in for treatment, entrances and exits of people in the client's life, and why the client system has come for therapy *now*. It is important to understand drug and/or alcohol use, suicidal tendencies, violent or homicidal tendencies, any past or current history of abuse, mental status, and physical health.

Current context. An assessment of the family's ecological system includes whether they have sufficient income to meet family needs, adequate food and shelter for stable family life, a safe and pleasant neighborhood to live in, access to medical and wellness care, adequate physical resources, meaningful social connections with family, friends, and neighbors. Does the client system engage with extended kin, participate in group activities, and share cultural or ethnic meanings or values with others? What are the positive or negative educational experiences for children and satisfaction with work or achievement?

Diagnosis. A comprehensive assessment is most likely to lead to a viable diagnosis. As noted earlier, diagnosis poses an interesting dilemma for the family psychologist. The family psychologist takes the accumulated information and synthesizes it into a cohesive diagnostic picture of the family, assigning a diagnosis for relevant individuals in the family, and a relational diagnosis for the family as a whole. The diagnosis should reflect the etiology of the disorder(s) and pathogenesis, or course of development for individual family members (Maxmen & Ward, 1995), but Gottlieb (1996) suggests the need for a relational diagnosis alongside personal diagnoses "when there is a dysfunctional pattern of interaction between two or more people within a system that leads to a reduced level of functioning for at least one member of the system" (p. 19). Patterson et al. (1998) have noted that "the practical, ethical, and logistical dilemmas of using both individual and family diagnosis have never been clearly delineated" (p. 173). In their argument of how to manage diagnosis, they propose the psychologist focus both on the individual diagnosis of the identified patient and relating family processes and on symptoms important to family functioning. They conclude that the exigencies of third-party payers frequently require individual diagnosis (e.g., treatment authorization and reimbursement), and, therefore, family psychologists must be knowledgeable about and assess for individual diagnosis. However, a contextual approach to family psychology will help family psychologists assess individual diagnosis while taking into consideration the family and its problems as a whole (Patterson et al., 1998).

Developing a treatment plan. The family psychologist should take all the information gathered through objective and subjective assessment and (1) explore other more manageable ways than those the family has used to describe or define the issues at play, (2) offer the family an initial assessment and recommendation for treatment, and (3) devise an evidence-based treatment plan (goals and interventions) that treats the family's presenting problem(s) and also treats the issues derived from the family diagnosis (Hanna & Brown, 2004).

A perusal of Ben's report cards through the years and speaking with his teachers indicated a possible pattern consistent with ADD, suggesting that a formal ADD assessment might be useful. The results of a formal assessment battery however seemed to rule out ADD, indicating elevated levels of trait anxiety and highly elevated levels of state anxiety. The psychologist began to look for family dynamics that might be contributing to anxiety in Ben's life and quickly settled on what appeared to be a strained relationship between his parents that was instilling fear of divorce in Ben.

Closing the loop. Meeting with the couple or family to discuss impressions, ideas, and suggested goals is a central step in building the alliance necessary for successful treatment. Rather than just a meeting to discuss diagnostic or clinical impressions, we think this session is actually a treatment intervention opportunity that is successful when goals of the couple or family and the therapist become aligned, where an open and inclusive process begins, and hope and expectation for success grow. It is important to remember that the typical attrition rate following first sessions is 30–40%; thus, this meeting is a therapeutic opportunity to:

- Join with the couple and gain information
- Describe the process of treatment and build alliances
- Find and reinforce common goals among family members
- Begin the process of helping the client(s) state a solvable definition of the problem
- Make plans for future sessions

WHAT THIS ALL MEANS AND WHAT IS NEXT?

The recursive and ecological nature of a systemic perspective can make the seemingly straightforward process of assessment, diagnosis, treatment planning, and intervention appear complex. Psychological practice is in fact complex in that each assessment can either inhibit or promote the core foundations of successful treatment. Taking a systemic perspective requires thinking of assessment as an integral thread that makes up the many aspects of successful treatment. As such, assessment in family psychology tends to be less linear and more relationally focused, developmental, and enduring throughout the course of treatment.

Our discussions in previous chapters have mapped out the interconnectedness between research and practice. In the next two chapters we will extend the map to focus on relevant therapeutic theories for couples and families in family psychology. Our focus will be on theories that are grounded in rigorous evidence-based research and that have found significant efficacy in evidence-based practice.

Chapter 7

Family-Focused Clinical Intervention Models

In theory there is no difference between theory and practice. In practice there is.

—Yogi Berra

Emerging out of the excitement of the revolution in systemic epistemology, the earliest family psychology treatment models were more clinical in nature, nonspecific, and built on the creativity and charisma of their founders. At the same time, these early ideas formed the foundation for future more specific approaches. More than mere relics of history, these models represent the common core of clinical practice when working with families and couples. As such, they provide a theoretical perspective that specifies and prioritizes ideas into comprehensive *lenses* that focus a clinician's understanding of clients, problems, and clinical change.

In the early days of family psychology, there were few methods or tools for evaluating family therapy interventions. Thus, earlier models tended to be more theory based. For example, structural and strategic models were one of the first generation of family therapy approaches. Other models (like MDFT and MST) have emerged out of a critical social need (adolescent substance abuse and delinquency) as illustrations of evidence-based approaches. Still others (like FFT) are traditional models first developed in the 1970s that have become evidence based through development and evaluation efforts via extensive and rigorous research. While each model is unique, they also share a common systemic focus on the family/couple as the core unit of analysis and a common epistemology for understanding clinical problems and clinical change (see Chapter 5). This means that seemingly individual problems are actually viewed as involving other family members, and interventions are directed to the whole family rather than an individual. Yet, these core traditional models differ with respect to their emphasis on (1) problem-maintaining behavior patterns, (2) problematic and constraining belief systems, and (3) historical, contextual, and constitutional predisposing factors.

In this chapter, we focus on five specific family-based clinical intervention models. We have chosen these models because they represent the range of ways in which couple and family psychology treatment is done. Some focus more on relational patterns, history, and context, while others focus on meanings and attributions (see Chapter 3). Two of these approaches, Structural/Strategic and Multigenerational, represent traditional approaches emphasizing theory rather than research—which is not to say they are not viable, but rather that there is little specific evidence to support outcomes of the proposed change mechanisms. The other three Multisystemic Family Therapy, Functional Family Therapy and Multidimensional Family Therapy represent the more current generation of evidence-based approaches, integrating the best research evidence with clinical experience, the most current and clinically relevant psychological theory, and client values (Institute of Medicine, 2001; Sexton & Gordon, 2009). The models covered in this chapter include the following:

1. *Structural and strategic* approaches that focus largely on behavioral transactions and patterns within family and couple systems.
2. Multigenerational approaches that focus primarily on the influences of relational history as the foundation of current transactions and interactions.
3. Multisystemic Family Therapy is a family-based model, aimed at helping delinquent and troubled youth, is largely integrative, and focused on the larger contextual and systemic issues facing families.
4. Functional Family Therapy (FFT) is a conjoint and systemic family therapy targeting adolescents with mental health and delinquent behaviors. FFT emphasizes engagement and therapeutic motivation, utilizing a family-focused approach to problem solving and behavior change.
5. Multidimensional Family Therapy (MDFT) is a strength-based, ecological, and integrative model that seeks to motivate and utilize family dynamics in the service of treating adolescent drug abuse and problem behaviors.

Whether traditional and theoretical or evidence based, all approaches are also *lenses* that we look through to understand individuals, couples, and families in order to plan and implement successful therapeutic change. What these approaches share is a focus on the necessary ingredients of any successful theory or clinical model: (1) a theoretical core that describes the functioning of both well-functioning and problem families, and (2) a clinical model or map that identifies the unique focus of assessment, change mechanisms, and techniques/interventions that are designed to help promote positive change. In this section, we describe the unique features that define each of the approaches.

There are some challenges inherent in devoting a single chapter to family-focused clinical interventions. No single chapter can do justice to the wide range of intervention theories and models let alone the plethora of manuals, training programs, books, chapters, articles, and journals, that are devoted to this topic (Gurman & Kniskren, 1991; Sexton et al., 2003; Sexton & Lebow, 2015; Bray & Stanton, 2009). In addition, treatments are comprehensive, systematic, and complex psychological interventions that can easily lose their dynamic and relational qualities when reduced to two-dimensional descriptions. Further, providing a snapshot of the breadth and scope of current family intervention models in a single textbook is an impossible task. The present chapter is not intended as a comprehensive list of approaches, but rather as a review of models that illustrate the integration of research, clinical wisdom, and good practice (Sexton et al., 2013; Sexton et al., 2011). In the following sections, we will address each model by considering:

- Theoretical principles that describe how families and couples function.
- The mechanism by which *clinical problems* develop.
- Primary *goals* of the intervention or what areas of family functioning are the primary targets.
- Clinical process and primary clinical interventions.
- Role of the therapist.
- Research support.

THEORETICALLY BASED MODELS

Structural/Strategic Clinical Models

Building on the early ideas of the Mental Research Institute (MRI) group and systemic thinking, Salvador Minuchin (1974) advanced the idea that family structure is essential to understanding and treating individual family member problems. He proposed a model in which structure encompasses the interaction between family subsystems as regulated by boundaries (Nichols, 2013). Structure develops within the broader sociocultural context that establishes role definitions and expectations. It takes on a unique design as a family operationalizes itself over time through patterns of behavior or arrangements; these patterns limit the range of available options, precluding adaptive responses to life challenges (Minuchin, 1974, p. 89). Structural family therapy (SFT) is one of the most widely practiced approaches in family therapy, and its principles have found their way into many of the more current and evidence-based treatment models (e.g., multidimensional family therapy).

Theoretical Foundations. Structural models focus on relational patterns and family relational structures as the primary dimensions for understanding couple and family relationships through their patterns of relationships (see Chapter 3). For example, hierarchical organization is necessary for positive family functioning (parental authority supersedes child power and authority), and smaller subsystems (e.g., parental or sibling subsystems) operate within the whole structure of the family. Boundaries determine the nature of interactions between subsystems and the larger system, ranging from rigid (limited interaction leading to greater subsystem independence or disengagement) to diffuse boundaries (frequent and intense interaction that results in closeness or enmeshment). The ideal boundary avoids the extremes and allows for appropriate responsiveness to the needs of other subsystems, as well as reasonable independence (e.g., a parent–child boundary that allows emotional connection and support while maintaining parental authority and spousal privacy; Nichols, 2013).

Family and relational structure can be seen only in movement—dynamic rather than static patterns over periods of time. The family operates through transactional patterns, repeated sequences of how, when, and who relates to whom, in which situations, and under what conditions. When these patterns are repeated over time, they become the preferred patterns for the family and part of its relational structure. These patterns become preferred because they work. These family structures and patterns of family interaction have a consistency to them that become rule governed and recursive. Some of the rules are *overt*, clearly stated (if not always implemented), while others are *covert*, never stated, and very rarely violated; for example, "if mother and father disagree, a child must misbehave to distract them from their conflict" is a covert family rule; in fact, the *recursive patterns* of family interaction are usually governed by covert rules, which may be inferred from observing repeated episodes of family interactions.

Structural intervention models are particularly interested in what are called alignments, the structural organization of different members of the family. One form of alignment, an *alliance*, is the sharing of common interest by two people not shared by third. A *coalition* is a relational process in which two join together against a third. Family structural alignments include those that are stable and provide consistency to the working of the couple and family, as well as more problematic alignments that create either *triangulation* (when someone is pulled into the conflict of another) or *detour triangulation* that prevent change. These two forces of stability and change reflected in the systemic foundation of any relational system are dialectical in nature (see Chapters 1 and 3). Normal families are not distinguishable from abnormal by the absence of problems—all families have problems. In fact, all well-functioning families are constantly transforming and changing as they adapt and restructure amid changing conditions and contexts. Family adaptation and change to internal and external stressors require boundaries that are both firm and flexible to allow for realignment and maintenance of family continuity.

According to this model, clinical problems of individuals within the family occur because of too rigid boundaries or conflict detour triangulation. These patterns not only help develop, support, and maintain problems such as depression and youth behavior problems, but also serve to maintain stability when one family member may be experiencing pathology. For example, conflict detouring triangulation occurs when both parents try, either covertly or overtly, to enlist the child's support against the other. This may also occur when parent–child coalitions—one parent sides with a child against the other parent—complicate the parenting process. Boundaries become problematic if the family system becomes too closed, making it difficult to grow up and leave the family, or to search for new ideas and resources to solve the normal problems of daily life. When they occur, coalitions disrupt family functioning by forcing the members to choose between three different paths: develop and/or continue with a relationship with high degree of connection and intention or involve a third party. That third party may be someone from another generation of the family or someone outside the family system.

Primary Goals of Clinical Treatment. The primary focus of SFT is to solve the presenting problems. While that might at first glance seem obvious, it illustrates the pragmatic approach of these models. Whether it is problematic school behavior, family conflict, or other clinical issues, behavior change comes from a change in the underlying family structure that maintains the problem. There are then four specific therapeutic goals to SFT: solve the presenting problems, change the underlying family structure that maintains the problem, reduce stress being felt by the family, and restore family equilibrium.

Process and Interventions. Structural family therapists are purposeful, active, and directive. Like all models, there are both specific clinical strategies and stages to the treatment process.

1. Accommodation/joining in which the therapist attempts to join the family system. This stage is one in which the therapist/ family alliance is built. From a structural approach, this occurs when the therapist adjusts to the family and relates to them in a way that is consistent with the rules and transactional patterns of the family.

2. Understanding/assessment stage is a time when the therapist observes family functioning in order to make hypotheses about boundary quality, flexibility, interactional patterns of subsystems, stage of family development, how the symptoms serve to maintain homeostasis, and the context in which presenting problems occur (stressors both internal and external impinging upon the family). Assessment is largely based on clinical observation of the family to ascertain where it fails to carry out its functions and identify behavioral patterns that get in the way of successful daily interaction.

3. Restructuring the family is the action part of the intervention. Here the structural family therapist actively intervenes to change the family structure. The goal is to create a directive that reorganizes the core family structure. This is not done through explanation but instead through instruction and direction of the therapist. Thus, the goal of any session for the family is to behave differently, rather than to gain awareness. To accomplish this, the therapist might block old transaction patterns, disrupt coalitions and triangulation, and push the family to realign and create new transactional sequences. To this end, the therapist uses a number of intervention techniques:

    •   Enacting—in which the therapist encourages family members to act out or engage in a type of central transactional pattern.
    •   Choreography—in which the therapist directs the family to act in a new sequence of patterns.
    •   Marking boundaries—in which the therapist identifies and has the family behave in ways that mark, acknowledge, and create new boundaries around subsystems and the family as a whole.
    •   Escalating stress—where the goal is to see and change core family patterns and structures by making them more apparent.
    •   Assigning tasks—where the therapist gives specific directions to the family members that change family structure.
    •   Making use of symptoms—through exaggerating, prescribing de-emphasizing the symptom or relabeling a symptom.
    •   Manipulating the mood—in which the therapist changes the focus from the problem or identified patient to the system as a whole in order to bring hope, focusing on strengths and family resources.
    •   Nurturance, education, and guidance.

4. Maintenance of change is the final step in the change process. Homoe-ostatic forces of stability that often reverse changes are attended to using clinical change techniques. It is this step that is intended to help the family make a second-order change or a change in the structure of the family.

Multigenerational and Bowenian Family Therapy

Multigenerational models highlight, as the name suggests, the role of *historical, contextual, and constitutional factors* in predisposing family members to adopt particular belief systems or engage in particular problematic interaction patterns. Multigenerational models are best illustrated by the work of Murray Bowen, a psychiatrist influenced by systems theory to conceptualize emotional disorder as a family process and the family as an emotional unit, extending beyond the nuclear family to the extended or multigenerational family (Hargrove, 2009).

Theoretical Foundations. Multigenerational models focus on the historical and contextual relational forces that impact couples and families (see Chapter 3). From this lens, it is the clients' family of origin relationships that predispose them to develop current life problems in their families of procreation. Family problems are viewed as multigenerational phenomena with patterns of family interactions or relationships replicated from one generation to the next through relational triangles, resulting in family members being unable to make their own decisions/choices.

Bowen (1978) considered families to be fundamentally, emotional systems. When threatened, family anxiety develops, and families engage in recursive, emotionally driven, problematic interaction patterns. Families differ in the amount of anxiety they contain; some families are relatively unthreatened and show little anxiety, while others feel extremely threatened and consistently experience high levels of anxiety. The amount of anxiety a family experiences determines the degree to which family members may display lack of differentiation. Highly anxious families are characterized by an undifferentiated ego mass—that is, they have extremely close emotional relationships characterized by enmeshment or fusion. Families containing little anxiety facilitate a high level of differentiation and autonomy in family members (Carr, 2012, p. 160).

It is through what Bowen described as the family projection process that symptoms of one generation are passed along to later ones. According to Bowen, psychopathology occurs because of family projection and the multigenerational transmission processes. Family projection occurs when parents project part of their immaturity onto one of their children, who in turn becomes the least differentiated family member and the most likely to become symptomatic. Some children avoid the impact of this projection while others, typically those who are most involved in their families' emotional processes and the least differentiated, do not. In turn, these children often select their own marital partners who share an equivalently low level of differentiation. As a result, they pass the problems of limited differentiation from the family of origin on to the next generation by inadvertently organizing family rules, roles, and routines in rigidly enmeshed and fused ways, cyclically preventing differentiation.

Others respond to the projection process by cutting themselves off emotionally from the family. Emotional cutoff is a way of coping with continual family pressure to become involved in a triangle *by* emotionally disconnecting from one or more family members. Emotional cutoff may involve physically making little contact and/or psychologically denying the significance of the unresolved family-of-origin relationship problems. The greater the degree of cutoff, the greater the probability of replicating the problematic family-of-origin relationship in the family of procreation. The solution to the anxiety projected on an individual is to be differentiated from this process. Differentiation of self involves separation of intellectual and emotional systems. When intrapsychic differentiation occurs, the individual does not impulsively act out strong feelings, but rather reflects upon these feelings and chooses a course of action. This intrapsychic differentiation frees the person to avoid repeating problematic, emotionally driven interaction patterns associated with the family of origin. Unresolved emotional reactivity to family and parents leaves us at risk and vulnerable to repeat family-of-origin relational patterns in new adult relationships and in our family of procreation.

"Differentiation is your ability to maintain your sense of self when you are emotionally and or physically close to others—especially as they become increasingly important to you" (Schnarch, 1997, p. 56). Lack of balance will lead to fusion/undifferentiation, defined as reacting to others, losing touch with our own goals, and becoming caught in others' agendas (Richardson, 1984). Fusion is the fantasy of "oneness" with another person. Undifferentiation requires that our sense of self be derived from others: their opinion. "We develop a contingent identity based on a 'self-in-relationship'" (Schnarch, 1997, p. 59). Being goal directed means being able to clarify one's own values decide what is important and be able to give their expression to others. Differentiation is the ability to separate feeling from thinking, to maintain oneself in the presence of important others and not become disengaged. It is the ability to maintain a sense of self in the face of an intense emotional relationship. Differentiation is the ability to relate in mutuality, that is, focusing on one's own self-development while being concerned with significant others' well-being.

Goals of Treatment. The goal of treatment is to achieve a balance between individual differentiation and the maintenance of intimacy with family members by managing anxiety and avoiding emotional cutoff and family projection (Goldenberg & Goldenberg, 2013; Hargrove, 2009). Failure to achieve this balance would result in symptoms that reveal "the struggle of the system to adapt to stressful conditions" (Hargrove, 2009, p. 292). Bowen family systems therapy views the therapist as a coach who helps the family curtail emotional responses to understand their own functioning objectively (Hargrove, 2009). In Bowenian multigenerational family therapy, couples are helped to:

- Become differentiated so that their understanding of family-of-origin processes prevents them from being inducted into recursive, emotionally driven interaction patterns.
- To develop person-to-person relationships in which they can speak directly to other family members about one another and avoid impersonal discussion or gossip.
- Recognize the degree to which they are experiencing fusion or lack of differentiation from their family of origin.
- Gain insight into how this is affecting their capacity to manage current life problems in their family of procreation.

Process and Interventions. Multigenerational and Bowen treatment approaches have the primary aim to promote differentiation of self for the individuals in the family. The objective is to create person-to-person relationships with one's parents in which the individual uses self-observation skills to reduce emotional reactivity and to "detriangle" from emotional family situations. To accomplish this, therapists often invite clients to bring their parents or siblings to therapy sessions or coach clients to set up meetings outside therapy with members of their families of origin. The purpose of these interactions is to renegotiate triangular relationships and replace fused or cutoff relationships with person-to-person relationships. In some instances, it may involve family-of-procreation meetings followed by couple sessions and finally family sessions, which are attended by members of the family of origin. In other instances, it may be conducted on an individual basis.

Many of the multigenerational models are designed to work with one member of the family, a family dyad, or many members of the family, all with the idea that changing one person in the family can infiltrate and change the whole family system. The therapist facilitates insight and change within the individual: the primary mechanism of change is to decrease anxiety and emotionality (reactivity) through the use of process questions, which slow people down as they shift from an emotive frame to one that is more cognitive. The therapist aims to short-circuit emotional reactivity, encourages rational thinking, and focuses on the process of their interaction rather than the details of the issue. The therapist helps clients use the "I" position rather than the "you" position by stating one's own beliefs instead of assigning blame and focusing on changing the self instead of the other. The therapist can use relationship experiments to identify and acknowledge the role that each member of the family fulfills in maintaining the system problem. For instance, the therapist may have partners recognize and identify their roles of distance/pursuer, pursuer/victim/rescuer, then have them change roles. The therapist can also use the "two-choice" dilemma by framing the problem as having choices for outcome from which the individual(s) may decide a course of action. One choice is the preferred, more differentiated one, while the less differentiated choice is one that is odious to the decision maker and therefore less likely to be pursued. Finally, in Bowen family systems therapy, the therapist models differentiated relating by demonstrating how to detach and stay out of triangles and refrain from emotional reactivity (Guerin, 1976). One clinical tool used in this approach is the genogram. The genogram is a pictorial representation of the client couple's family trees, going back three generations. On the basis of the data generated by the genogram and the discussion following, the therapist makes hypotheses about the issues going on in the relationship.

Role of the Therapist. The therapist acts as a coach, emphasizing calm rationality, seeking to create a therapeutic triangle between her/himself and the couple. A stable triangle is formed because the therapist is not emotionally entangled, which then aids in dissipating relational tensions. This stable triangle is based on process, not content. Sessions should be lively enough to be meaningful, but cool enough to be objective. The therapist assesses the degree of emotionality in the couple relationship: mild, moderate, or high degree of emotionality. When feelings are running high, questions are asked to get family members to think more and feel less.

EVIDENCE-BASED CLINICAL INTERVENTION MODELS

Multisystemic Therapy (MST)

MST is a family- and community-based treatment model with its roots in family systems theory. It is theoretically designed to address chronic behavior problems, and serious emotional disturbances in adolescents. MST was initially developed in the late 1970s to address the clinical needs of juvenile offenders and their families (see, e.g., Henggeler et al., 1986) and has been used to treat serious emotional disturbances in adolescents, youth violence and criminal behavior, juvenile sex-offending behavior, alcohol and drug abuse, and child maltreatment. Research evidence supporting the model is the strongest when it is used with youth presenting serious antisocial behavior in conjunction with their families. MST has been widely implemented in community settings and is one of the most researched family-based approaches (Henggeler & Lee, 2003; Sheidow, Henggeler, & Schoenwald, 2003).

Theoretical Foundations. There are nine principles that guide case conceptualization and the development and implementation of intervention strategies (for a more complete description of the core principles, see Henggeler & Lee, 2003; Sheidow, Henggeler, & Schoenwald, 2003):

- Finding the fit: understanding the "fit" between the identified problem(s) and the broader systemic context.
- Positive and strength focused: therapeutic interactions emphasize strengths as mechanisms for change.
- Increasing responsibility: interventions are designed to promote responsible behavior among family members.
- Present focused, action oriented, and well defined: interventions target specific and well-defined problems, and criteria are established to track progress.
- Targeting sequences: interventions target sequences of behavior that maintain the identified problem(s), and treatment is designed to change family interactions and increase prosocial support.
- Developmentally appropriate: interventions are appropriate to the developmental needs of the youth and emphasize building youth competencies in peer relations, academics, and so on.
- Continuous effort: interventions are intensive and require daily and weekly effort on the part of the family.
- Evaluation and accountability: effectiveness is continuously evaluated from multiple perspectives.
- Generalization: interventions are designed to produce long-term maintenance of change by empowering caregivers to cope with family members' needs across multiple contexts.

MST service delivery is based on a model of home-based intervention, which has proven effective at engaging families in treatment and preventing dropout. The therapists who deliver MST typically have master's level training and carry caseloads of four to six families. The MST therapists work in small teams of three to five full-time therapists and a supervisor. Services are delivered either at home or in a community-based setting such as school or a neighborhood center in order to minimize barriers to treatment. The treatment is time limited, typically lasting between 3 and 6 months, to promote self-sufficiency and cost effectiveness. Therapists are available 24 hours a day and 7 days a week to provide services as needed and to respond to or prevent crises. For a complete description of clinical procedures, please see Henggeler, Schoenwald, Borduin, Rowland, and Cunningham, (1998).

Primary Goals. The primary goal of MST is to help families develop skills to effectively manage and resolve a youth's serious clinical problems. In addition, MST strives to empower families to prevent potential problems likely to occur during adolescence. Acknowledging the multisystemic nature of causal and sustaining factors that affect youth, MST therapists utilize resources within families' ecologies to develop their capacity to cope. Therapists intervene at the family level to reduce conflict, improve communication, improve family cohesion, and increase behavioral monitoring. Treatment may also address parental or marital functioning if they contribute to the youth's problems, and caregivers are considered essential to treatment generalization. MST therapists may also address peer-level factors that contribute to the youth's problems such as association with deviant peers and poor socialization skills. However, much of the therapist's attention is focused on helping the caregiver learn to manage the adolescent's interaction with his or her environment, especially the school environment (Sheidow et al., 2003).

Process and Interventions. Because MST is individualized to each youth and family, it can't be characterized as step by step or session by session. The caregivers are the primary targets of assessment and intervention. MST emphasizes specifying problems, being present focused and action oriented, and utilizing behavioral and cognitive-behavioral treatment techniques. MST treatment is a collaborative process between therapist and family. Using the MST principles, therapists select and integrate interventions in ways hypothesized to maximize their synergistic interaction. Throughout MST, therapists obtain information via observation, interaction, interview, and official records where applicable (e.g., school attendance records, probation violations). The "process" of MST can be best described by the following steps:

- Therapist gathers the desired treatment outcomes of each family member and stakeholder, and then helps the participants develop consensus on the overarching goals of treatment and how these can be measured in tangible ways.

- The therapist assesses the family and other systems to develop an understanding or "fit" of the referral behaviors and how these behaviors make sense in the context of the systems (i.e., home, school, peer, community) in which the youth and family live. Family assessment is often described as the MST Analytic Process (a "Do-Loop") used to guide therapists through the interrelated steps of case conceptualization, planning, implementing, and evaluating impact.

- Family members and clinical team prioritize the hypothesized drivers of the clinical problems and develop interventions targeting these drivers. These interventions are subsequently implemented, their implementation is monitored, and barriers to their implementation as intended are identified.

- Finally, the therapist gathers multiple perspectives on the effectiveness of each intervention. If the information gathered suggests the intervention was not successful, the therapist and team start back at the top of the Do-Loop and work with the family and other participants to reconceptualize the "fit" of the behavior and generate new hypotheses about potential drivers of the problem and subsequently new interventions.

Research Support. As an evidence-based model of treatment, MST has an extensive research foundation measuring outcomes in clinical trials and community settings. Findings from eight published studies composed of seven randomized clinical trials and one quasi-experimental design provide the evidence that supports the effectiveness of MST. The first MST outcome study was quasi-experimental (Henggeler et al., 1986), and it evaluated short-term effectiveness of MST with juvenile offenders. Findings indicated improved family relations, decreased youth behavior problems, and decreased youth association with deviant peers. This study was followed by three randomized clinical trials with chronic and violent juvenile offenders. Henggeler, Melton, & Smith (1992) found that when MST served as a community-based alternative to incarceration, at post-treatment, MST was more effective at improving family and peer relations than the usual juvenile justice services. Among the youths treated with MST, recidivism was reduced by 43% and out-of-home placement was reduced by 64% at the 59-week follow-up. In another randomized clinical trial with chronic juvenile offenders, Borduin and Schaeffer (1998) found that MST was more effective at decreasing youth psychiatric symptomatology at post-treatment, and at a 1.7-year follow-up, it produced a 50% reduction in incarceration than the usual juvenile justice services. Two randomized clinical trials with substance abusing youth have demonstrated short-term reductions in adolescent substance abuse (Henggeler et al., 1992a; Henggeler, Pickerel, & Brondino, 1999). Another study has demonstrated long-term reductions in substance-related arrests (Borduin et al., 1995). MST was also found to be successful in treating youth with serious emotional disturbance (Henggeler, et al., 1999b).

In addition to randomized clinical trials, MST researchers have developed a quality assurance system designed to maintain the internal validity of the model as it is disseminated to community provider organizations across the country. Several empirical studies have examined the relationship between adherence to MST treatment principles and clinical outcomes (Henggeler, et al., 1999; Schoenwald, Sheidow, & Letourneau, 2004). These studies indicate that therapist adherence and organizational climate predict parent-reported child outcomes immediately post-treatment.

Functional Family Therapy (FFT)

FFT is a systematic, evidenced-based, manual-driven, family-based treatment program that has been successful in treating a wide range of problems affecting youth (including drug use and abuse, conduct disorder, mental health concerns, truancy, and related family problems) and their families in a wide range of multiethnic, multicultural, and geographic contexts (Sexton & Alexander, 2002: Sexton 2006; Sexton, 2010; Sexton, 2015). FFT has evolved over the past 30 years and is built on a foundation of integrated theory, clinical experience, and empirical evidence. The model is now a systematic and comprehensive clinical model designed to treat at-risk youth aged 11–18 with a range of maladaptive behaviors including delinquency, violence, substance use, risky sexual behavior, truancy, conduct disorder, ODD, disruptive behavior disorder, and other externalizing disorders.

Like many models, FFT is built on the principles of good clinical practice (create a therapeutic relationship, be client centered, etc.) and contains all of what we would today call the "common factors" of successful therapies. The primary focus of treatment is on the family relational system, with an emphasis on the multiple domains of client experience (cognition, emotion, and behavior) and the multiple perspectives within and around a family system (individual, family, and contextual/multisystemic). As a treatment program, FFT is a short-term family therapy intervention that ranges from 8 to 12 sessions of 1 hour for mild to moderate cases and up to 30 hours of direct intervention for more serious situations. The program also works as a preventive measure in diverting the path of at-risk adolescents away from the juvenile justice or mental health systems (Alexander, Pugh, Parsons, & Sexton, 2000).

Theoretical Foundations. A number of theoretical, clinical, and research-based constructs guide the intervention program. The FFT clinical model focuses on the relational patterns that are represented by serious acting-out behaviors as the basis for therapeutic intervention. From this perspective, the specific problem behaviors of the adolescent are the manifestation of enduring family behavioral and relational patterns. While some family relational patterns provide protective factors for the adolescent, others represent risk factors. These risk and protective factors are together the target for change. The guiding principles provide a framework for understanding family functioning, the etiology of clinical problems, the driving forces and motivating factors behind change, and the direction on how to deal with each family in a way that meets each family's unique needs (Sexton & Alexander, 2003).

FFT is based on the principle that all behavior is part of a multisystemic relational system with multiple, mutually interactive components including the youth, parents, family system, community, and extended family, among others. From this perspective, specific problem behaviors are embedded within a relational pattern and are influenced by the many systems of a multisystemic context. The family is the primary entry and assessment point for the initial work in FFT. Working from the inside of the family, FFT initially addresses within family barriers to change and helps identify specific new prosocial behaviors to build. FFT is built on five core principles (Sexton, 2015):

1. *Behavior is best understood in a multisystemic context.* FFT is based on the principle that all behavior is part of a multisystemic relational system with multiple, mutually interactive components including the youth, parents, the family system, community, and extended family, among others.
2. In FFT, the family system is the primary focal point for understanding and intervening.
3. *Alliance-based motivation* is a core part of the clinical change process. Motivation is an outcome of the type of therapeutic alliance described earlier in which successful change process is built on an atmosphere, which is shared by the family, of hope, expectation of change, a sense of responsibility (internal locus of control), and a positive sense of alliance.
4. *Meaning change through reframing.* In FFT, reframing is a family-focused method to create alternative cognitive and attributional perspectives that help redefine meaning events and thus reduce the negativity and redirect the emotionality surrounding the events. Reframing then challenges clients (implicitly at first, then explicitly

later in therapy) to identify new directions for future change and link family members to one another, such that each shares in the responsibility for the family struggles.

5. *Obtainable change goals.* The FFT model seeks to pursue obtainable outcomes that "fit" the values, capability, and style of the family, rather than to mold families into someone's version of "healthy" or to reconstruct the "personality" of the family or individuals therein.

6. Evidence-based clinical decision making results in better community-based outcomes. In real-life clinical settings, clinicians must make decisions adapting treatment to the needs of clients they serve.

Process and Interventions. FFT is more than a series of "intervention techniques." Instead, it is a systematic, theoretically based clinical change process with specific clinical and theoretical principles and a systematic clinical protocol ("map") that guides therapeutic case and session planning. The clinical model synthesizes a theoretically integrated set of guiding principles and a clearly defined clinical "map" that specifies within-session process goals, linked in a phasic model to guide the therapeutic process. The process of change is guided by four theoretically integrated and clearly articulated principles: (1) change is predicated upon fostering alliance-based motivation; (2) behavior change first requires meaning change, primarily through the relationally based process of reframing that includes validation and a reattribution of meaning; (3) behavioral change goals must be obtainable and appropriate for the culture, abilities, and living context of the family; and (4) intervention strategies match and respect the unique nature of each family.

The FFT change "map" or clinical protocol is a systematic and temporally organized set of core mechanisms, specific goals, and relational outcomes that result from doing FFT as a clinical process. FFT has three phases of clinical intervention. Each phase has specific goals and intervention strategies designed to address these goals. FFT phase goals are "proximal goals" or intermediate steps to lasting family change. The FFT model is a phase-based clinical change model consisting of three specific phases of therapeutic intervention:

(1) *Engagement and motivation phase.* Engagement and motivation begins with the first contact between the therapist and family. This phase has three primary objectives: build a balanced alliance (between the family members and between each family member and the therapist), reduce between-family blame and negativity, and create a shared, family-focused problem definition in order to build engagement in therapy and motivation. The desired outcome of these early interactions

is for the family to develop motivation by experiencing a sense of support in their position, emotions, and concerns; a sense of hope for change; and beliefs that the family psychologist and therapy can help promote those changes. When negativity and blaming is reduced, more positive interactions among family members foster hope.

(2) *Behavior change phase.* The primary goal of the behavior change phase is to target and change specific risk behaviors of individuals and families by building specific protective skills within the family. Changing risk behaviors involves targeting the behavioral skills of family members in order to increase their ability to competently perform the myriad of tasks (e.g., communication, parenting, supervision, problem solving, conflict management) that contribute to successful family functioning. Risk factors are reduced as family members develop more protective behaviors for use in these common family tasks. This phase is not curriculum based (like many other approaches) but instead conducted in a manner in which the goals are accomplished from within the family by applying new skills to salient issues presented by the family. The behavior change phase has four primary goals: (1) changing individual and family risk patterns, (2) in a way that matches the unique relational functions of the family, and (3) in a way that is consistent with the obtainable change of this family, (4) in this context, with these values.

A behavior change plan targets the risk factors common in many families (see earlier discussion of risk and protective factors) in the population of at-risk adolescents. These targets frequently include changes in communication, problem solving, conflict management, and parenting.

(3) *Generalization phase.* In the generalization phase, the focus of attention turns from changing family behaviors to extending the application of these changes to other areas of family relationships. In this phase, the primary attention is on the family's interface with the external world. Once again, the therapist accomplishes the phase goals by engaging in the discussion of salient issues of the family rather than using predetermined curricular-based ways. There are three primary goals in this phase: *generalize* the changes made in the behavior change phase to other areas of the family relational system; *maintain* changes made in the generalization phase through focused and specific relapse prevention strategies, and *support* and extend the changes made by the family by incorporating relevant community resources into treatment. The desired outcomes of the generalization stage are to stabilize emotional and cognitive shifts made by the family in engagement and motivation and the specific behavior changes made to alter risk and enhance

protective factors. This is done by having the family develop a sense of mastery around its ability to address future and different situations.

Role of the Therapist. In practice, FFT is a dynamic, highly interpersonal, relationally focused, and emotionally therapeutic experience. Even with its strong evidence base, FFT depends on the therapist to successfully translate the model from ideas to actual practice. Much of what happens in FFT takes place in the interaction between the therapist and the family. In that interaction, the therapist follows a model (or a map) and is guided by core principles (or a lens) yet dependent on their own creativity to match the unique structure, functioning, and interaction style of the family. This is why so much recent attention has been focused on helping clinicians implementing FFT to make creative, model-focused, and client-centered clinical decisions. Inevitably, despite all the theory, change mechanisms, research, and tools for decision making, it is the creativity that occurs within the structure of FFT that results in good outcomes for some of the most difficult clinical cases. Thus, over time, FFT has evolved to a treatment model that blends both structure and creativity into a systematic approach for working with some of the most difficult types of clinical cases.

FFT is unique in that it also developed a model-specific measurement feedback system (FFT–CMI: Sexton, 2010) that allows for reliable, session-by-session measurement of symptoms, model impact, and progress. The system is part of a web-based feedback tool that provides specific evidence from which to make clinical decision and session plans. The combination of case planning and measurement tools allows for an evidence-based practice of FFT and accomplish what Strikler (2007) called "becoming a local clinical scientist." The goal of all of the implementation tools is to help equip the therapist with all the necessary tools to be both model specific and client centered in his or her implementation and delivery of FFT. FFT treatment manuals and supervision processes have been described at length in other descriptions of FFT (Sexton, 2010; Sexton & Fisher, 2015; Sexton, 2015).

FFT–Care4 is an FFT-specific measurement feedback system that integrates an existing battery of process, progress, and case planning measures (of youth symptoms, family functioning, session impact, and progress). The FFT–Care4 is composed of two components: (1) clinically sensitive measures that are administered regularly throughout treatment to collect ongoing information concerning the process and (2) progress of treatment and timely and clinically useful feedback about the progress and process of treatment to aid in clinical decision making. In actual practice assessment, treatment planning and individualization of treatment are difficult. The goal of the FFT–CFS is to *provide information that helps clinical decision making by* prioritizing and therefore individualizing the process more quickly and effectively; giving youth and families a voice in treatment where they are safe to express it if necessary; multisystemic perspective considering multiple points of view; and a way to monitor the therapeutic process and progress in real time.

Research Support. FFT has proven effective in reducing recidivism between 26% and 73% with status-offending, moderate, and seriously delinquent youths when compared with no-treatment and to juvenile court probation services (Alexander, Pugh, et al., 2000). In addition to reduced recidivism rates, other studies have used other dependent measures such as the number of crimes committed and severity of crimes. Barton, Alexander, Waldron, Turner, and Warburton (1985) conducted a series of three small studies of different severity of youth delinquency. FFT conducted by undergraduate students resulted in significant reduction of 1-year recidivism rates of 26% for youth in the FFT group as compared with 51% base rated on the juvenile justice jurisdiction.

Gordon and colleagues used a model of FFT that emphasized problem-solving and specific behavior change skills. They found FFT to have much lower re-arrest rates at both 24 months and 5 years post-treatment. Compared with juveniles who received regular probation services ($n = 27$, 67% recidivism rate), clients in the FFT group had an 11 % recidivism rate at 2-year follow-up. At 5-year follow-up, the group that received FFT had a 9% recidivism rate as (as compared with 41% recidivism rate for the comparison group). Waldron and colleagues (Waldron, Slesnick, Turner, Brody, & Peterson, 2001) studied the impact of FFT on drug using youth and found that a combination of CBT and FFT led to significant reductions in percentage of days using marijuana, from pretreatment to 4 months following initiation of treatment.

The largest FFT was conducted in Washington State and is the first to study FFT in a true community-based setting. The project results have been reported by Barnowski (2002), Sexton and Alexander (2004), and Sexton and Turner (2010) in varying forms and with different subsets of participants. When compared with a "no-treatment" control, FFT had a 31% reduction in criminal behavior and a 43% reduction in violent recidivism. However, the positive effect of FFT was not universal; in fact, those therapists who delivered FFT with high fidelity (i.e., how it was designed) had the outcomes noted earlier. The most recent published studies of FFT were conducted in Ireland. The first was a retrospective study of FFT's effectiveness indicating that adolescent behavior problems improved in cases treated with FFT. The best outcomes occurred when receiving treatment from therapists who conducted FFT with a high degree of fidelity (Graham, et al., 2013). In the second randomized trial (Hartnett, Carr, & Sexton, in press), those families who participated in FFT reported significantly greater improvement in adolescent conduct problems and family adjustment than the comparison group. Among the FFT cases, 50% were classified as clinically recovered after treatment compared with 18.2% of cases from the waiting-list control group. Improvements shown immediately after treatment were sustained at 3 months of follow-up. The cost saving of FFT in community-based systems has also been studied. These comparisons of cost support the cost findings of the Washington Study. Using the algorithm developed by Aos and Barnowski (1998), FFT saved the Washington State system $16,250 per youth in court costs and crime victim costs. Total savings from the first year of the FFT program amounted to $1,121,250. This same algorithm suggests that for every $1 invested in delivering FFT, more than $14.67 is saved.

Multidimensional Family Therapy (MDFT)

MDFT was developed as a systemic treatment for adolescent drug abuse and behavior problems. It is a "therapy of subsystems" (Liddle, 2009, p. 349), that is, both phasic and flexible in design and implementation. A therapy of subsystems is one that is ecological, targeting interventions at the individual, relational (parent/child, parent/parent, siblings), family, and social systems levels. MDFT is integrative in the sense that it uses techniques derived from various family therapy theoretical orientations including structural family therapy (the use of enactment to shape positive family interactions), cognitive behavioral family therapy (to move away from blaming to a focus on strengths and problem solving), self-efficacy theory, developmental theory, and transactional theory (Liddle, 1999).

MDFT is phasic in its adherence to a stepwise process. The model emphasizes establishing therapeutic alliances with members of the various stakeholder subsystems. This in turn fosters a process-oriented unfolding of relevant therapeutic content and themes that provide motivation for action steps and change strategies. MDFT is flexible in that the course, pace, and content of therapy are shaped collaboratively with the adolescents and parents and shift in response to clinical need. Sessions may occur one or more times during the week and can take place in a variety of settings including homes, schools, and the juvenile system.

Theoretical Foundations. The MDFT model follows a number of theoretical assumptions regarding individual and family functioning:

1. Teen drug abuse and related problems are multidimensional.
2. Individual, family, and environmental factors contribute to drug use and related problems.

3. Positive family functioning is instrumental in creating lasting change for adolescents.
4. Motivation for change can be fostered, and change can occur.
5. Therapists create working relationships with the adolescent, parents or caregivers, and collaborating professionals (mdft.org, 2015).

MDFT recognizes that the outcomes of a drug abuse lifestyle often include drug abuse, delinquent behavior, mental health issues, academic challenges, problematic family functioning, and risky sexual behavior. These outcomes are often the result of a plethora of linked causes, and effective treatment requires that they all be addressed in a systematic fashion. Variables that affect drug abuse and drug treatment are ecologically linked at the micro, meso, and macro systems levels, comprising subsystems that affect one another in a reciprocal fashion (Bronfenbrenner, 1979).

A primary focus of MDFT treatment involves interventions aimed directly at eliminating the adolescent's drug use through developmentally appropriate individual sessions that promote motivation for change, as well as monitoring via drug testing. The therapist develops an individual treatment plan that includes methods for stress reduction, effective problem-solving and decision-making skills, and the promotion of new skills to ameliorate possible comorbid disorders such as depression and anxiety. MDFT assumes that the family is capable of providing a natural healing environment. Therapy is meant to enhance family functioning by decreasing blaming and fault finding and promoting positive and supportive interactions between family members. The therapist troubleshoots school problems and interfaces with the juvenile justice system when needed in order to coordinate the development of intervention plans that minimize overlap or gaps in aid to the adolescent and his or her family. The therapist helps facilitate meetings with school personnel and the juvenile justice system, and coaches parents regarding their interactions with these systems. The meetings provide a strategic opportunity for discussing conflict de-escalation and creating action plans. Through these meetings, important stakeholders in the adolescent's life collaborate to promote the most positive outcomes for prosocial behavior and academic achievement.

Process and Interventions. There are five assessment and intervention modules that structure the MDFT approach. The model also allows for flexibility in sessions in order to reflect the unique and individual needs of the adolescent and the family. Individual work with adolescents accounts for about 25–30% of the overall therapy, while 20–30% of therapy time is spent with parents alone, 30–40% is spent doing family therapy, and 10–20% is spent working with the outside community (Rowe et al., 2012). MDFT is a stage-specific model, and the content of a given session will be dictated to some degree by the stage of therapy the family is in. The five assessment and intervention modules are as follows:

- Individual assessment and interventions with the adolescent.
- Individual assessment and interventions with the parents.
- Assessments and interventions to change parent–adolescent interactions.
- Assessments and interventions with other family members where needed.
- Assessments and interventions with systems external to the family (mdft.org, 2015).

Treatment is phasic in structure, following a developmental model. There are three stages of treatment, representing the introduction of treatment, the heart of treatment, and termination/maintenance of treatment gains (Liddle, H. A., 2014). The stages of treatment are as follows:

- Stage 1 focuses on building the therapeutic alliance with the individual members of the family, with the parent–child dyad/triad and with the family as a whole. During this stage, the therapist uses the interview process to instill hope, define the parameters of the problem, identify individual and corporate strengths and weaknesses, identify where parenting skills might need to be enhanced, identify themes that define the family and that contribute to the abnormal or chaotic functioning, and motivate parents toward commitment to their child.
- Stage 2 seeks to move the adolescent and the family toward normal stable functioning by utilizing the structural family therapy technique of enactment (Minuchin, 1974). The therapist and family members work on identified themes to increasingly shape "positive and constructive family interactions" (Liddle, 2009, p. 349). To facilitate such movement, the therapist helps the family work on their communication skills by decreasing negative attributions and instead using more collaborative, problem-solving approaches. Stage 2 will also work to provide a firm but non-recriminating structure for drug screenings. Comorbid disorders are also targeted for treatment during this phase of treatment.
- Stage 3 of treatment is organized around moving toward termination. Attention is paid to the maintenance of gains in the normalization of individual and family lives, as well as strategies to handle potential relapse.

Role of the Therapist. Effective use of the MDFT model requires a therapist with unique skills beyond what is needed to do effective substance abuse treatment with adolescents. The therapist's attitude must be positive, and she or he must be patient in working with different subsystems. He or she must be skilled at joining with the various constellations of the family to promote hope to all involved parties (Liddle, 2009). Motivation for change is usually necessary for positive treatment outcomes, so the therapist should have the skills necessary for motivating, encouraging, and negotiating with stakeholders in ways that promote the treatment plan. One of the main goals of MDFT is creating a normative lifestyle intrapersonally, interpersonally, and contextually for individuals and family members. The therapist must be able to provide a therapeutic context that is non-chaotic and structured, but one that also provides room for flex in response to the situational needs of the individuals and family. The therapist should be adept in skills associated with individual and family therapies. She or he should also be able to comfortably direct multiple family participants in a therapy session.

The therapist should have a commitment to collaboration in developing interventions. A collaborative mind-set is just one marker of an attitude of respect and care for all the individuals in the family and for the family as a whole. The therapist is likely to serve as an advocate for both the adolescent and the parents, as well as for outside parties like the school system, the legal/justice system, friends, and outside family members. The therapist may be working with all these parties to create a streamlined plan of approach to maximizing positive gains for both the adolescent and the family. Tact and negotiating skills are useful in assuring that all requisite stakeholders feel buy-in to the direction of therapy and that all parties feel their particular expectations are being taken into account.

Research Support. The research record on the efficacy of MDFT as a family-based, /developmentally oriented, comprehensive treatment for adolescent drug abuse and antisocial behavior is impressive (Liddle, 2015). There have been between 7 and 10 studies that have found strong evidence for the efficacy of MFDT. Studies have been conducted in a variety of settings such as juvenile detention settings, day care centers, drug court, and clinics devoted to diversion programs. Vaughn and Howard (2004) conducted a meta-analysis of substance abuse programs to assess outcome findings. MDFT and cognitive-behavioral group treatment were among the strongest models tested. Liddle and colleagues (Liddle, Rowe, Dakof, Henderson & Greenbaum, 2009) compared multidimensional family therapy with a peer group intervention among a population of clinically referred low-income adolescents. Both treatments utilized manual formats, lasted 4 months, and were delivered through a community agency. Latent growth curve modeling analyses suggested that MDFT provided a superior model of treatment for both substance abuse and delinquency.

CONCLUSIONS: WHAT IS NEXT?

As psychologists, we are not independent of the system(s) that we are intervening in or trying to understand. What this means is that we, the psychologists, bring something beyond the client that shapes and organizes how we understand client problems and subsequently how we decide to intervene. As we noted earlier, theories and intervention models are like *lenses* to be looked through, bringing some elements into particular focus while letting others fade into the background. At the broadest level, systems epistemology is the primary organizing lens for family psychology. Yet, those broad epistemological ideas are not always actionable and specific enough to clinically intervene to help a client, couple, or family best improve their situation or resolve the personal issues with which they struggle.

The family-based clinical intervention models presented in this chapter are representative of the two domains of clinical approaches for taking a family approach: theory based and evidence based. The evidence-based approaches tend to be the more current approaches in part because ongoing research and evaluation have only recently become a routine part of practice in the development of clinical models. As noted in the chapter, this movement is part of a culture-wide shift for the inclusion of research evidence in medicine, education, and mental health (among other areas). While each focuses on a unique element of the family (relational patterns, history and context, or beliefs), each also shares a focus on the core or necessary ingredients of any theory or clinical model (see Chapter 3): (1) a theoretical core that describes the functioning of both well-functioning and problem families, and a (2) clinical model, "map" that identifies the unique focus of assessment, change mechanism, and clinical change model, or techniques/interventions that are designed to help promote positive change.

In the next chapter, attention turns to those approaches that focus on couples. Similar to family-based models, those in the couple domain have both theoretically and research-based models. Family clinical intervention models also have a different history than intervention models that focus on couples (see Chapter 8). While couple intervention models have used more behavioral directions, family intervention models have retained a more traditional systemic focus (Sexton et al., 2013). This makes sense given the history of family psychology. The initial applications of system epistemology were focused on the family as a whole. The couple was often seen as a subset of the family and, therefore, was treated along with the larger family systems. As you will find out in the next chapter, couple approaches have emerged out of an interest in the unique transactional and behavioral interaction within couple relationships.

Chapter 8

Couple-Focused Clinical Intervention Models

Emotionally intelligent couples are intimately familiar with each other's world. I call this a richly detailed love map.

—John Gottman

The pioneering early clinical models in family psychology were frequently more family oriented than couple oriented. Couples were viewed as alternative subsystems of the family (e.g., structural family therapy) or an extension of the intergenerational transmission process. It was through the work of the psychodynamic and more behavioral thinkers that couples therapy and now couples psychology has emerged. Through the work focused on couples, we have discovered that while couples are truly a subsystem of the larger family, they are also unique relational units that work differently from the family as a whole. Some have suggested that because coupling is a choice (rather than biological as with family), that unique variables play a part in the functioning of this relational unit and in the development of clinical issues. In fact, some of the most current clinical intervention research suggests that the couple relationship might in fact be the most efficient and effective place to focus individual substance abuse or depression treatment (Whisman, Johnson, Be, & Li, 2012).

Couples therapy has as its primary unit of analysis the couple dyad. In some cases, coupling is demonstrated by formal marriage and in other cases by a relational connection alone. Like family therapy, couples work focuses on (1) problem-maintaining behavior patterns, (2) problematic and constraining belief systems, and (3) historical, contextual, and constitutional predisposing factors (see Chapter 3). In addition, couples clinical models take the same risk and protective factors approach. Distressed couples evidence lower rates of positivity in their relationships, they do not spend time in pleasurable activities together or in building pleasant memories (Weiss, Hops, & Patterson, 1993), and they have ineffective communication and conflict management skills (Halford & Sanders, 1990; Jacobson & Follette, 1985; Weiss & Heyman, 1990). Additionally, distressed couples think about their partner in negative ways and focus on negative behaviors as personality traits rather than expressions of temporal situations and therefore develop negative relationship schemata, and these schemata often result in negative generalizations about their partner or relationship (Buehlman, Gottman, & Katz, 1992; Halford, Osgarby, & Kelley, 1996). A distressed couple's behavior is often more hostile, forming escalating negativity loops, accumulating criticism, hostility, excuses, denial of responsibility, withdrawal, and complaints about the other's personality (Weiss & Heyman, 1990).

A variety of protective characteristics are present in healthy couples. For example, the belief in relative rather than absolute truth, which means they understand that there is more than one point of view on any given issue, being able to operate under the assumptions that the partner has good motives underlying his or her actions or communication, and that differences will be resolved are all protective factors in couples (Beavers, 1985; Sperry & Carlson, 1991). In a similar way, taking responsibility in the relationship, having goals that are in alignment, mutually encouraging one another, having open communication, sharing in joint conflict resolution, and adhering to a commitment to relationship equality are also protective factors. Gottman suggests that friendship is the main factor in happy marriages, "a mutual respect and enjoyment of each other's company" (Gottman, 1999, p. 19).

In this chapter, we focus on five couple-based clinical intervention models. Just as in the previous chapter, we have chosen these models because they represent the range of ways in which couple and family psychology treatment is carried out, with some theories focusing more on relational patterns, history, and context, while others focus on meanings and attributions (see Chapter 3). Two of these models represent traditional approaches that have tended to emphasize theory rather than research, while the other three represent the more current generation of evidence-based approaches that integrate the best research evidence with clinical experience, the most current and clinically relevant psychological theory, and client values (Institute of Medicine, 2001; Sexton & Koop-Gordon, 2009). Some of these approaches are used in family-based applications as well as couples work (e.g., solution-focused therapy and psychodynamic therapy). We have chosen to include them here because of their contribution to understanding couple functioning and their unique perspective on intervening in couple relationships. Two models of couple's therapy have particularly strong empirical support for treatment. In a meta-analysis of the couple and family literature, cognitive behavioral couples therapy (CBCT) had an effect size of .78 and emotionally focused therapy (EFT) had an effect size of .87 (Sexton et al., 2012, p. 622). A variant of CBCT, integrative behavioral couples therapy (IBCT; Jacobson & Christensen, 1996), integrates emotion with behavior and, over time, has proven to be a more efficacious modality even than CBCT.

In the following sections, we focus on the following five couple-oriented clinical intervention models:

1. *Psychoanalytic/psychodynamic* approaches emphasize the internal mechanisms of an individual with an emphasis on the evocation of affect, on bringing troublesome feelings into awareness, and on integrating current difficulties with previous life experience, using the therapist–patient relationship as a change agent.
2. *Solution-focused* approaches focus on pragmatic ways to solve problems.
3. *Acceptance and commitment therapy (ACT)* seeks to help couples focus less on cognitive and behavioral relationship change and more on relationship flexibility leading to increases in understanding and acceptance of one another.
4. *IBCT* is the next generation of behavioral couples therapy.
5. *EFT* is an approach that focuses largely on theoretical notions of attachment and the primacy of emotion in helping a couple improve their relationship.

As we noted in the last chapter, both traditional and theoretical or evidence-based concepts are lenses that we look through in order to understand couples and implement successful therapeutic change. What these approaches share is a focus on the necessary ingredients of any successful theory or clinical model: (1) a theoretical core that describes the functioning of both well-functioning and problem couples, and (2) a clinical model or map of assessment, change mechanisms, and techniques/interventions that are designed to help promote positive change. In this section, we describe the unique features that define each of the approaches.

As in the previous chapter, there are challenges in providing a comprehensive snapshot of the breadth and scope of complex couple intervention models in a short chapter—much less as sections of a chapter. Most couple intervention theories and models are comprehensive, systematic, and complex psychological interventions that can easily lose their dynamic and relational dimensions when reduced to parsimonious descriptions. A detailed understanding will come from the treatment manuals, training programs, books, chapters, articles, and journals that are devoted to specific couple treatment models. Thus, this is not a comprehensive list of approaches, or explanation of any one given model, but is instead illustrative of the integration of research, clinical wisdom, and good practice (Sexton et al., 2013; Sexton et al., 2011). In the following sections, we will address each model by considering the following:

- Theoretical principles that describe how couples function
- The mechanism by which *clinical problems* develop
- Primary *goals* of the intervention or what areas of couple functioning are the primary targets for change
- Clinical process and primary clinical interventions
- Role of the therapist
- Research support

THEORETICALLY BASED MODELS

Psychoanalytic and Psychodynamic Models

Many of the early pioneers of family therapy had been trained as psychoanalysts, and some retained a psychodynamic approach as they extended the model to include families. Nathan Ackerman was a prominent early voice for extending his orientation from "the inner life of the person, to the person within family, to the family within community, and finally, to the social community itself" (Ackerman, 1972, p. 449). Conflict or symptoms could arise at any level of the system and resound across all system levels, with a kind of interlocking pathology (e.g., an individual symptom may be symptomatic of a marital or family problem; improvement in one part of the system may trigger symptoms in another part). Role definition was an important element of family dynamics because role clarity could facilitate system functioning. The successor to the earliest attempts to extend psychoanalytic theory to the family was object relations family therapy. Drawing on the work of Melanie Klein and other members of the British Middle School, and influenced by the adaptations of Fairbairn, this approach was adopted in the United States by Lyman Wynne, James Framo, Jill Savege Scharff, and David Scharff (Goldenberg & Goldenberg, 2013).

Theoretical Foundations. The term "psychodynamic" refers to a broad domain of therapies including, but not limited to, Adlerian, object relations, developmental, self psychology, Neo-Freudian, and attachment theory. Klimek (1979) defines the term "psychodynamic" as "the forces, motives, and energy generated by the deepest of human needs" (p. 3). This definition arises out of the Greek for "psyche," meaning soul or heart, and "dynamics" meaning energy or force. Paolino and McCrady (1978) noted that "dynamic factors in the mind are often in conflict. The psychodynamic functional anatomy of the mind always includes specific identifiable factors that are often in conflict and are psychological, powerful, usually unconscious, motivating forces of human behavior" (p. 92). These conflicts and the defenses that are erected to mediate them are at the core of psychodynamic theory, that is, the ability to recognize and interpret basic impulses and the defenses that mask them.

A core theoretical principle of these models is the interplay of psychical forces at the heart of human nature, sex, and aggression, which motivates much of human behavior—frequently called drive theory. It is the tension between drives and defenses that define human conflict, both intrapsychic and interpersonal. Healthy people have flexible defenses and so can gratify impulses to some extent. In neurosis, excessive fear of punishment leads to rigid defenses, resulting in a blocked life, with energy drained off by repression, resulting in symptoms of anxiety or depression.

Psychodynamic family therapy recognizes that present relationships and early experiences interact recursively. Interestingly, while the treatment may be individual in nature, the core roots of anxiety and depression are found in four prototypic traumatic and *relationally based* experiences: (1) abandonment, (2) loss of love, (3) powerlessness, and (4) self-condemnation (Nichols, 1987). Defense responses to these events include repression, denial, projection, introjection, internalizing aspects of others, reversal, displacement, and isolation. Thus, it is the ghosts of prior relationships that shape current relationships and also the conversations inherent in those relationships (Scharff and Scharff, 1987). Symptoms are manifestations of family stressors and are transactional in nature (Framo, 1970).

Psychodynamic family therapy approaches focus on the role of relational processes in development as a way to understand clinical problems. From this lens, it is the quality of the first human relationship that becomes the prototype for all other intimate relationships (Horner, 1984, p. 3). How children relate to others in the future is determined in large measure by how they respond initially to patterns in their environment. Children have an inborn, autonomous biological affinity for organizing experiences into patterns (Horner, 1984, p. 9). These patterns, or mental pictures, are organized into patterns of patterns, then schemas, which become consolidated and stabilized through repetition. A schema is a mental representation, which, when generalized, becomes an internal working model, or internalized object, a basic structure of the mind that is fundamental to establishing a sense of self. Schemas of self and others are developed through interpersonal transactions between infant and caregiver, which mediate the psychological tasks of child development, that is, attachment, self–object differentiation, internalization of the good/bad mother, development of object constancy, and basic structuring of the psyche. Object relations focus on the importance of attachment in the development of perceptions of self and others. Object relations create rule sets for the organization of information that is relevant to attachment-related experiences, feelings, and perceptions (Main, Kaplan, and Cassidy, 1985).

Attachment, then, is a major issue in development, determining the infant's ability to separate/individuate from the caregiver. In the course of normal interaction with the caregiver, the child will experience relational tension and friction, that is, experiences of gratification and frustration, union, and separation. If environmental demands are greater than developmental proficiencies, or if environmental resources are inadequate, the child will experience a deficit in organization, leaving areas of experience unpatterned. Under stress, the child will disintegrate, with schemas failing to knit together, resulting in developmental arrest. A bad object is a working model of an attachment figure to whom are attributed characteristics such as inaccessibility, unwillingness to respond helpfully, or who offers a hostile response. A good object is a working model of an attachment figure conceived of as accessible, trustworthy, and ready to help when called upon. If an infant experiences a secure attachment, that is, if the child's experiences are developmentally appropriate and not too disruptive, then the child will develop the cognitive structures to accommodate the development of more mature structures (Bowlby, 1969 pp. 37–38). The fundamental goal in attachment and individuation is the ability to be intimate with another.

Goals of Treatment. The two major goals in dynamic therapy are to (1) uncover the projective identification style of the couple and (2) expose the transference between the couple and the manner in which the couple relates to each other on the basis of the transference (parataxic distortion). Once the projective identifications and transferences can be understood, then corrective measures can be taken to establish a greater sense of true intimacy between the couple.

The underlying rationale for psychodynamic therapy is that "the thoughts and feelings expressed gradually make explicit what the patient is doing which is self-hurtful and may, therefore, need to be changed"

(Luborsky, 1984, p. 10). If couples had a better idea of what their behavior was and the unconscious motivations for that behavior, the assumption is that they could then be in better control of their relationship. Further, working with conscious motives for behavior, and current and immediate interactions tends to facilitate first-order change only, rather than second-order dynamic change, which is deep and lasting (Framo, 1970). As was stated earlier, internal working models are heuristic guides that color perceptions, behavior, and reality itself. Internal working models will not change unless the client system is given corrective experiences that are different from that which have been known.

Treatment Process and Clinical Interventions. The focus of psychodynamic therapy is on the dynamic aspects of relationship, both intra- and interpersonal. Psychodynamic therapists encourage and facilitate client sharing of experiences; help clients identify recurrent patterns in experience or behavior; point out the use of defensive maneuvers used to stifle threatening information or feelings; draw attention to unacceptable thoughts or feelings, or thoughts and feelings not clearly in awareness; and overall promote the client system's experience and processing of affect (Luborsky, 1984). The therapeutic process is characterized by several different intervention foci (Skynner, 1976).

1. *Setting the stage.* The therapist provides a frame for therapy: time, space, and structure. The frame should be flexible, but strong. The therapist puts the couple at ease, building a sense of trust and security so that the dyad is willing to examine defenses. Support can be encouragement and modeling, leading to an exploration of unexpressed feelings about the symptom/problem, with the therapist enquiring of each person what would improve the problem. The therapist recognizes that there are several family systems and subsystems in the therapy room: the couple's families of origin, the therapist's family (countertransference), the therapist, and the partners themselves. Disagreements and other dynamic dyad material will be exposed, and transference and countertransference will begin to manifest. There will be movement between the here and now and the past that is in the present.

2. *Interpretations.* The dynamic aspect of therapy occurs as the therapist absorbs the projective system of the dyad, suffers the dilemma of not knowing, just as the couple does not know, and arrives at interpretations tailored to the exact defensive structure of the couple. Interpretation of material involves the process of helping the couple understand their dynamics, as the therapist seeks to understand. Interpretations are based on helping the couple understand the inner logic of a partner's thoughts, feelings, or actions.

3. *Sequences.* Projective identification is the dynamic between a couple where one person splits off an aspect of self, projects it onto the other, and then treats the other as if the other possesses that trait. For example, if one person unconsciously feels like he or she is a weakling, then he or she will split that intolerable aspect off of self and project it onto the significant other and then treat the other with disgust or disdain.

4. *Developmental affect.* The initial stages of Erickson's psychosocial development include trust/mistrust (fear), shame/autonomy (shame), and guilt/competence (guilt). Often, couples through problematic interpersonal or environmental experiences are emotionally arrested in these initial stages of development. The person then spends the rest of his or her life in a repetition compulsion, using significant others to paradoxically, at one and the same time, attempt to escape from debilitating feelings of guilt, shame, and fear and at the same time reinforce those primitive feelings over and over again. Such feelings include insecure attachment feelings, fear of abandonment, fear of being unloved, fear of punishment, shame (feeling like nothing), guilt (can't do anything right).

5. *Themes.* Psychodynamic couple therapy is very much focused on process. A clear understanding of process recognizes it to be thematically oriented. Psychological and relational themes are played out within session, between sessions, and from one session to the next. There is a dynamic unity to the material that is presented in session; it is up to the therapist to unveil the theme within each session and between sessions in order to move therapy along. There is also a thematic continuity from the beginning of a session to its end. The therapist seeks to understand the underlying dynamics in each session from the point of what other therapists might consider light chitchat at the beginning of the session through the middle to the end of the session. Everything that is said and done in session or outside of sessions when the couple is working on their relationship has thematic significance and may be mined for emotional residue that can be used in the service of the corrective emotional process.

6. *Transference and countertransference* are primary areas of clinical intervention. Transference has to do with emotional stress skewing and distorting the feelings for contemporary significant relationships based on past significant others in the client's life; the client then relates to the contemporary other as if he or she were the person from the client's past. Countertransference occurs when the significant other reacts to the transference as if it were real. In couples therapy, the couple may relate pathologically (unrealistically) out of mutual transference and countertransference at an unconscious level. Transference

and countertransference may also take place between one or both of the members of the dyad in relation to the therapist. The therapist's countertransference may reflect how the client(s) experiences others, how others experience the client(s), or may simply be the therapist's own personal pathology triggered by the client or client system.

7. *The corrective emotional experience*/process is a major change mechanism in both couple and family psychodynamic treatment. The information the therapist brings out is usually uncommunicated pain or fear that partners have denied and repressed. Evocation of affect, bringing troublesome feelings into awareness, integrating current difficulties with previous life experience, and using the client/therapist relationship as a change agent are all aspects of the dynamic stage of couple therapy. The therapist utilizes the dynamic therapeutic relational connection between self and the couple and also between the partners to mine unconscious material where each partner experiences the force of repressed feelings and can then process those feelings in the safety of the therapeutic environment. What makes these relationships therapeutic is the therapist's treatment of each partner in new novel healthy ways when this emotional material emerges, and helping each partner treat the other in new ways that neither has experienced before. Just as one's metabolism continues in an excitatory state for hours after the actual exercising itself has ceased, so too does the process of emotional excitation and correction continue well beyond the limits of the session hour.

Role of the Therapist. Psychodynamic couple therapists use probes, clarification, and interpretation in uncovering and explaining those unconscious feelings, beliefs, and expectations contributing to current observable couple difficulties (Snyder and Wills, 1989). The therapist seeks to make overt what is covert, thoughts, feelings, and beliefs that are either totally or partially beyond awareness, so that these can be restructured or renegotiated at a conscious level. Emphasis is placed on the interpretation of underlying dynamics that contribute to the current observable relational difficulties and then a working through or processing of those difficulties at behavioral, cognitive, and affective levels (Snyder and Wills, 1989).

Solution-Focused Therapy (SFT)

Solution-focused therapy (SFT) is a brief therapy approach that emphasizes client strengths and attempts to produce desirable solutions to the couple's presenting problems. SFT originated in the early

1980s at the Brief Family Therapy Center in Milwaukee through the work of Steve de Shazer and his associates (Friedman & Lipchik, 1999; O'Connell, 1998; Visser, 2013). The contextual framework for the solution-focused approach is the constructivist postmodern paradigm (Hoyt & Berg, 1998), and it represents those models that focus on meaning and attribution, relational patterns, and a pragmatic orientation to problem solving.

Theoretical Foundations. Following the postmodern paradigm, the solution-focused approach focuses on how individuals construct meanings about their experiences, relationships, and future plans. The meanings that a couple ascribes to situations and events are changeable, and the therapist helps couples develop adaptive perceptions of life experiences (O'Connell, 1998). In fact, much like the early Mental Research Institute (MRI) notions, the lens of the solution-focused approach focuses on the future and develops more adaptive perceptions of life experiences for the client system. The therapist focuses primarily on solutions and not problems, does not emphasize the past, except in relation to present and future solutions, and validates the resourcefulness of clients (De Jong & Berg, 1998; Friedman & Lipchik, 1999; O'Connell, 1998). There is an a priori solution-oriented assumption, that is, individuals can draw on existing resources to aid them in building solutions to manage problems (De Jong & Berg, 1998; Walter & Peller, 1992). Hoyt and Berg (1998, p. 204) summarize the basic rules of SFT as:

1. If it ain't broke, don't fix it: The therapist only works on the material the couple have identified as problematic in their relationship.
2. Once you know what works, do more of it. Discover what the couple is doing right in their relationship and have them do more of it.
3. If something doesn't work, don't do it again; do something different. Couples tend to do the same problematic behaviors over and over hoping for a different outcome. The therapist stops couples from re-enacting fruitless behaviors and has them do something different where they are more likely to achieve relationship success.

Change is a major focus of the solution-focused approach, and change occurs when couples focus on solutions and competencies (Walter & Peller, 1992). Although change can occur at any time, the solutions that lead to change may not be directly or obviously related to problems (O'Connell, 1998). Solution-focused theory is based on the assumption that small changes produce larger changes (Friedman & Lipchik, 1999; O'Connell, 1998; Walter & Peller, 1992). In the most basic terms, change occurs when the client does something different (Quick, 1996, p. 7).

Goals of Treatment. The goals of SFT are to emphasize client strengths. The therapist validates the resourcefulness of clients and attempts to help them produce desirable solutions to their problems. De Shazer (1991) has written that workable goals have these characteristics: (1) small rather than big changes, (2) should be salient to client needs, (3) should be described behaviorally and concretely, (4) practically achievable, (5) should be the result of hard work, (6) are a beginning point, not an ending point, and (7) should result in new behaviors, not merely the extinction of old behaviors (p. 112).

Goals are an ongoing dynamic property of the therapy process, open to constant negotiation, moving toward possibilities, rather than fixed targets (Walter & Peller, 1992). Establishing goals requires negotiation between a couple who may have very different ideas about the nature of the interpersonal issues. However, by placing the emphasis in therapy on resources, on the here and now, and on solutions, the therapist provides a context for more likely mutual agreement on how to proceed forward (Friedman & Lipchik, 1999).

Process and Clinical Interventions. SFT interventions lie in the relational interactions between the therapist and the client. In general, the common focus is not on problems, but on available solutions. For example, instead of asking a couple, "What are the problems in your relationship?" A solution-oriented practitioner might ask, "If problems didn't exist, what would your relationship look like?" (O'Connell, 1998). Practitioners must be particularly attentive to the language they use to address couples in therapy as the language used by the therapist can orient the therapeutic conversation toward either problems or solutions (Friedman, 1993). In addition to general solution-oriented questions, practitioners can employ three specific types of questions:

1. *The miracle question.* When used in therapy, the miracle question asks clients what their experiences would be like if a miracle were to occur that resolved all of their problems (O'Connell, 1998). The miracle question helps elicit information about each partner's vision for the marriage. The practitioner should follow the miracle question with a detailed exploration of the miracle, being particularly careful to use the client's language (Quick, 1996). The miracle question can aid couples in developing a clear picture of their vision for their relationship, particularly when the miracle is explored fully (O'Connell, 1998; Walter & Peller, 1992). As the miracle question can be used to elicit each partner's optimal vision of the marriage, an unlimited number of possibilities for the marriage may develop (De Jong & Berg, 1998). For example, Janet and Dean were a couple in their

mid-40s with two children living on the West Coast. Janet worked in public relations and Dean worked in the biotechnology sector. Janet had for years wanted to move closer to her parents in the Midwest, while Dean always held off for fear that he would not be able to find work. Their division had led to consistent squabbling about Janet's perceived unrelenting pressure and Dean's perceived recalcitrance. The therapist asked them what their life would look like if a miracle were to occur that resolved all of their problems. Janet immediately stated, "We would live in Kansas City near my parents, the kids would be in private school, Dean would have the job of his dreams and I'd be working for a strong PR firm." It turned out that Dean's perception was not that different from Janet's, which began a conversation about how they could make the dream a reality. They began with blue-sky brainstorming, which led to a detailed plan and timetable with which each of them was comfortable.

2. *Scaling questions.* Scaling questions can be used throughout therapy to help couples identify their position in relation to their goals (O'Connell, 1998). A general example of a scaling question that can be used in premarital therapy might be, "On a scale from one to ten, how confident do you feel that your marriage will be satisfying?" A specific application of scaling questions to communication skills is, "On a scale from one to ten, how comfortable do you feel in telling your partner your feelings?" If a partner's answer was seven, a follow-up question could be, "What would need to be different in order for you to answer with an eight?" Scaling questions provide the therapist with baseline information related to each couple's unique needs (Quick, 1996). The use of scales can help clarify what couples can do to produce small changes in their relationship, and couples can see change over time when scaling questions are revisited in subsequent sessions; thus, scaling questions can help highlight a couple's progress toward their goals (Hoyt & Berg, 1998; O'Connell, 1998).

3. *Exception questions.* Therapists ask questions that help couples identify times when problems they experience are not present (De Jong & Berg, 1998). Exceptions are highlighted to help the couple become aware of spontaneous and/or purposeful times when problems in their relationship do not exist (Clark-Stager, 1999). An example of an exception question that may be used in premarital counseling is, "Can you tell me about a time when you have not felt nervous about getting married to your fiancé?" Because couples may experience exceptions spontaneously or deliberately, it is important that the therapist explore fully the exceptions that are discovered (De Jong & Berg, 1998; Quick, 1996; Walter & Peller, 1992).

Typical SFT interventions also include goal setting, homework tasks, and amplifying exceptions. For example, a couple may indicate that they feel closer to each other when they have spent time talking. The therapist may assign a "sharing time" homework task where the couple spends 15 minutes every other night sharing about their relationship. Finally, in SFT, the therapist provides the client system with a form of feedback toward the end of the session. This feedback focuses primarily on couple strengths and on the progress they have made in therapy. In addition, feedback includes a task for the couple to complete that is designed to help them move toward positive change (De Jong & Berg, 1998; O'Connell, 1998; Walter & Peller, 1992). An example might be, "In the coming week, write down each time your partner does something you consider thoughtful."

Role of the Therapist. Initially, the role of the therapist is one of *questioner*, as she or he ascertains the nature of the clients' problems, the solutions they have tried in the past to rectify their problems, both those that have worked and those that haven't, and the mutual strengths they bring to bear in the service of the relationship. Questioning serves to elucidate and punctuate for clients those points in their relationship where what they have done has worked. The goal is to move clients away from a problem-saturated narrative to (1) create a positive valence for client interactions and (2) facilitate a sense of cooperation between them in the pursuit of positive relating.

To that end, the role of the therapist is also that of *facilitator*, endeavoring to aid the client system to see their relationship as more than a problem, to look for resources rather than deficits, and to help clients identify goals that will enable them to create a different story for their lives. Problems may be initially highlighted in order to help clients identify patterns and repetitive cycles, but the greater focus is on the identification of solutions, exceptions, and the "difference that will make a difference." The therapist acts as a *consultant* to "influence the clients' view of the problem in a manner that leads to a solution" (Berg & Miller, 1992, p. 70). The role of consultant is one where, when the clients come seeking expertise when they have run into seemingly insurmountable roadblocks, the therapist opens up new possibilities by identifying interpersonal patterns, exploring strengths and resources, and promoting positive coping skills inherent in the couple's relationship. The therapist *encourages* clients to experiment with new approaches to achieving small successes in problem management, through a counterintuitive emphasis on strengths rather than the problems themselves. While the therapist may have clients talk to him or her during the assessment phase, increasingly, there is an emphasis on clients talking and strategizing together, highlighting the solution-focused value that the clients are the experts of their own lives.

Acceptance and Commitment Couples Therapy (ACT)

ACT is a model designed to increase a couple's understanding and acceptance of one another. It bridges the gap between the cognitive behavioral evidence-based models (e.g., IBCT; see later) and experiential models (e.g., EFT; see later). ACT (Hayes, Luoma, Bond, Masuda, and Lillis, 2006) is founded on the principles of behavioral marital therapy, one of the earliest behaviorally based approaches to couples therapy. ACT is akin to many of the third-wave behavioral therapies developed during the period of the 1980s and 1990s (DBT, Linehan et al., 1991; ACT, Hayes, Strosahl, & Wilson, 1999). It acknowledges that many issues couples struggle with are essentially unresolvable; therefore, it focuses on enhancing both partners' ability to empathize with one another and respond in a more accepting way, thus building intimacy around the problem.

Theoretical Foundations. The core concepts of ACT is that psychological suffering is usually caused by experiential avoidance, cognitive entanglement, and resulting psychological rigidity that leads to a failure to take needed behavioral steps in accord with core values. As a simple way to summarize the model, ACT views the core of many problems to be due to the concepts represented in the acronym FEAR:

- Fusion with your thoughts
- Evaluation of experience
- Avoidance of your experience
- Reason-giving for your behavior

The healthy alternative is to ACT:

- Accept your reactions and be present
- Choose a valued direction
- Take action

These principles suggest that instead of focusing attention on changing the behavior of the "wrongdoer" in a conflict, "acceptance" focuses on modifying one's own response to the other partner's behavior. Acceptance means letting go of the struggle to change the other partner in order to turn toward more fully understanding and experiencing empathy for him or her. A couple's disagreement can result in argument, unhappy resignation, or a third option: mutually sharing their feelings of frustration and experiencing increased intimacy and closeness as a result (Jacobson & Christensen, 1996). In many cases, as this increased intimacy naturally leads to more caring behaviors, couples find that they have a decreased need for traditional behavior change. At the same time, many couples also find that increased intimacy accelerates their motivation to change their own behaviors as their partners had originally desired (Jacobson & Christensen, 1996). It is important to note that emphasizing acceptance does not mean couples are expected to embrace the status quo in their relationship, as this would be unlikely to improve relationship satisfaction (and may, in some cases, be extremely unfair to one partner; Jacobson & Christensen, 1996).

Goals of Therapy. ACT's general goal is to increase psychological flexibility—the ability to contact the present moment more fully as a conscious human being, and to change or persist in behavior, when doing so serves valued ends. Psychological flexibility is established through core ACT processes. Acceptance is taught as an alternative to experiential avoidance. Acceptance involves active awareness, an embrace of those private events occasioned by a couple's mutual history without unnecessary attempts to change their frequency or form, especially when doing so would cause psychological harm. Cognitive diffusion techniques attempt to alter the undesirable functions of negative or interfering thoughts and other private events, rather than trying to alter their form, frequency, or situational sensitivity. Said another way, ACT attempts to change the way one interacts with or relates to thoughts by creating contexts in which their unhelpful functions are diminished.

Goals of Treatment. ACT promotes ongoing nonjudgmental contact with psychological and environmental events as they occur. The goal is to have couples experience the world more directly so that their behavior is more flexible and thus their actions are more consistent with the values that they hold. This is important in part because from this standpoint, one can be aware of one's own flow of experiences without attachment to them or an investment in which particular experiences occur. Thus diffusion and acceptance are fostered, and self in the context is fostered through mindfulness exercises, metaphors, and experiential processes. A major component of ACT is to aid couples in relational value clarification, chosen qualities of purposive action. That is, relational values are the mutual beliefs a couple believes strongly enough in to act on. Finally, ACT encourages the development of more generalized patterns of effective action linked to a couple's chosen values.

Clinical Process and Interventions. The first stage of ACT is assessment. Over the course of one conjoint and two individual sessions (one with each partner), the therapist assesses the couple's present difficulties, relationship history (including any history of intimate partner violence), and level of commitment to the relationship (including the presence of any affairs). Then, the therapist meets with both partners to summarize the results of the assessment and provide them with a formulation of their presenting problem. As the therapist describes various aspects of the formulation, he or she invites the couple to revise as they see fit. If the couple adopts the formulation as descriptive of their problems, it can alter their understanding of the problem into one that is more interpersonal and less blaming. The therapist then describes treatment as focusing on incidents and issues related to their formulation, with the therapist being active in helping them discuss these incidents and issues in a constructive way.

There are five phases that characterize the therapeutic process. In the first phase, couples are brought into contact with the reality that previous struggles to control their inner and interpersonal experiences have been unsuccessful. In the second phase, couples are helped to see that not only have their previous struggles to control private events been unsuccessful, but also that these struggles have actually made matters worse. The third phase of ACT emphasizes attempts to help couples delineate between their personal and interpersonal selves and their cognitive, emotional, and physiological experiences. In the fourth phase, couples are asked to willingly experience the aversive private and interpersonal events that they have previously avoided to accomplish their goals not yet reached. Finally, the fifth phase of ACT involves securing a commitment from the couple for implementing behavior change strategies.

The process of ACT is data driven. Sessions often begin with each partner completing the weekly questionnaire (Christensen, 2010) to give the therapist a quick view of the couple's week. The couple then answers questions to identify (1) the most important positive and negative or difficult events since the last session, (2) any upcoming event that will be challenging for them, and (3) any issue(s) of concern. They then rank order these in terms of what they feel is most important to discuss in therapy. Typically, the therapist reviews the positive events and creates an agenda based on the incidents or issues that the couple has identified, preferably ones related to earlier formulations (Jacobson & Christensen, 1996). The therapist then engages the couple in a discussion of the identified incidents or issues, actively intervening to promote any of three interrelated aspects of acceptance: empathic joining, unified detachment, or tolerance building. Sequencing of these interventions (or the addition of the more change-oriented CBCT interventions) is based on the formulation, the current presentation of the couple in the room, and the therapist's clinical judgment.

One of the primary goals of the early stages of treatment is what Jacobson et al. call empathic joining, a process in which the therapist guides the couple to increased levels of emotional intimacy by having them describe their deepest feelings to one another and expressing empathy for the other's distress (Jacobson, Christiansen, Prince, Cordova, & Eldridge, 2000). Once one partner has expressed soft emotions about the problem (e.g., fear of rejection), the therapist models empathy for that disclosure and may encourage the other partner to respond. The therapist will most likely need to take an active role in eliciting vulnerable feelings from each partner early in therapy, validating emerging emotions, but the experience of being responded to compassionately is expected to be naturally reinforcing of the behavior of self-disclosure. The approach also focuses on initiating new, more effective behaviors, providing the couple with constructive feedback, and asking them to practice these behaviors together outside the session. Communication training focuses on improving dyadic communication by expressing one's subjective views rather than making seemingly objective blaming statements. The therapist teaches the couple that listening and speaking are separate roles that should be alternated during a conversation.

EVIDENCE-BASED APPROACHES

Cognitive Behavioral Couples Therapy (CBCT) and Integrative Behavioral Couples Therapy (IBCT)

CBCT recognizes that non-distressed partners exchange more pleasing and less displeasing behaviors than distressed couples (Thibaut & Kelly, 1959; Gottman, 1993). The couple is interviewed in order to gain an understanding of individual functioning, relationship strengths and weaknesses, how the couple expresses affection and sexuality, how they view the future, and how the relationship is affected by the greater social environment. Assessment is utilized for the purpose of ascertaining the ways in which rewards and punishments are exchanged between the couple (Nichols & Schwartz, 2001). Therapy begins with the therapist identifying the presenting problem or problems. The therapist wants to understand the couple's complaints, the reinforcers for perceived problematic behaviors, the antecedents and consequences for problematic behaviors, and when behaviors occur or fail to occur.

The therapist often employs various objective assessments in the functional analysis of the relationship. These various areas of assessment reflect an ecosystemic approach to understanding the couple's relationship, including individual assessment, couple assessment, family assessment, and perhaps even an assessment of how personal resources are enhanced or eroded by community commitments through the use of an eco map. Using individual assessments, the therapist may want to rule out individual mood and anxiety disorders or evaluate overall personality with a personality assessment, such as the Millon Clinical Multiaxial Inventory-III (MCMI-III; Millon, Millon, Davis, & Grossman, 2009). Couple assessments might evaluate overall marital satisfaction using the Dyadic Adjustment Scale (Spanier, 1976) and more specific relational factors with the Marital Satisfaction Inventory-Revised (MSI-R; Snyder & Aikman, 1999). The MSI-R has 11 scales that assess couple interactions on a range of relationship factors including problem-solving communication, affective communication, sexual dissatisfaction, conflict over parenting, family history of distress, aggression, and global distress. The therapist would be especially interested in a couple's problem-solving acumen as well as their scores on overall global distress.

Goals of Treatment. The therapy goals of CBCT are to aid couples in modifying behavioral exchanges in the relationship by having couples exhibit more desired behaviors, help couples use conflict as a problem-solving tool, correct faulty attributions in interactions, educate couples in the use of self-instructional procedures to decrease destructive interactions, and help couples improve overall communication. Interventions are specific and behavioral, along with communication training to increase a couple's ability to express their thoughts and emotions clearly, clarification and listening techniques, problem-solving training, and contingency contracts. Contingency contracts aid in identifying specific problems in the couple's relationship that require a solution through the use of contingency contracts in dyadic negotiations (Nichols & Schwartz, 2001).

Process and Interventions. CBCT is based on the core principles of a therapeutic working alliance and a caring and supportive therapeutic relationship. The CBCT model emphasizes the need for coaching and active practice of new behavioral, cognitive, and emotional responses (Epstein & Baucom, 2002). The therapist coaches couples in rehearsing communication skills, cognitive restructuring skills for modifying negative and unrealistic relationship cognitions, and enhancing or regulating the experience and expression of emotions. In addition to teaching specific skills, CBCT therapists guide couples in increasing particular types of behavior patterns (e.g., forms of mutual social support) to meet partners' basic needs more fully (Epstein & Baucom, 2002). More specifically, CBCT mechanisms of clinical change focus on:

- Social relationship skills via problem-solving skills. When a therapist frequently coaches couples in constructive problem-solving techniques, couples often experience an improvement in relationship satisfaction (Baucom & Epstein, 1990; Christensen et al., 2005; Epstein & Baucom, 2002).

- The acknowledgment in behavioral exchanges of reciprocal positive and especially negative actions in the couple's patterns. Change is assumed to occur more easily when both members of a dyad acknowledge their roles in a negative pattern and take responsibility for making some changes.
- Training in such communication guidelines is a core component of traditional and enhanced CBCT. The more that members of a couple express their thoughts and emotions to each other in constructive ways (e.g., acknowledging the subjectivity of one's feelings, conveying empathy for the listener's position) and the more that the listener engages in nonjudgmental reflective listening, the greater the partners' satisfaction with their relationship.
- Psychoeducational interventions contribute to new learning by introducing new concepts (instituting cognitive change) and instructions to guide new responses. For example, psychoeducation regarding negative effects of particular destructive forms of communication and positive effects of constructive communication skills can increase clients' motivation to change their behavior and also guide them in how to do it.

Role of the Therapist. The role of the therapist in CBCT is one that toggles between didactic training and process support (Wood & Jacobson, 1985); therefore, the therapist must have the ability to flex with the needs of the unique client system. The role is a directive one, especially in the initial phases of therapy when gathering data for a functional analysis of the client system. Later, the therapist will act more as a guide and facilitator of the client change, "reducing his/her influence in order to foster the couple's competency and confidence in continuing to make positive, global changes in their relationships after treatment has ended (Baucom, Epstein & LaTaillade, 2002, p. 42).

The therapist relates to the client system on three levels, with each member of the dyad and with the couple as a whole. Each part of the client system needs to feel the therapist's support and advocacy. This may entail shifts in alliances during the course of therapy in the service of therapeutic goals, which requires an adroit touch on the part of the therapist (Wood & Jacobson, 1985). Finally, the therapist acts as a motivator, especially during guided behavior change interventions, where there is no overt quid pro quo. The goal is to get each member of the client system to participate fully and collaboratively and to own the sessions and work as theirs, not the therapist's (Epstein & Baucom, 2002).

Integrative Behavioral Couples Therapy (IBCT) developed in response to the emphasis in traditional CBCT on behavioral exchange, which produces sharp immediate reduction in relational distress, but poor durability in long-lasting change (Dimidjian et al., 2002). CBCT seems most useful for couples that are less distressed, younger, and not experiencing co-occurring individual pathology (Jacobson & Addis, 1993). It has also been found that some couples experience the rote nature of behavior exchange as artificial and off-putting.

IBCT suggests that relationship problems are a result of how couples respond to their dyadic difficulties, not the fact that couples have disagreements, difficulties, or conflicts. Jacobson and Christensen (1996) discuss the erosion over time of partners' willingness to accept and tolerate the idiosyncratic behavior of the other with three types of problematic responses: mutual coercion (criticizing, withdrawing, stonewalling, contempt; Gottman, 1999), vilification (making of each other opponents rather than allies), and polarization (unsuccessful attempts to reform the other leading to greater relational distance).

Six questions are used to guide the assessment phase: (1) How distressed is the couple?, (2) how committed to the relationship is the couple?, (3) what are the dividing issues between partners?, (4) why are these issues such a problem?, (5) what are the couple's strengths?, and (6) how can treatment help them? (Dimidjian et al., 2002, p. 257). The fundamental treatment goals for IBCT are for couples to be more understanding and accepting of one another as well as developing a collaborative set to improve the quality of their relationship. Techniques of IBCT treatment include promoting greater acceptance, encouraging greater tolerance, and facilitating relationship change.

Acceptance is promoted through the use of a rational approach to relationship problems, empathic joining (couples hearing each other without accusation), and soft disclosures (emphasizing hurt and vulnerability over anger and resentment). Couples are encouraged to become more tolerant of each other's ways of relating, rather than constantly trying to change the other. The therapist helps the couple find the positive places in the relationship to emphasize and reinforce. Tolerance accrues as a by-product of self-care. Each partner seeks to satisfy his or her own needs rather than relying on a partner over whom one has little control. This notion of self-care through self-control underlies the technique of behavior exchange where couples are encouraged to focus on changing their own behaviors in order to provide greater pleasure for their partners. Behavior exchange is a method that consists of communication training and training in problem-solving techniques. Couples are encouraged to share their feelings, to employ listening skills in the service of process sharing, and to take a collaborative approach with regard to generating solutions to problems as allies rather than opponents (Dimidjian et al., 2002).

Research Foundations. There is a healthy history of research to support the efficacy of cognitive and behavioral couple treatment models that emphasize mindful acceptance, understanding, and commitment (Carson, Carson, Gil & Baucom, 2004; Peterson, Eifert, Feingold & Davidson, 2009). In fact, the so-called third-wave models of acceptance and commitment seem to have greater efficacy over time than more behaviorally oriented models. Wimberly (1998) demonstrated that eight couples randomly assigned to a group format of IBCT were significantly more satisfied than nine wait-listed couples at the end of therapy. Jacobson, Christensen, Prince, Cordova, and Eldridge (2000) compared CBCT and IBCT; effect size data and clinical significance data favored IBCT. The most extensive data in support of the efficacy of the dimensions of acceptance and commitment come from a large, two-site randomized clinical trial of CBCT and IBCT (Christensen et al., 2005). In an average of 23 therapy sessions over the course of approximately 36 weeks, 134 married couples participated. The 2-year follow-up to this study suggested that change in satisfaction after the end of treatment did not occur linearly (Christensen, Atkins, Yi, Baucom, & George, 2006). Instead, couples' trajectories followed a "hockey stick" pattern of decline in the weeks immediately following termination and then a reversal in which satisfaction again began to increase (Christensen et al., 2006).

During the four 6-month assessments through the first 2 years of follow-up, IBCT couples showed significantly greater satisfaction than CBCT couples (Christensen, Atkins, Baucom, & Yi, 2010). At the 2-year follow-up assessment, 69% of IBCT couples and 60% of CBCT couples were reliably improved or recovered, a considerable number given the initial distress of this population (Christensen et al., 2006). At 5-year follow-up, treatment group differences in marital satisfaction were no longer significant (Christensen et al., 2010). Half of couples continued to show reliable improvement or recovery, but a quarter of them were separated or divorced. The authors suggested that with this population of seriously and chronically distressed couples, additional booster sessions might have been needed to maintain gains over the long term (Christensen et al., 2010).

Two studies have examined particular mechanisms of change in IBCT. Cordova, Jacobson, and Christensen (1998) found that IBCT and CBCT couples did not differ on the amount of detachment or soft emotion (e.g., fear or sadness) demonstrated in early therapy sessions, but IBCT couples displayed significantly more of each in the middle and late sessions. Across groups, increases in soft emotion and detachment, as well as decreases in problem behaviors, correlated with improvements in marital satisfaction. These results suggest that IBCT produces more significant changes than CBCT in couples' tendencies to discuss problems in a non-blaming, empathy-inducing way, behaviors that are then associated with greater relationship satisfaction (Cordova, Jacobson, & Christensen, 1998). Doss, Thum, Sevier, Atkins, and Christensen (2005) found that CBCT led to greater changes in the frequency of targeted behaviors (those rated as important to either partner) early in therapy, but IBCT led to greater changes in the acceptance of targeted behaviors both early and late in therapy. Moreover, change in behavioral frequency was strongly related to improvements in satisfaction early in therapy, while emotional acceptance was more strongly related to changes in satisfaction later in therapy. Self-reported communication patterns also improved over the course of treatment (Doss et al., 2005). Both CBCT and IBCT couples increased their incidence of mutually positive interactions and decreased their incidence of mutually negative and demand–withdraw interactions; each of these changes was associated with improvements in marital satisfaction for both husbands and wives. Together, these studies suggest that IBCT's focus on acceptance is a strong mechanism of change in couple relationship satisfaction, possibly explaining its comparatively greater effect on satisfaction through 2-year follow-up (Doss et al., 2005).

Emotionally Focused Therapy (EFT)

Emotionally Focused Therapy (EFT) (Johnson, 1996) is a brief integrative approach that focuses on helping partners in close relationships create secure attachment bonds. EFT integrates an experiential humanistic perspective that values emotion as an agent of change with a systems view of reciprocally reinforcing patterns of interaction, grounded in attachment, and is built on the groundbreaking work on emotions done by Greenberg & Paivio (1997).

Theoretical Foundations. EFT is integrative, combining an experiential focus on self with a systemic focus on interaction. The theoretical perspective of EFT combines research on the nature of relationship distress, with research on the attachment perspective of adult love and relatedness. EFT integrates an experiential/gestalt approach with an interactional/family systems approach. The roots of EFT lie in systems theory, humanistic psychology, and attachment theory. A key principle of EFT is that attachment needs are normal, healthy, and adaptive. While attachment needs have their roots in the child/caregiver relationship, adult emotional bonds also address adaptive needs for security, protection, and connectedness. The task for adults is to develop a secure interdependence that nurtures both partners. Marital distress is "the failure of an attachment relationship to provide a secure base for one or both partners" (Johnson, 1996, p. 124).

The primary focus of EFT is the way in which distress occurs—through the repeating and escalating negative cycles that maintain disconnection and limit responding to needs for comfort and support. The EFT perspective focuses on how the power of absorbing states of negative affect and negative interaction patterns, such as criticize/demand followed by defend/distance, generate and maintain each other in a reciprocal negative feedback loop. The negative affect is attachment related and is thus associated with perceived unmet primal needs for comfort and closeness in the face of threat, danger, and uncertainty. EFT emphases: the power of negative affect, as expressed in facial expression, for example, to predict relational distress and dissatisfaction; the importance of emotional engagement and how partners communicate, rather than the content or the frequency of arguments; how cycles such as demand–withdraw are potentially fatal for close relationships; and the necessity for soothing, comforting interactional cycles that lead to greater relationship satisfaction and stability.

EFT targets the experience and expression of emotion and uses these avenues to shift couple interactions toward accessibility and responsiveness. Emotion is the primary agent in organizing attachment behaviors and determining how self and others are experienced in intimate relationships. Emotional communication allows a degree of predictability for individual behavior on the part of a couple and is therefore a key regulator of marital interaction (Johnson, 1996, p. 125).

Therapy Goals and Interventions. EFT interventions focus on the emotional experience of the client and how that experience is impacting interactions and relationships. The therapist–couple relationship is a collaborative alliance, which offers partners a secure base from which to explore their relationship. The clinician's initial task is to identify whether a partner's emotion is secondary or primary. Secondary emotion, such as anger, represents a defensive posture, while primary emotion, such as hurt, represents greater vulnerability. Once the therapist has established secondary and primary emotions in the relationship, he or she can utilize these emotions to address the inner experiences of each partner, which are contributing to their defensive posture in the relationship. Additionally, the therapist will aim to identify the specific relationship events that have shaped the couple's degree of attachment and have coalesced into hardened relationship patterns (Johnson, 1996, p. 122). After de-escalating the couple's negative relational patterns, the therapist aims to create new interaction patterns that aid in developing more secure attachment. The emotional climate of early childhood (primitive developmental feelings, i.e., fear-mistrust, shame-inadequacy, guilt-insecurity) is re-experienced in the adult couple relationship. By helping partners identify, express, and restructure their emotional responses at different points in the interactional cycle, the EFT therapist helps the couple develop new responses to each other and a different frame on the nature of their problems (Johnson, 1996, p. 223).

As established by EFT, change occurs not through insight or negotiation, but through new emotional experiences in the present attachment relationship (i.e., new secure bonding). Therefore, the therapy process needs to facilitate the expression of underlying emotions of partners as well as de-escalate negative interaction patterns and reactive emotions. Shaping new positive interaction cycles for the couple will be evidence of the couple making strides forward in the change process.

The therapist moves recursively between three tasks, monitoring and actively fostering a positive alliance, expanding and restructuring key emotional experiences, and structuring enactments that either clarify present patterns of interaction or, step by step, shape new more positive interactions. EFT interventions are identified as follows: the EFT therapist is always *tracking* and *reflecting* the process by which both inner emotional realities and interactions are created. The therapist also *validates* each partner's realities and habitual responses so that partners feel safe to explore and own these. Internal experience is expanded by *evocative questions* that develop the outline of such experience into a sharply focused and detailed portrait. *Heightening of emotion* may be done with images or repetition, or the therapist may go one step beyond how clients construct their experience with an *empathic conjecture*, such as wondering if someone is not, as they say, simply "uncomfortable" but actually anxious. The therapist also *reframes* interactional responses in terms of underlying emotions and attachment needs and *choreographs enactments*.

The EFT therapist is a process consultant, helping partners expand constricted inner emotional realities and interactional responses, thereby shifting rigid interactions into responses that foster resiliency and secure connections (Lebow, Chambers, Christensen, & Johnson, 2012).

Research Foundations. There are 16 outcome studies and 9 process research studies that support the EFT model. EFT was found to achieve the most positive outcomes of any approach to couple therapy, in terms of both helping clients reach recovery from distress and maintaining these results over time (Johnson, Hunsley, Greenberg, & Schindler, 1999; Lebow, et al., 2012). No other empirically validated approach has yet exceeded its effect size of 1.3 and been found to be stable over time (Clothier, Manion, Gordon, & Johnson, 2001; Halchuk, Makinen, & Johnson, 2010). Couples who have gone through EFT have shown increased improvement after therapy ends (Johnson & Talitman, 1996), and a meta-analysis of research found that 70% of couples found distress relief after 8–12 EFT sessions (Johnson, 1996).

EFT is not recommended for all couples; therefore, the clinician should be aware of the boundaries for utilization. When a couple presenting for therapy is planning to divorce or is experiencing domestic violence or sexual dysfunction, EFT is not the appropriate therapy model. It is also contraindicated as a modality when alcoholism, psychosis, or attempted suicide is present. EFT is appropriate for couples hoping to increase intimacy, for example, couples that report problems with communication or where one partner desires more intimacy than the other.

THOUGHTS, COMMENTS, AND WHAT'S NEXT?

One of the biggest challenges in any type of clinical practice is to choose the best treatment for each client system given the issue(s) they present, the context in which they live, and their unique individual characteristics. This challenge presents itself at many levels. For the clinical practitioner, the challenge is to identify and then tailor a specific intervention or treatment protocol to the individual client. For program administrators and policy makers, the difficulty is choosing which types of treatments to support in their agency or clinic in order to achieve the highest likelihood of positive outcome for the broadest range of clients. For professional educators and professional organizations, the burden is to identify and develop sound policy and relevant current clinical curricula based on the best available practices. As in all other areas of psychotherapy, family psychology has two major domains to consider in decisions like these.

The profession of family psychology has a vast store of clinical experience and practice-based theory that has been developed over the years. At the same time, there is a robust and systematic array of clinically focused research to guide practice in family psychology. Inconveniently, these two domains do not always point in the same direction. The dilemma is how to integrate relevant science, clinical experience, and theory in such a way that it can improve practices and lead to the best treatments (Sexton & Gordon, 2009).

In the next section, the focus turns to the broader domain of the specialty of family psychology. In the next chapter, the focus is on training specialists in the profession, the role of clinical supervision, and the ethics that guide and inform theory, research, and practice.

Section III

The Professional Context of Family Psychology

Chapter 9

Specialty Areas of Family Psychology

The scientist rigorously defends his right to be ignorant of almost everything except his specialty.

—Marshall McLuhan

Like all professions, family psychology has developed specialties (or subspecialties in this case) that fall under the larger umbrella. These specialties are areas of practice that are unique in either clinical problems (e.g., sex therapy) or their setting (e.g., collaborative health care), while others have to do with scope (international family psychology). These areas have a common center founded in the systemic epistemology (see Chapter 2) and clinical and research knowledge base of the field. Here the focus is on the most prominent of these domains: sex therapy, international family psychology, collaborative health care, and family forensic psychology (FFP). The following pages will provide an overview of these subspecialties.

SEX THERAPY

In its first iteration, family psychology was referred to as marriage, family, and sex therapy, recognizing the close relationship between family psychology and sex therapy. The fields drifted apart over time, reflecting a parallel process that had come to define the field of sex therapy itself. One aspect of sex therapy, human sexuality, was primarily the purview of psychology researchers and the other, sexology, the clinical practice of sex therapy, was primarily the purview of nonpsychologist clinicians. This divide between sexology and human sexuality was decades long. From the time of Kraft-Ebbing through the work of Kinsey and Masters and Johnson continuing on to contemporary research, human sexuality has taken a positivist position with a focus on empirical research of specific factors related to sexuality. On the other hand, while popular culture often associates sexology with the empirical approach of Alfred Kinsey (Bullough, 1998), the formal discipline of sexology was first articulated by Iwan Bloch as an integration of social, literary, philosophical, biological, and medical disciplines (Farmer & Binik, 2005).

Bloch's original vision of a multidisciplinary sexology approach freely combines the qualitative sexual information from literature and philosophy with the quantitative sexual information from biology and medicine (Money & Herman, 1978). The scientific divide between the positivist ideals of psychology and the value-laden science of sexology has reinforced the differences between the two disciplines. It is clear that the early science of sexology reflected a postpositivist bias—integrating empirical evidence with historical, comparative, and philosophical interpretations to form a "value-aware" explanation of observations (Munck, 1999; Reiss, 1993).

In Europe, human sexuality's focus was on long-term psychodynamic therapy examining underlying causes of sexual difficulties, while in the United States, Terman offered a more focused analysis of sexual behaviors, practices, and preferences in the context of marriage. Terman was specifically interested in the role of a couple's sexual relationship on marital adjustment and headed one of the first research groups to study in detail such aspects as the frequency of intercourse and passion of spouses (Terman, Buttenwieser, Ferguson, Johnson, & Wilson, 1938).

In recent years, Tiefer (1994) has recommended a postpositivist, sexology-oriented conceptualization of human sexuality in which the biases of psychologists are as equally important in understanding sex research as raw participant data. We have argued throughout much of this book for the recognition that science and practice are mutually recursive, and this is no less the case in sex therapy. The research orientation of human sexuality and the clinical focus of sexology find common ground in a systems epistemology that values quantitative and qualitative data, as well as value awareness of relationships. In a similar fashion, an ecological perspective recognizes that a couple's sexual relationship is a subsystem of their relationship as a whole and that when a couple presents for therapy, both their overall relationship and their sexual relationship will likely require attention and intervention. The goal of a systems sex therapy then is consistent with the overall goal of creating and/or restoring couple relationship satisfaction, and the work of sex therapy is the creation and restoration of mutual sexual comfort and satisfaction between a couple (Wincze & Carey, 2001). In one study, "feeling close to my partner before sex" was the top factor correlated with sexual satisfaction (Ellison, 2000). Our model of sex therapy is based on sex as experience rather than as work or performance, where couples create erotic experiences through a stepwise transitioning into intercourse. To this end, intercourse and orgasms become choices not requirements, and the best relationships tend to exhibit a variety of sexual experiences.

Sexual experience begins with mutual consent, the freedom to say no or yes. In fact, low sexual desire may be partly explained by the absence of a sense of consent. In one survey, 67% of women reported being too tired for sex and 64% too busy at least some of the time for sex. When a couple does express mutual interest in pursuing a sexual experience, a shift in attention and consciousness occurs as couples develop an intimate trance. "When couples think of sex as creating erotic pleasure, then sex is a continuum of possibilities and there are many ways they can express their affection through sexuality, even when tired," such as low-key sexual relaxing (Ellison, 2000, p. 174).

There are three components to contemporary sex therapy: (1) coordinating couples therapy with sex therapy through the intersystem sex therapy approach, (2) reducing anxiety in the couple relationship and increasing partner differentiation through a Bowen family systems approach, and (3) treating particular sexual disorders through a cognitive behavioral treatment approach.

Intersystems sex therapy model. The intersystems sex therapy paradigm is informed by Sternberg's triangular theory of love (1986) (the balance between eroticism, friendship, and companionship in a relationship) and the theory of interaction (how aspects of communication are negotiated in a relationship) (Hertlein & Weeks, 2009; Strong & Clairborn, 1982) and is organized around promoting passion, commitment, and intimacy. There is a dynamic aspect to a sexual relationship where couples make attributions regarding how each partner defines the relationship and predict how the other person will think, feel, or behave around issues of sexuality. The interactional component in a sexual relationship comprises a kind of social intercourse, which includes (1) congruence—the degree to which couples agree on how events are defined; (2) relational interdependence—the partner's perceptions of the other's ability to meet emotional and sexual needs, that is, the sense that partners can depend on each other; and (3) attributional strategies—the manner of ascribing meaning to a sexual event. Couples may have problematic linear attributional styles where they relate in terms of cause and effect, that is, "she makes me mad," or circular attributional styles where couples examine the impact of their behavior in a reciprocal or interlocking way, that is, "I bruise you, you bruise me." Sex therapists use reframing to move from linear negative blaming styles to more circular positive styles.

The intersystems sex therapy approach has several components for assessing sexual dysfunction. The first component functions at the level of the individual—psychological and biological, with a focus on each partner's individual health status (physical and biopsychological) and medical concerns and how those concerns might affect the sexual relationship. An individual and psychological component will include assessment of personality, psychopathology, intelligence, temperament, developmental stages, attitudes, values, and defense mechanisms. The second component assesses the couple relationship. Assessment is aimed at understanding how the couple defines the relationship in incongruent ways, how they make negative attributions about the other, and how they regulate intimacy. The therapist seeks to understand the couple's relational fears, problematic communication patterns, conscious and unconscious expectations, and the management of conflict. The real or underlying problem often is not the sexual issue, but another relational component of which the sexual issue is a symptom. Third, the intersystem sex therapy model explores family-of-origin issues, seeking to ascertain each partner's level of differentiation in the relationship. The therapist is looking for messages given by family that are covert, overt, internalized, and/or expressed in the relationship. The final component of the model examines the impact of society, culture, history, and religion on the couple's sexual relationship. Assessment of values and beliefs as well as customs and rituals is ascertained primarily through interview (Hertlein & Weeks, 2009).

The course of sex therapy includes the formulation of a treatment plan that flows out of a thorough assessment. Once a diagnosis has been made, the therapist will recommend a course of treatment that may include biomedical interventions, cognitive behavioral techniques, and couple/individual psychotherapy. Biomedical interventions include medications (e.g., treating erectile dysfunction with Viagra), surgery, or injections. Individual therapy may also be used to treat trauma or issues of addictive or compulsive behaviors.

Couple therapy may include Bowen family systems therapy to address intrapersonal and interpersonal anxiety. Schnarch (1997) has suggested that sex therapy should not be so much about increasing eroticism as decreasing anxiety. Undifferentiated anxiety often manifests as performance anxiety with a focus on the pleasure/orgasm of the other as a way of feeling good about self. Bowen family systems therapy can be used to increase differentiation of self in each member of a sexual dyad, allowing the couple the opportunity to focus on self-pleasure, rather than performance, and on other erotic aspects of the sexual relationship besides orgasm.

Cognitive behavioral couples therapy can provide tools to modify the behaviors inherent in particular disorders. Psychoeducation provides information on sexual myths, adequate preparation for the sexual trance, and can be the cornerstone for communication training. Behavioral therapy can offer training in sensate focus (focusing on the erotic sensations of pleasure) and graduated exposure techniques with a focus on the joy and the utility of foreplay. A family systems approach to sex therapy offers a holistic approach that grounds sexual satisfaction in relational satisfaction and educates and trains couples in individual differentiation, communication interaction, and sexual technique.

INTERNATIONAL FAMILY PSYCHOLOGY

The increased mobility of psychologists and other mental healthcare professionals on a global level, and the increased use of professional psychological treatment worldwide, has begun to raise the profile of psychological delivery on an international scale. The field of international psychology is young and vigorous with many vibrant agendas, theories, and perspectives. Historically, the dominant epistemology has been the clinical pathology model reflecting a Western focus on individualism and personality, tending to lead to what Pupavec (2006) has called "the psychologization of human experience" (p.17). A Western sensibility, with its focus on individuals and emotion states, is shared by relatively few people groups worldwide; in fact, several authors report that as psychology expands in non-Western countries, a process of indigenization is taking place, integrating Western individualistically oriented ideas with a stronger focus on families and communities (Church & Katigbak, 2002; Clay, 2002; Mpofu, 2001; Pettifor, 2004). The looming question in international psychology is whether non-Western cultures simply adopt Western psychology or forge their own unique folk psychologies.

There are three perspectives that guide the shaping of an international psychology: an absolute perspective that sees no differences between cultures, a relativist perspective that requires that each culture develop its own standards of treatment and ethics, and a universalist approach that suggests that while underlying treatment and ethical issues may be similar from culture to culture, they will be apprehended differently by each culture and therefore require similar, but unique theoretical and ethical perspectives (Pedersen, 1995).

International psychology also raises the question: how do clinicians from other countries or cultures practice internationally? The apparent conflict between universality of principles and respect for diversity by practitioners raises crucial questions: How do we as practitioners adhere to our own treatment and ethical guidelines and not disregard the local values and norms of those served? How do we practice without disrespecting or disregarding local values? How do we ensure respect for local culture and peoples, yet remain true to effective, evidence-based treatment protocols and those ethical guidelines that are universal (Okasha, Arboleda-Florez, & Sartorius, 2000)?

Family psychology provides a multimodal approach to international psychology by using a systems psychology perspective as a contextual bridge between the intrapersonal clinical pathology model and an interpersonal community mental health model that emphasizes individual strengths and community resources. What emerges is an ecological approach that is greater than the sum of its parts and able to bridge the divide between Western models of psychology and folk models of psychology. Family psychology also provides a platform from which to practice across borders. When clinicians recognize the intertwined social ecologies of individual, family, and community subsystems, and when they embrace both a pathology model and models that emphasize individual strengths and community resources, they become less dependent on traditional Western norms (Wessells, 2009).

The international community is served by several noteworthy organizations that seek to promote international psychology and international family psychology. The International Council of Psychologists (ICP) was established in 1941 with the intent of promoting world peace and "to advance psychology and the application of its scientific findings throughout the world" (ICP Bylaws 1.3). Programs, projects, publications, and public information are focused on educational and scientific psychology and its application for well-being (Certificate of Incorporation, State of Connecticut). The founding members of the ICP had a vision to pull together academic institutions that share a common global interest in psychology. The ICP is dedicated to promulgating the science of psychology and its application for the betterment of individuals, groups, and societies. The overarching commitment of ICP is to further world peace and promote human rights through collegial global collaboration among mental health professionals and social scientists (http://icpweb.org/).

The International Union of Psychological Science (IUPsyS), a tripartite union of the IUPsyS, the International Association of Applied Psychology, and the International Association for Cross-Cultural Psychology has drafted universal principles for ethical international psychological practice (IUPsyS, 2014). The mission of the IUPsyS is to articulate principles and values that provide a common moral framework for psychologists throughout the world, and that can be used as a guide for the development of differing standards of psychological conduct as appropriate for differing cultural contexts (IUPsyS, 2014; Russell, 1984).

The IUPsyS consists of 71 member nations and lists 44 member ethical codes (Leach & Harbin, 1997). While every country's individual ethical standard has aspirational values and codes of conduct, each varies according to culture. Leach and Harbin (1997) conducted a study analyzing the various country codes in relation to similarities with the APA's code of ethics (APA, 2002). The IUPsyS lists the 44 codes according to percentage of similarities, and, as might be expected, Leach and Harbin (1997) found that Western countries were most similar to APA's code of ethics, whereas Eastern or developing countries' codes were least similar. For example, in contrast with the more individualistically oriented West, Asian cultures tend to prioritize ethics in terms of the nation, community, family, and, lastly, the individual (Pettifor, 2004).

The IUPsyS is seeking through a strategic plan to develop an international code of treatment and ethics focusing on the commonalities of people from diverse regions of the world. Commonalities exist for current codes worldwide, including respect for the dignity and rights of persons, caring for others and concerns for their welfare, and competence, integrity, and professional, scientific, and social responsibility (Gauthier, 2005). Building on this, an international code of psychological ethics must focus on character rather than principles, health as well as pathology, transcultural ideals of collectivism, and community as well as individual support (Pettifor, 2004; Thoburn, Mauseth, McGuire, Adams, & Cecchet, 2015). However, the efforts of the IUPsyS have been undertaken with the recognition that historical and cultural differences may hinder or delay the development of a unified code of ethics.

The International Academy of Family Psychology (IAFP) is a nonprofit, worldwide scientific organization of academic and professional psychologists (scientists, therapists, teachers, graduates, etc.) interested in the field of family psychology. The founding members launched IAFP in 1990 as a noncommercial global scientific organization. In 1994, the directorate was replaced by a board of directors serving an academy that seeks to promote the ideals of a systems psychology approach worldwide. The goal of IAFP is to improve basic and applied psychological research on the structure and development of diverse forms and lifestyles of individuals in families as well as the family as a whole. The IAFP seeks to promote training and further education in the area of family psychology and family interventions based on empirically validated research.

COLLABORATIVE HEALTH CARE

Advances in our understanding of physiology, nuclear medicine, bio-technology, neuroscience, and brain anatomy, coupled with new medi-ums for healthcare delivery and a more global cooperation on the part of healthcare providers, have led to a more systemic approach in the West to the mind/body dichotomy and a greater focus on biopsychosocial approaches to patient treatment and care. The complexity of modern-day pathologies has required a response in our own field of family psychology giving renewed primacy to epistemology over populations. We have seen a vibrant and vitalized science of family psychology with evidence-based treatments engendering a greater respect for our discipline from other fields in the scientific and healthcare communities.

The driving force behind the felt need and subsequent development of collaborative healthcare teams are the twin engines of cost and qual-ity of care. There has been an explosion in knowledge and skills in all fields of healthcare creating a milieu of niche expertise by healthcare providers emphasizing pathology-specific treatment models and struc-tures for the provision of treatment and care. The result is that today's healthcare environment is too often characterized by fragmented service delivery, human resource shortages, service duplication, and unneces-sary interventions (BPharm & Wood, 2010). An alternative response has been more holistic, with the goal of creating "large, vertically integrated, regional healthcare centers that are fully capitated, that is, providers are paid for managing patients' overall health, not providing specific services" (McDaniel, Campbell, & Seaburn, 1995, p. 283). While the skills and knowledge to serve the complex needs of a given patient may be beyond the range of an individual, patient goals can be achieved by synchronized teams working toward a common goal, thereby enhancing clinical effec-tiveness and patient outcomes, providing integrated and seamless care that is also cost-effective (BPharm & Wood, 2010; Mooney, 2011; Sautz, 1995; Wagner, Austin, & Von Korff, 1996).

Collaborative health care, also known as multidisciplinary health care or interprofessional health care depending on what continent or island you live on, has to do with a biopsychosocial approach to the provision of health care through the use of teams of clinicians representing medical, behavioral, social work, and case management disciplines (Amundson, 2001). The key element is collaboration between individual professionals with differing areas of knowledge and skill for the purpose of managing the complexity of clinical practice (Grosz, 1996). Team members are part-ners in a participatory, collaborative, and coordinated approach to shared decision making around health issues (Orchard, Curran, & Kabene, 2005).

To be effective, collaborative healthcare teams must move beyond the traditional mind/body split, recognizing that every psychosocial issue has some biological component and every biological issue is embedded in psychosocial dynamics. "Collaborative family health care is based on an integration of systems theory and the biopsychosocial medical model first developed by Engel" (McDaniel, Campbell, & Seaburn, 1995, p. 286). In Canada, integrated health networks are becoming a new way of caring for people with complex, chronic health conditions (Mable & Marriott, 2002; UKCC, 1994). In Japan, the Japan Inter Professional Working and Education Network (WHO, 2013) was established by leading universities engaged in health professions education, and in the United States, the Agency for Healthcare Research and Quality is promoting collaborative care research and development.

Collaboration occurs in different contexts; for example, clinicians may reside in different health organizations such as community health centers, hospitals or public health centers, or private practice, while mental health services often are located in outpatient facilities such as private practice, community mental health centers, or social service agencies (Amundson, 2001). Interestingly, mental health complaints tend to be made first to primary care providers (McDaniel, Campbell, & Seaburn, 1995), and 70% of primary care visits include a psychosocial issue; depression is the most common psychological diagnosis first seen in primary care (Miller, Kessler, Peek, & Kallenberg, 2013). On the other hand, most severe and persistent mental illness is seen in mental health clinics, but there is a significant need for medical services for this population (Daumit, Pratt, Crum, Powe, & Ford, 2002; Thoburn, Hoffman-Robinson, Shelly, & Sayre, 2009).

One substantive question that arises when viewing health care in its varying contexts is, who leads the collaborative healthcare team? In one hospital-based study, 73% of all interactions took place between physicians and nurses; 60% of mental health interactions from mental health professionals were with nurses and physicians, and 40% of mental health professional interactions were between the mental health professionals themselves (Patela, Cytryna, Shortliffeb, & Safranc, 1997). The preponderance of interactions had physicians and nurses playing a central role and therefore might seem to argue for a model where collaborative teams are physician led. However, while this may be the case in a hospital venue, it is not always the case in every healthcare setting. One question that must be asked when determining leadership is, what is the primary presenting problem—medical or behavioral? Another question is, where is the patient's treatment primarily located—in a primary care or hospital setting or in a mental health setting? Answers to these questions will help determine the leadership structure of any given team.

Another, more provocative question considers what part, in a truly systemic approach to collaborative health care, the patient and patient's family plays in treatment and care? Today's patients tend to be sophisticated, often having researched and self-diagnosed their complaint from online resources before making an appointment to see a clinician (Mooney, 2011); therefore, we might easily see the patient as part of his or her care team. Even beyond the healthcare team/patient dyad is the healthcare team/patient/family triad (Doherty & Baird, 1983), a triangular model of medicine that recognizes the impact that families have on patient health and on how the patient relates to the healthcare system. Family may be seen as the first responders in an individual's healthcare crisis, and while patients might not have expertise on a given health condition, they do have expertise on themselves, so a solid argument can be made that a truly systemic approach to collaborative health care will include patient and family in the team process (McDaniel, Campbell, & Seaburn, 1995).

The collaborative healthcare team model is novel enough to warrant specific education in relevant skills to ensure the greatest likelihood of success. The development of interpersonal skills that enhance working together effectively is as vital as the acquisition of knowledge about how to interact with other clinical fields and disciplines. More than anything else, education in collaboration is about relationship building, having respect for the contributions of all team members, having an egalitarian attitude, and having a willingness to listen in order to work together to maximize performance (BPharm & Wood, 2010; Koyama, 2011). A collaborative healthcare curriculum will focus on the dynamics of team formation, including the stages of team development, the roles of various clinicians within the team, and meeting preparation and common problems in team functioning (Amundson, 2001).

Education will emphasize the necessity for a clear definition of roles. Collaborative healthcare teams operate within organizational scaffolds in order to optimize decision making and output through command and authority structures. Collaborators need to be socialized in the "knowledge, skills, values, roles and attitudes" (Orchard, Curran, & Kabene, 2005, p. 5) associated with various clinical disciplines. The goal is acculturation and the ability to recognize one's role in the overall structure of the team. Recognizing one's place on the team allows the collaborator to accept his or her place in levels of responsibility. One kind of team structure may be the managed care structure where the primary caregiver will naturally carry most of the responsibility for clinical treatment and care and therefore carry the leadership role as well. Another structure may be the group home for the long-term care of severe and persistent mental illness where the responsibility and leadership role will be assumed by the mental health professional. Ultimately, embracing structure allows the collaborator to put role out of mind as it becomes a normal part of team relating, so that the more overt focus can be on relationship building. In all cases, responsibility needs to be clearly defined, thus, the need for clear effective communication. The best communication occurs when both parties are attuned to listening rather than telling. Each team member listening to the expertise of other team members engenders a sense of mutual respect and trust, which gives a sense of common mission to the collaborative effort. The collaborative healthcare team becomes a community of caring marked by humility and professional altruism (Axelsson & Axelsson, 2009).

Finally, education will emphasize the need for a respect for cultural differences. Every discipline and field has its own vocabulary and its own customary way of operating in the service of patient care. Often, medicine and behavioral health have different practices and styles, so each must understand the language of the other and the differing practices. For example, medical clinicians and behavioral health clinicians often have different ideas about confidentiality. Understanding, respecting, and developing team protocols that uphold cultural standards are important to team effectiveness. There are intercultural differences as well that need to be understood when building teams. For example, in one Japanese study, medical doctors were expected to display strong leadership for effective interprofessional collaboration, a standard that would likely be different in the United States, where there is a greater desire for egalitarian relating (Koyama, 2011).

There are factors that inhibit effective team collaboration. First, a hierarchical mind-set, especially when combined with a dominating style, will likely inhibit team effectiveness. A second problematic factor is that of territoriality, where the team member is relating more according to professional role than to personal relationship and is subsequently guarded in collaborative relationships. Leadership styles can also affect collaboration. Under some conditions, medical personnel may be more action oriented, while behavioral health personnel may be more oriented toward hypotheses generating and testing, reflecting differences in training backgrounds (Patela, Cytryna, Shortliffeb, & Safranc, 1997). There may also be differences in pay and status, organizational boundaries, and underlying prejudices that can affect team building. Finally, a particularly significant barrier to collaboration can be a restriction of the resources necessary for education and implementation of collaborative treatment teams, inhibiting an overall holistic treatment approach (Kvarnström, 2008).

While there are challenges in the effective provision and implementation of collaborative health care, the benefits far outweigh those challenges. New wine requires new wineskins, and the new emerging fields and knowledge bases in biomedicine, nuclear medicine, and neuroscience all require new structures and models for generating new science and for delivering informed treatment and care to patients. Family psychology, by virtue of its expertise in systems psychology, has the opportunity to lead the way as new, more holistic models of patient treatment and care are developed.

FAMILY FORENSIC PSYCHOLOGY

Family forensic psychology is a subspecialty of both forensic psychology and family psychology. The recently revised Specialty Guidelines for Forensic Psychology (Committee on the Revision of the Specialty Guidelines for Forensic Psychology, 2011) define forensic psychology as any practice applying psychology to assist in a legal matter (Varela & Conroy, 2012, p. 413). However, the American Board of Forensic Psychology is more specific in its definition:

Professional practice by psychologists within the areas of clinical psychology, counseling psychology, school psychology, or another specialty recognized by the APA, when they are engaged as experts and represent themselves as such, in an activity primarily intended to provide professional psychological expertise to the judicial system.

(ABFP, 2014, p. 2)

The key factor in the second definition is that forensic psychologists offer expert practice to the judicial system. While many psychologists may testify in court as part of their clinical work, forensic psychology offers psychological expertise to the courts. This is noteworthy because forensic psychology is a specialty requiring specialized education and training. Psychologists must have accumulated 1,000 hours of qualifying experience in forensic psychology over a minimum of a 5-year period after the date of their doctoral degree and 100 hours of specialized training in forensic psychology after the date of the doctoral degree in psychology (ABFP, 2014, p. 3). The competencies for forensic psychology are organized around knowledge, skills, and attitudes of the specialty. There are six functional domains of forensic psychology including assessment, intervention, consultation, research, supervision training, and management administration (Varela & Conroy, 2012, p. 410).

The subspecialty area of FFP focuses on particular areas of legal concern, matters of child custody, child dependency, and juvenile delinquency, and the emerging areas of family business planning and elder law (Welsh, Greenberg & Graham-Howard, 2009). As noted earlier, FFP is primarily engaged with the welfare and well-being of children. Child custody cases involve disputes about parenting time and decision making on behalf of a child. Between 1977 and 1997, an estimated 2 million children entered family or probate court over custody issues (Ackerman & Ackerman, 1997). In a research study of 201 mental health professional evaluators, all evaluators conducted interviews with both parents, 75% used psychological tests with both parents and children, 84% used the MMPI-2, and 31% used the Rorschach (Hagen & Castegna, 2001). Juvenile dependency cases involve the state through Child Protective Services alleging that one or both parents are unfit to care for a child as a result of abuse (physical, emotional, sexual) or neglect, or that the child might be in danger of suffering abuse or neglect. Family forensic psychologists act as expert witnesses, mediators, expert therapists, evaluators, and parenting coordinators (Welsh, Greenberg, & Graham-Howard, 2009). Juvenile delinquency court often seeks evaluative information on the disposition and treatment of minors. The court wants to know why the minor has engaged in criminal behavior, about the family stressors on the minor, and what the evaluator recommends. Other cases involve diagnosis and treatment evaluations, competency to stand trial, and risk assessment (Welsh, Greenberg, & Graham-Howard, 2009).

The role of a family forensic psychologist is challenging; in fact, it has been recommended that only those who plan to pursue FFP fulltime should pursue the specialty. The rationale is that there are so many details involved in the various evaluative and treatment roles, and that it is easy to make mistakes of both omission and commission if the work is undertaken with inconsistent engagement (Wall, 2007).

CONCLUSIONS: WHAT IS NEXT?

The specialties of the field of family psychology illustrate the diversity with which systems epistemology and the core knowledge and clinical practice of the profession can be applied. The domains reflect diverse contexts (international), unique clinical problem areas (sex), and unique organizational settings (health care). The specialties of family psychology also illustrate how the core research and the systemic epistemology of the field can be used in unique settings and with unique problems. Consistent with the developmental and evolutionary nature of the profession, these unique applications will help push the core of family psychology to grow and adapt yet further. It is likely that in the future, there will be additional applications of family psychology that also meet unique social needs while stretching and adapting the field. We would hope that a next edition of this volume would include other, diverse applications of family psychology to add to this group.

Chapter 10

Training, Supervision, and Ethics in Family Psychology

Catch someone doing something right.
—Kenneth Blanchard and Spencer Johnson

As a profession matures, it creates internal structures to set standards and criteria for professional practice. In fact, the sign of any mature profession is not only a body of scientific and clinical knowledge but also professional standards for training, practice (in the form of ethics), and professional supervision. Each of these domains represents the movement of the knowledge base of the profession into its praxis. With the emergence of family psychology as a specialty, so too emerged training guidelines to shape the development of new professionals entering the profession, ethical guidelines that guide the practice of the profession, and training programs that incorporate both the core of psychology and the unique features of the specialty of family psychology. Training of clinical skills requires a clinical supervision model that develops and guides the trainee to utilize appropriate professional practices for clinical decision making that brings together research, practice, and theory into an integrated treatment plan.

The specialty of family psychology differs from other specialties within psychology because of the unique perspective from which family psychologists are trained to consider the biopsychosocial problems of their clients. It is not that family psychologists treat populations different from other professional psychologists, nor even that a family psychologist's clients present with vastly different problems. Rather, the epistemology of the family psychologist differentiates him or her from the more traditionally trained professional psychologist. The family psychologist is trained to approach client issues from an ecosystemic perspective, providing a vastly different conceptual model from which to view the complex presenting issues of families and their constituent members. Family psychologists are trained to utilize key systemic concepts such as reciprocity, self-organization, complexity, adaptability, and social construction (Nutt & Stanton, 2008). Whether the client is a family, a couple, or a single member of a family, to the extent that the client's presenting issue intersects with family or systemic functioning, a specialized conceptual model and related interventions are required.

For this reason, specialized training, uniquely nuanced ethical guidelines, and systemically focused supervision practices in family psychology are quite different from what is offered in general counseling and clinical psychology training programs. For example, none of us would go to a physician who was not specifically trained in cardiology to have our chest pains diagnosed. Many clinical psychologists, social workers, or mental health counselors take the good work they do with individuals and apply it to couples and families. Unfortunately, like the physician, cardiology is a specialty with a unique body of knowledge, specialized research tools, and purposeful clinical interventions. The ethics of family practice are not the same as those in traditional individual treatment. Who is the client (the individual, the couple, or the family?), and how does confidentiality work with couples and family members? There are unique ethical and legal considerations in the practice of family psychology. Family psychologists must be familiar with laws and regulations regarding issues such as custody and visitation; child, spouse, and elder abuse; and ethical relationships with attorneys. If planning to engage in active courtroom work, the family psychologist must be trained in family forensic psychology. In supervision, a similar systemic focus is essential. Thus, while psychologists in many specialties may upon occasion treat families or couples, the depth and breadth of their coursework and training with families and couples and thus their expertise in treatment will not parallel that of family psychologists.

Our goal in this chapter is to provide an overview of these three crucial domains of the profession of family psychology: professional training, ethics, and clinical supervision. In these areas, the systemic epistemology continues to be the primary organizing principle for the unique challenges that surround how best to train clinicians who are competent in a specialized field, who practice in a complex multirelational context and must do so ethically, and who have received specialized clinical supervision. It is our assertion that trained couple and family psychologists are the best practitioners for couple and family work.

TRAINING IN FAMILY PSYCHOLOGY

Education and training in family psychology builds on the core foundations of training as those of clinical psychology (e.g., biological bases of behavior, developmental, abnormal, learning, and cognition), but goes beyond traditional coursework and training to capture the unique aspects of a systems psychology and multisystemic theoretical orientation. Bringing a systemic way of thinking to the core areas of clinical and counseling psychology (cognitive, developmental, etc.) is more difficult to develop than it might appear. For example, the 2-year postdoctoral fellowship in family psychology at the University of Rochester spends 1 year focused on how to consider assessment, diagnosis, and treatment from a systems psychology paradigm (McDaniel, 2010). It takes effort, commitment, and time to learn to think systemically. In addition to thinking systemically, family psychologists are trained in:

- Biological Foundations. Family psychology systems are composed of individuals whose behavior has *a biological foundation*. Understanding the principles of anatomy and physiology and the interaction between the biological, individual, family, and environmental (social) variables as determinants of behavior is essential. Specific areas, which are most relevant to family psychology, would be the effects of drugs and neuropsychological problems on family interaction, developmental disabilities, and organically based psychological problems. Another important area would be the impact of chronic illness and/ or long-term disability on the family. Current scientific knowledge of biological issues in parenting, both mothering and fathering, is essential to family psychology, as are the biological components of sexuality and sexual dysfunction.
- Social Bases of behavior. A family is a social system within a larger social system. It is important for the family psychologist to understand the principles governing social systems and their interactions. Therefore, a strong scientific foundation in the social bases of behavior is particularly critical for the family psychologist. Knowledge of social influence theory, attribution theory, attitude change, interpersonal attraction, small group interaction, family-of-origin dynamics, emotional triangles, underfunctioning and overfunctioning family systems, multigenerational transmission of relationship patterns, and

impact of genograms as interventions are essential. Problems such as teenage gangs, violence and abuse, parenting and stepparenting, and school issues would be examples of the application of social bases of behavior.

- Individual Differences. The psychological functioning of the individual and the family or other social system is interactional, so understanding interactions requires a thorough grounding in the scientific bases of development, personality functioning, and individual psychopathology. In addition, facing one's own individual resistance to change helps the family psychologist avoid pathologizing clients. Working on one's own family inspires humility in a family psychologist and increases the probability that the psychologist will not judge the family or blame any members of the family for the behavior of other members. The ability not to blame any one individual member is the essence of achieving a systemic perspective.

- History and Systems. Family psychologists must be well versed in the philosophical and historical origins of the discipline of psychology and of the perspectives which have shaped contemporary psychology. Thus, they must have completed coursework that includes the various schools of thought associated with the field of psychology and the impact of these schools on contemporary practice in psychology. Within the context of history and systems, the history of family psychology may be seen as emerging from a synthesis of empiricism, systems thinking, and clinical psychotherapy.

- Assessment. Competence is needed in family assessment that goes beyond individual measures and test batteries. A family psychologist should be able to construct new tests or use current instruments to measure family functioning, carry out validation studies, and administer and interpret test results. Evaluating how a family functions requires the ability to assess relationship patterns in both current functioning and prior generations. The ways in which a family manages emotional closeness, distance, and conflict are central to the work of a family psychologist as well as understanding how relationship patterns are transmitted across generations. Family psychology assumes that sets of categories exist along continua by which families and larger systems can be assessed to be healthy and functional or unhealthy and dysfunctional. Assessment also may describe types of dysfunction. Various schools of thought in family psychology view problems through their own theoretical perspectives. Some focus on the structure of the family or group, while others focus on sequences that maintain symptoms. Others look at variables such as communication, patterns, cohesion, and affection. Overall, family psychologists must be able to assess dysfunction in a multitude of situations and problems.

Competency in Family Psychology. Competency includes attitudes, behaviors, and skills in both foundational and functional competency domains. Foundational competencies usually include assessing the student's level of professionalism, reflective practice, scientific knowledge and methods, relationships, individual and cultural diversity, ethical and legal standards, and policy and interdisciplinary systems. Functional competency involves assessment, intervention, consultation, research/evaluation, supervision, teaching, administration, and advocacy (Kaslow, Grus, Campbell, Fouad, Hatcher, & Rodolfa, 2009).

Existing doctoral psychology programs that emphasize family psychology employ a variety of mechanisms for measuring student competence. Students are required to achieve developmentally appropriate competence in the core clinical competencies as defined by the National Council of Schools and Programs of Professional Psychology (Peterson, Peterson, Abrams, & Stricker, 1997). Competencies in family psychology are assessed in eight family-specific domains (Kaslow, Celano, & Stanton, 2005): the application of scientific knowledge to practice, psychological assessment, psychological intervention, consultation and interprofessional collaboration, supervision, professional development, ethics and legal issues, and individual and cultural diversity. These competencies may be assessed through written and oral comprehensive examinations, a clinical dissertation, assignments and tests in courses that cover subject matter, and case conceptualizations demonstrating the knowledge of family psychology.

Practicum, Internship, and Postdoctoral Fellowships. Education and training value both didactic and experiential components. Didactics are encouraged, and they occur not only in educational coursework, but also in practice, internship, and postdoctoral fellowships. In like manner, experiential training is as encouraged in the educational setting as it is in practice, internship, and postdoctoral settings. Because of the difficulty of achieving a systemic perspective and because of the number of clients with whom a family psychologist works, advanced training in this specialty requires more live supervision than is typical of most other fields of psychology. The development of this supervision model and research evaluating its effectiveness are critical to family psychology.

Students in family psychology often have the opportunity to work in clinical settings that conceptualize cases systemically and intervene directly with couples or families. While the predoctoral internship provides generalist training, the student of family psychology will seek out internships that offer a rotation or emphasis in couple or family work. A typical 1-year full-time predoctoral internship with a family psychology emphasis should include a balance of clinical experiences and didactic offerings. The predoctoral internship needs to have an emphasis on the integration of theory and research into the practice of family psychology. In addition, the integration of theory, research, and practice in applied psychology generally, and family psychology more specifically, needs to be central to the professional socialization of the predoctoral intern. Interns need to be provided with a diversity of clinical experiences in assessment and intervention with couples and families. In addition, the intern needs to have substantial opportunities for training in systems assessment and treatment of individuals and interpersonal psychopathology and/or organizational problems. Both individual and group supervisions need to be offered. One-way mirror, co-therapy, or videotape supervision is preferred over exclusive reliance on verbal case report. In addition to the core seminar topics important for interns, family psychology training at the internship level must include seminars in family and systems-oriented work with individuals, couples, families, and groups. Such seminars may include topics such as clinical assessment with diverse couples and families, theory-driven clinical interventions, and family process and outcome research. Live supervision family therapy seminars are highly recommended.

Understanding the systemic nature of behavior is difficult because we naturally experience other people's behavior as emanating from a specific source; thus, achieving a systemic perspective is counterintuitive. Systemic principles can be taught at the beginning level through readings and classroom instruction; however, at a more advanced level, the student's training must be experiential. Two experiential training techniques that are used to provide advanced scientific and theoretical preparation for family psychologists are work on the student's own family of origin and live supervision of work with families and/or larger systems.

Working on one's own family of origin provides a concrete experience of such systems concepts as emotional triangles, the underfunctioning/overfunctioning couple, and the multigenerational transmission of relationship patterns. Although psychoanalytic training also requires working on the self, family-of-origin work differs from the kind of work a psychoanalytic trainee might do. Family-of-origin work involves interactive interviewing of family and extended family members, rather than simply talking about these people in a therapist's office. In family-of-origin work, the focus is on relationship patterns (rather than intrapsychic processes), for example, pursuing and distancing, triangling, fusion, and communication patterns.

In addition to work on one's own family, beginning family psychologists need extensive supervision as they try to achieve advanced scientific and theoretical knowledge in their clinical practice. When working with a family, it is easy to become overwhelmed by the multiple members. Conflict can escalate, and members can be scapegoated. Because of the powerful nature of family systems, inexperienced family therapists can make things worse rather than better. Live supervision provides a safety net for the beginning family therapist and is more extensively used in family psychology than other specialties. Live supervision involves a supervisor, and sometimes other students and colleagues, observing a session behind a one-way mirror. Clients are informed that this observation is occurring and usually are taken behind the mirror to see the room that the "team" will be in. In some training sites, the team is introduced to the family as well. The team might interrupt a session with a telephone call to the therapist suggesting another line of questioning, or the team might send a message to the family directly. In this form of supervision, the "team" becomes a version of co-therapist. As a family psychologist becomes more experienced, supervision usually changes to videotapes of sessions.

When family psychologists are working with larger systems, apprenticeship with an experienced family psychologist on-site replaces live supervision behind a one-way mirror. For example, in family–school consultation or collaboration with family practice physicians, training typically includes a year of shadowing and observing more experienced family psychologists, and then working with the more experienced person as a co-consultant, similar to the way a co-therapist might work in a therapy session. The co-consulting provides a forum in which the beginning family psychologist can be given live supervision.

Postdoctoral training is based on the premise that the doctoral resident holds a doctorate in professional psychology from a program that is accredited by APA/CPA or designated by ASPPB/National Register. It is assumed that the resident applicant has obtained a doctorate with a focus in clinical, counseling, or school psychology and has had some coursework and predoctoral internship experience in family/child psychology. If an applicant has not obtained a doctorate with such a focus first, he or she should be directed to a respecialization program. It is further assumed that the resident applicant has completed a predoctoral internship accredited by APA/CPA or approved by the Association of Psychology Postdoctoral and Internship Centers. Each postdoctoral training program in family psychology will be responsible for determining criteria and procedures to assess an applicant's competence in basic areas of applied psychology, either directly through the program or in some other acceptable academic/clinical forum whenever necessary. Supplementation of any existing deficiencies of the applicant may be required by the program as a condition of admission (Williams, Kaslow, & Grossman, 1994). A full-time postdoctoral residency (1 or 2 years) or a part-time postdoctoral externship

(2–4 years) in family psychology is needed to consolidate mastery of the specialty. The nature and duration of the residency experience is determined in part by the nature and amount of prior training in family psychology (e.g., individuals who have had minimal predoctoral training in family psychology will require longer, more intensive postdoctoral training that will need to include clinical, didactic, and research training to remediate their deficiencies in family psychology education).

In addition to ongoing weekly clinical supervision, preferably using a one-way mirror, videotape, and/or co-therapy, the following is a proposed model for postdoctoral training in family psychology (Williams, Kaslow, & Grossman, 1994). Training should be offered in (1) professional and ethical issues in family psychology, (2) marital and family systems theory, (3) assessment in family psychology, (4) couple and family intervention skills and strategies, (5) educational skills, (6) sex therapy, (7) family law, (8) family research, (9) supervision and consultation, and (10) management (administration).

SUPERVISION IN FAMILY PSYCHOLOGY

The objective of supervision is to train new psychologists to be competent and effective professionals as assessors, diagnosticians, and clinicians and help through ongoing support for family psychologists to develop and maintain their levels of competence. Competence is defined as "the habitual and judicious use of communication, knowledge, technical skills, clinical reasoning, emotions, values, and reflection in daily practice for the benefit of the individual and the community being served" (Epstein & Hundert, 2002, p. 226). In recent years, psychology education and training has been primarily organized around the concept of competency, with a competency-based approach to supervision providing a general "framework and method to initiate, develop, implement, and evaluate the processes and outcomes of supervision" (Falender & Shafranske, 2004, p. 20).

There are numerous approaches to supervision, but all are organized around the idea that the therapist/supervisee can provide sufficient data to the supervisor such that the transfer of knowledge and skills can take place from trainer to trainee to provide competent treatment and care for the cases under consultation. Psychotherapy-based approaches to supervision continue to dominate the field as supervisors train supervisees in particular theoretical orientations (Frawley-O'Dea & Sarnat, 2001; Milne & James, 2000; Mahrer & Boulet, 1997; Storm, Todd, Sprenkle, & Morgan, 2001). Developmental models are organized around increasing ~nomy on the part of the client/supervisee as he or she moves toward independent functioning (Falender & Schafranske, 2004). Process-based models, such as the discrimination model, emphasize process, conceptualization, personalization skills development, and professional behavior (Bernard, 1997; Lanning, 1986). Holloway (1995) put forward a systems model that links the various factors inherent in the supervisory relationship that contribute to process and outcome. "All of the other factors—that is, the client, supervisor, trainee, institution and the functions and tasks of supervision—interact dynamically and influence the supervision relationship" (Falender & Schafranske, 2004, p. 18). Within this framework, clinicians understand that each individual trainee will have unique features, goals, and objectives, necessitating a strong emphasis on the development of the supervisor–supervisee relationship.

The best family psychology supervision embraces the recursive nature between theory, practice, and research. Supervision aids in the acquisition and enhancement of skills—the clinical tools necessary to meet client need. However, Nichols (1988) suggests that family psychology supervision is more than applying techniques to the treatment of persons; it also involves the study and investigation of human behavior. That is to say, the supervisory process involves practice, study, and research with the family psychology supervisor recognizing the systemic nexus of theory, practice, and research, directing the student to draw upon relevant research and theory as a way of ensuring the best in client system care. The linkage of praxis with academia ensures the ongoing growth and development of the therapist as a skilled clinician. This same recursive effect is also at work in the therapist/supervisor relationship, reflecting the fact that different theoretical orientations will affect how supervision is done (McDaniel, Weber, & McKeever, 1983).

There are features of family psychology supervision that all skilled supervisors hold in common, no matter the theoretical orientation. In particular, there are seven features of supervision that define a growth-oriented family psychology orientation: a systems perspective, isomorphism, supervisee's family projection process, ethics, dialectic, development, and a shared learner model. Family psychology supervision is:

- *Systemic.* A systems perspective recognizes the relationship between entities. Relationship has to do with the process of human interaction, and supervision, like therapy, is a relationship context in which various meanings are shared (Anderson & Goolishian, 1988). Systems are nested entities, each affected by and affecting the others. The client system is a subsystem of the therapist/client system, which itself is a subsystem of the supervisor/therapist/client system. Each of these systems impacts the other and cannot be viewed apart from one another.

Nichols (1988) notes that a supervisee's life experience within his or her own family of origin, extended family, and social system underlies systemic education. He states, "Those experiences and their residue, along with the effects of present involvement in individual and family life cycles, form a mosaic against which theory and current therapeutic involvement with families are perceived and interpreted during the student's clinical work" (p. 111). Of course, there is debate about how much emphasis is placed on past and present, but little debate that these elements are part of a systemic paradigm of training.

- *Isomorphic.* The word isomorphic applies when, "two complex structures can be mapped onto each other in such a way that to each part of one structure there is a corresponding part in the other structure, where 'corresponding' means that the two parts play similar roles in their respective structures" (Hofstadter, 1979, p. 49). There is general recognition in family psychology supervision that the relationship between the therapist and the client, and supervisor, therapist, and client systems is interconnected and interrelated. Training and therapy interact recursively, coevolve over time, and are themselves subsystems within other contexts that are also isomorphically related (Liddle & Saba, 1985). The importance of isomorphism cannot be overstated; Schwartzman and Kneifel (1985) have noted that "family patterns will not be resolved by a treatment/service system that repeats these problems at the helping level" (p. 104).

- *Contextual.* Contextual variables may be defined as "the ever present aspects of supervisors, supervisees and clients and the unique aspects of the environment in which supervision and therapy occur" (Storm et al., 1997, p. 9). Contextual variables range from multicultural, ethnic, gender, age, values, and religious differences to differences in theoretical orientation between therapist and supervisor. These variables impact the way that both therapy and supervision takes place, and the supervisor must be sensitive to the many variables that affect the supervisor/therapist/client system. At the heart of family psychology, supervision is Constantine's (1976) notion that family therapists are grown, not made. Growth requires time, patience, nurturing, structure, encouragement, and an unshakeable belief in the supervisory process. Beyond technique and study is the primary element of growth—relationship. If, as Fairbairn notes, psychopathology is the result of broken relationship, then wellness arises out of the restoration of relationship (Delisle, 2011). Buber explains that the "I" of personhood arises out of the "we" of relationship. Health within individuals occurs as a result of health between individuals (Kramer, 2003). Psychotherapy is as much about the promotion of healthy relating between the therapist and client system as it is the application of evidence-based treatment technique. What makes psychotherapy therapeutic is when the therapist treats the client in a way he or she has never been treated before.

- *Contingent.* New client responses require appropriate affective processing, new cognitions, and new behaviors, which are then generalized out to the client's relational world. The skill of relating responsively and therapeutically is a growth skill, first experienced in the supervisor/therapist relationship, then generalized out to the client/therapist relationship. Supervision with growth as a goal explores the issues of therapist countertransference. The supervisee unconsciously responds to specific traits of the clinical family, which trigger similarities with or a repetition of dynamics within his or her own family of origin (Halperin, 1991). Supervision further explores the supervisee's reactions to the client system's dynamic albeit unconscious attempts to manipulate reactions from her or him (Nichols & Everett, 1986). Framo (1965) has noted that it is almost impossible not to get caught up in the drama of the family.

- *Interpersonal.* Maintaining a therapeutic posture requires that supervisees examine the hidden motives or issues of their own lives that might impact the therapeutic process. Some of the issues dealt with in supervision include power, idealization, self-esteem, competency, and feelings of inadequacy. Supervision explores the immediate relationship between supervisor and supervisee in light of transference, countertransference, and projective identification issues. Ferber, Mendelsohn, and Napier (1972) suggest that the supervisor's task is not to help the supervisee solve his or her family's problems, but to teach him or her to cope with and be aware of the secret presence of his or her own family in the treatment room.

- *Dialectic* is a concept that has its Western roots in Hegelian philosophy where one concept serves as thesis over against a seemingly contradictory concept that serves as antithesis. The goal is to find truth and utility through synthesis or integration of concepts to form a new concept that is closer to the truth than either one concept provided alone. For example, relational process and theoretical content are relatively orthogonal concepts in psychotherapy, yet when synthesized provide a complex scaffold for effective treatment. Research and practice are generally seen as disparate elements of psychology, yet when synthesized provide a continuous backdrop of scientist practitioner. Science and art are generally segregated forms of academic endeavor, yet the basis for art is science (see mathematics and music), and science is sterile without the touch of human emotion. Evidence-based science brings to human problems the latest in research, and evidence-based practice recognizes the unique aspects that every individual, relationship, and family brings to therapy. The growth-oriented supervisor must be willing to hold disparate elements of psychology in dynamic tension and aid the supervisee in doing the same, to learn to sit with chaos in order to obtain clarity, and to hold lightly the tensions of oppositional forms in order to provide the best in evidence-based practice.

- *Developmental.* The main task of supervision is to facilitate supervisee movement from dependency to autonomous functioning (Hess, 1986). Watkins's (1992) discussion of the four different types of autonomy/dependency issues for psychology supervisees informs the main task of teaching, which is the preparation of the student to inhabit the professional role of psychologist. The supervisor must regulate the relationship with his or her supervisee in order to foster a sense of secure base. The supervisor fosters nurturance and encouragement and is more directive initially, meeting the cognitive, behavioral, and emotional needs of the supervisee. The supervisor models nonreactive, non-anxious behavior in relation to the supervisee's scientific and applied work. As the supervisee gains confidence, she or he moves into what developmental theory calls the practicing period, where the supervisor helps the supervisee "think outside the box," that is, explore ways to think and practice that particularly resonate with whom the supervisee is. It is important for the supervisor to encourage the supervisee's attempts to step out on his or her own, all the while guiding the supervisee in ethical and professional directions. The supervisee will begin to gain a sense of identity as a professional psychologist and will increase the ability to recognize and manage transference/countertransference issues.

Because of this focus on growth, the relationship between supervisor and therapist is a naturally hierarchical one. There has been debate over the issue of the power inherent in the supervisor/supervisee relationship. Ackerman (1973) thought that the relationship should be egalitarian, but recognized the difficulties. Others, such as Ard (1973), have suggested a developmental stage model, from greater hierarchy in the early stages of training, to a more collegial relationship as the therapist matures in the profession. Nichols (1988) advocates for a more hierarchical approach, but believes that the supervisor should find ways to level the playing field. For example, Ackerman (1973) asserts that the important tool at the supervisor's disposal is empathy, the supervisor's ability to understand the supervisee's experience. The supervisor can also reduce the evaluation process and humanize it through communicating that he or she believes in the supervisee's potential to be a good therapist. He or she can search for active strengths, rather than deficits, and can accommodate self to the supervisee's learning style, rather than vice versa. The supervisor can communicate that his or her sense of identity is not dependent on the supervisee's competence. The supervisor can communicate that mistakes and growth are to be expected. The techniques that are used in therapy are also used in training, that is, modeling and self-disclosure, reframing and refocusing, as well as exploration of both present and past to elucidate family patterns of living (Sullivan, 1954). The supervisor should provide a frame and structure for supervision while keeping an open mind, free of expectations that might impose a structure on the information shared in the supervision session. The supervisor should work to put the supervisee at ease, building a sense of trust in the relationship. The supervisor should encourage the supervisee in the process of becoming a professional, discovering the orientation that most represents who she or he is and helping the supervisee in the development of a skill set. The supervisor should model respect for the supervisee's autonomy, a stance characterized by a seeking to discover, rather than knowing in advance, displaying an empathic, neutral, nondirective stance. Palmer (1998) has advocated for a shared learner model between teacher/trainer and student/trainee. In this model, there is clearly a teacher, but both student and teacher take the role of learners. The supervisor understands that the supervisee is the expert on his or her own life. The supervisor participates as a co-learner as they discover ways to improve as therapists. This models for the supervisee the notion that the client system is the expert with regard to itself. This way of training, while not eliminating hierarchy, helps reduce the impact of the power differential between supervisor and supervisee.

Evidence-Based Supervision. With the advent of evidence-based practice, the process of clinical supervision is also changing. Sexton (2010) and Sexton, Alexander, and Gillman (2004) outlined how supervision changes within evidence-based models—with the model as the core "yardstick" and goal for a relational change process. Their focus was on supervision process in the evidence-based treatment model FFT; however, the model illustrates how clinical supervision changes and adjusts when an evidence-based treatment model is used. In this description, the model allows for the development of adherence (good clinical skills) and competence (the application of those skills in ways that fit the client and match the model).

- *Model focused.* It is the clinical model (its central core principles and clinical protocol) that is the primary basis for quality assurance and quality improvement; therefore, it is the yardstick by which the therapist is assessed and the outcome goal to which the supervisor directs all interventions. Supervision is based on attention to model adherence (the prescribed goals and intervention strategies of the model) and competence in meeting these goals and using treatment strategies.

- *Relational.* The relational process between a supervisor, individual therapist, and a working group of therapists is reflected in the phasic nature of the supervision model. The relational process is founded on respect for the individual; it acknowledges the unique differences, strengths, and characteristics of each therapist. In addition, it is a relational process built on alliance in which the supervisor and the therapist work together to the same end.
- *Multisystem.* Supervision requires attention and action in multiple domains: the therapists, the service delivery system, and the working group.
- *Phasic.* The supervision process unfolds over time, parallel to the treatment phases. Each phase has a set of goals, related change mechanisms, and supervisor interventions most likely to activate those change mechanisms.
- *Databased or evidence based.* Specific supervision interventions and goals are based on monitoring the therapist's service delivery patterns and consulting specific measures of therapist activities related to adherence and competence. Monitoring, goal setting, and ultimately interventions use data from multiple sources and perspectives. Throughout the phases of the supervision process, the supervisor constantly assesses adherence, competence, and the developmental status of the working group.

ETHICS IN FAMILY PSYCHOLOGY

There are ethical issues and dilemmas unique to family psychology. The family psychologist must truly embrace the APA's aspirational principles as well as the relevant codes in order to make ethical decisions when working with a client system on issues such as (1) determining who the client is, (2) confidentiality, and (3) disclosure. We will comment briefly on several of the unique ethical issues we experience most frequently in the practice of family psychology.

1. Determining the client. The family psychologist must have a clear sense of how he or she personally views systemic therapy prior to entering into a therapeutic alliance with the familial unit or each individual within the familial unit. The APA's 2002 Ethics Code states,

When psychologists agree to provide services to several persons who have a relationship (such as spouses, significant others, or parents and children), they take reasonable steps to clarify at the outset (1) which of the individuals are clients/patients and (2) the relationship the psychologist will have with each person. (p. 15)

The psychologist must determine who the primary client will be. The questions must be asked: will the client be the couple as a unit or the family as a whole, or will the individuals within the family serve as collaborative support of an individual client or client dyad (Dishion & Stormshak, 2007; Fisher, 2003; Lambert, 2011)? At the very least, the therapist must make sure that improvement in one family member does not occur at the expense of another family member (Snyder & Doss, 2005).

Marriage and family therapists consider the family to always be the client, no matter what constellation of the family is being seen at any given time. For example, marriage and family therapists would view a child's acting out in terms of family dynamics and deal with it therapeutically on that basis. In fact, some family therapists will only see the entire family (Napier & Whitaker, 1978). Whether the child is being seen individually, the parents are being seen for couple issues, or the whole family is being seen together—the family is the client, and the marriage and family therapist advocates for the whole. To advocate for individuals within the family, unless it is strategic, is to skew the course of effective systems treatment from a marriage and family perspective.

Family psychology, on the other hand, sees the client in more traditional psychological terms. For example, when a therapist sees a child who is acting out, he or she does assessment at multiple ecological levels and, depending on the diagnosis, decides whether or not to see the child as an individual, to see the child with the parents, or to see the entire family. If the therapist sees the child individually, then meets with his or her parents for parent training that is adjunctive to work with the child, the child remains the client. However, if the therapist's systems assessment returns a relational diagnosis of parental discord as the primary reason the child is acting out, the therapist may choose to see the couple for therapy rather than the child, and if so, his or her client will shift from the child to the couple relationship. However, if the psychologist determines that both the child and parents should be seen for therapy, the therapist will in most cases see the child individually (as the child was his or her initial client), see parents as adjunctive to the child's treatment or refer the parents out to another therapist for couples work.

Snyder and Doss (2005) suggest four approaches a psychologist can take in order to prevent ethical dilemmas when determining who exactly constitutes the client. First, the psychologist can treat each family member as if he or she were an individual client. The therapist would see one member of the family, and if others wanted to be seen, they would be referred to other therapists. Second, the psychologist could view only the marital or familial system as the client and consequently refuse to form an alliance with any single individual, as the focus would be on the marital relationship or familial relationships for treatment. If an individual wanted to be seen for therapy, the therapist would refer him or her out. Third, the psychologist has the option of shifting her or his alliances between subsystems of the family based on the psychologist's judgment. A final option that the psychologist could utilize is to strictly follow the family's or couple's goals and formulate a treatment plan based on those specific goals. The family psychologist must make it clear to the client(s) if the psychologist decides to switch his or her view of who constitutes the client during the course of treatment.

A major problem occurs when a psychologist sees one subsystem of the family and ostensibly completes therapy, and the family then wants another subsystem to be seen. This occurs with some frequency when an individual completes therapy and then requests that the psychologist see his or her partner. The problem is making the determination that therapy with the initial client is complete. It is not uncommon for clients to complete a phase of therapy, but return later as further issues crop up or as they move through the life cycle. Seeing another member of the subsystem can hinder an initial client from returning to therapy with the psychologist when the need arises. Consider the therapist who saw Mr. and Ms. X for couples therapy. As the couple's relationship improved, Mr. X began to act out and was determined to be going through a manic episode. At his request and the couple's agreement, the therapist chose to see Mr. X individually for a time. After several sessions in, Ms. X requested to be seen following a fight with Mr. X, and the therapist agreed. Mr. X was livid that the therapist had seen Ms. X when he thought he was being seen individually. Mr. X refused to return to therapy. From a psychology perspective, it seems the better part of wisdom to ascertain who the client is at the beginning of therapy and not deviate from that position. If other subsystems want to be seen for therapy, the psychologist should refer them to another psychotherapist. Doing so will keep the boundaries clear, clean, and free of confusion.

2. Confidentiality and disclosure. Confidentiality has to do with a client holding the privilege concerning with whom the therapist can share the content of therapy. In most cases, the therapist cannot share the content of therapy with anyone without the client's written permission. Of course, there are exceptions: if an issue of child or elder abuse

comes up during therapy, if a client intends to harm self or others, or if a judge orders the contents of a therapy session to be turned over to the bench. The issues of confidentiality become more complicated when the client is a system, that is, two or more persons.

In the case of a couple, each person "owns" the contents of the therapy session. Details of the session cannot be revealed unless both parties agree in writing. This becomes problematic during dissolution of marriage court cases or during custody battles when one of the clients wants the contents of therapy to be made public, but the other does not. What course of action should the therapist take, especially when he or she has been subpoenaed by one of the client's attorneys?

The therapist may request that both parties agree in writing to the submission of a treatment report from the therapist, rather than submission of the full contents of the progress notes. The report would be seen by both before being made public. A treatment report allows the therapist to retain greater control of the publication of therapy by his or her interpretation of the progress notes. The therapist may decide that he or she will turn over only those contents of therapy that have to do with the client who made the request and will redact any information on the partner. This tends to be problematic in that much of a couple's personal information is intertwined and not easily parsed, and it is often labor intensive to carefully go through all the notes and redact all information having to do with the non-consenting partner. Finally, the therapist may inform the parties that he or she will not disclose the contents of therapy because the contents cannot be parsed apart and move to quash the subpoena. It is best if the therapist makes his or her position clear prior to the start of therapy verbally and in writing.

A second question of confidentiality and disclosure that often comes up in family psychology is what to do with information the therapist obtains from a minor. Therapy information cannot be shared with anyone without parental consent and the assent of the minor, but how does confidentiality operate between parent and child? Parents technically have a legitimate right to know what occurs in therapy with their children, but children also have a right to privacy as much as do adults. Typically, the therapist walks a fine line trying to honor the rights of both parties. When the therapist is seeing a minor, it is best to clarify prior to the beginning of therapy what he or she will keep confidential from the parents. Often, the therapist will provide the parents with the broad themes of therapy while retaining confidentiality around details of the minor client's story, unless the minor is at risk.

3. Confidentiality and secrets. There is perhaps no greater ethical dilemma faced by family psychologists than how to deal with the disclosure of family secrets during the course of therapy. Snyder and Doss (2005) suggest four different methods for dealing with confidentiality within couple and family therapy. First, the psychologist can decide to treat all information disclosed individually as confidential. A second approach is to consider no information, regardless of whether shared individually or in the course of joint therapy, as confidential. Another alternative is for the therapist to keep certain information confidential as a matter of privacy due to the sensitive nature of the disclosure. A final approach to confidentiality is for the psychologist and the client(s) to agree to keep certain information confidential until a later date. In order to avoid ethical dilemmas, the psychologist must inform the client system of how he or she will handle confidential disclosures. Patterson (2009) argues that when working with couples and families, it is important to keep separate records for each person with whom a family psychologist is working. By recommending that separate records be kept, Patterson is suggesting that each person within the couple or the family be treated as an individual client. Furthermore, Patterson suggests that when individual interviews or sessions are held with clients who are also engaging in family psychotherapy or couple therapy with the same psychologist, all information obtained during the course of the individual session remains confidential. This suggestion poses a number of potential ethical dilemmas for a psychologist if a secret is disclosed. For example, the disclosure of a secret during the course of an individual session may interfere with the psychologist's ability to effectively work with the couple or the nondisclosing individual. Yet, Patterson argues that by disclosing secrets, the psychologist may be inflicting undue harm on the family or the non-disclosing individual (Lambert, 2011; Patterson, 2009).

While Patterson's position is a legitimate one and supported by many in the field, Thoburn (2009) has argued that family psychologists should not keep secrets at all. He suggests that many couple problems have their core issues caught up with secrecy. As Pittman (1990) has noted regarding infidelity, "the problem of infidelity is not so much who one lies with, its who one lies to" (p.53). The problem here is that the client may possibly feel betrayed by the therapist and discontinue treatment. Of course, a hard-and-fast policy about disclosure can be problematic in and of itself. For example, if a spouse discloses an affair that occurred 20 years ago, does it make therapeutic sense to report that to the other spouse, that is, how would such disclosure further or inhibit the course of treatment? On the other hand, if a spouse discloses a recent infidelity and the psychologist's policy is to keep such disclosures secret, then it is quite likely that treatment will be inhibited. Atkins's (2005) research makes it clear that when an ongoing affair is kept secret, couples therapy will likely make little progress.

Since it is apparent that psychologists who work with couples and/or families, at times, hold individual breakout sessions, it would be helpful to establish guidelines for appropriate use of individual sessions in this context. When a psychologist is comfortable holding individual breakout sessions, the psychologist has thought through many of the guidelines suggested earlier and has established some form of clear policy on how to handle individual breakout sessions. Psychologists who hold breakout sessions should be able to articulate the value of the sessions and also explain how they handle situations and information that impact the individual not participating in the individual breakout session. It is recommended that psychologists have a written policy expressing how information in individual sessions is handled. Individual breakout sessions without clear rules, policies, or guidelines can lead to the psychologist becoming uncomfortable with, and thus unsure how to handle, disclosures made at those sessions. Moreover, individual breakout sessions without clear rules or guidelines may lead to ethical dilemmas and/or violations.

The answer for how to proceed is perhaps best found in the decision tree. The decision tree offers a flexible, considered, and rational approach by providing guidelines for determining a course of action regarding determination of who the psychologist's client is, and if and when to make disclosure of individually reported information (Lambert, 2011, pp. 122–124).

First, the therapist must clearly define who the client is and explain who constitutes the client(s) to all parties involved. The therapist must decide if the client will be the same if individual breakout sessions are to be held. If, during individual breakout sessions, the individual is considered a separate client from the couple or family, it will be necessary for the psychologist to consider how viewing one individual as part of a client couple or family and an individual client will impact the couple or family as a whole. The therapist must decide whether or not to allow individual breakout sessions during couple and/or family therapy, then the psychologist must decide what information should be disclosed during joint sessions following an individual breakout session. Should all disclosures that impact the couple or family be disclosed? Or should only specific types of disclosures (i.e., money matters or relationships outside the couple) be disclosed? If all or certain types of disclosures relevant are to be brought back to joint sessions, the psychologist should decide if there is a limit to how long it is appropriate to proceed with joint therapy without discussing the disclosures from individual sessions. Do the disclosures need to be introduced at the next joint session? Is it appropriate to wait more than one joint session before discussing the disclosure? It will probably be helpful for psychologists to have an upper limit on the number of sessions they are willing to wait for a disclosure to be shared.

Psychologists need to decide how they wish to bring disclosures back to couple or family sessions. Is it the obligation of the individual who disclosed the information to bring it back to the couple or family session? Is it the psychologist's job to bring the disclosure up in a future joint session? If the disclosure from individual therapy is never brought back to the joint therapy, the psychologist must decide how he or she will proceed. Does the psychologist need to terminate with the couple or family if the disclosure is not shared after a certain period of time? Psychologists need to consider how to handle communications made outside of sessions when they are working with couples or families. Should the psychologist share the details of all conversations? Should the psychologist play messages for all participants in therapy to hear? Psychologists should consider when, if ever, it is appropriate to change the format of therapy.

Based on research, the following suggestions might serve as useful guidelines for psychologists working with couples and/or families to follow if they decide to allow individual breakout sessions.

1. Always understand who the client is.
2. Develop a policy around the changing of therapy formats.
3. Consider what the role of the psychologist is.
4. Consider what the goal of therapy is.
5. If individual breakout sessions will be part of therapy, achieve a shared comfort level with the decision to allow breakout sessions.
6. Consider when individual sessions are contraindicated.
7. Consider developing a distinction between information revealed that needs to be shared with the couple or family and information that the psychologist is able to contain without needing to disclose it to the spouse or family (i.e., secrets *vs.* private information).
8. At all times, always be clear around boundaries and information that will need to be disclosed to the other individual(s) in the couple or family (Lambert, 2011, pp. 124–126).

CONCLUSIONS AND REFLECTIONS

Family psychology has emerged from its early more turbulent days as a profession with not only a substantial knowledge base, a wealth of clinical wisdom, and comprehensive practice and theories, but also one with benchmarks for training, practice, and clinical supervision that are systemic in nature. These domains set the scaffolding and structure for how and in what way family psychologists are trained, the rules for professional and ethical practice, and the unique methods of supervision. Within the scaffolding of each are various approaches all united around the ideas of systemic practice and linked through the epistemology of systemic thinking. The existence of these domains illustrates the maturity of the field of family psychology.

Epilogue
The Art of Science, Practice, and Theory in Family Psychology

This book began with our invitation in the preface to take a "view through the looking glass" at the unique epistemology and practices of family psychology. The chapters that followed described a specialty field of psychology that integrates the intrapersonal, interpersonal, and contextual elements of human behavior creating a multidimensional foundation of theory and research, and unique couple and family clinical interventions built on a common set of principles about clinical practice, assessment, and treatment planning. As you can see, family psychology plays an important role in the landscape of applied psychology bringing strong research findings, a unique way of perceiving people and their problems, and multisystemic treatments that have demonstrated outcomes with a wide variety of clinical problems for individuals, couples, and families. Yet, underlying the science resides the covert art of family psychology. Consider the daunting task facing a family psychologist; as the individual couple, or family tell their story; the therapist must respond in a personal, yet therapeutic fashion and orchestrate new ways of relating between members of the client system, meeting the phase-based relational goals of the therapeutic model in order to move therapy forward. Whether evidence based or more traditionally theoretical, every successful intervention must be conducted in a relational way that is artful, personal, and at the same time systematic and model focused. When conducting research, the application of the basic rules of the scientific method needs to be creatively adapted, adjusted to answer the requisite research questions in a systemic way while being reliable and valid so that the results contribute to the overall knowledge base.

This means finding tools to measure, deciding when to measure, determining the core change mechanisms to investigate, among many other tasks. In both research practice and theory, family psychologists balance a number of tensions that are inherent in the field (Sexton, 2010): being purposeful and creative, being contingent and responsive, and being client focused and model driven. Therein lies one of the paradoxes of good therapy, sound research, and constructive theory building—balancing clinical relevance with structure and flexibility, all at the same time.

As the profession matures and practices become more standardized and as the research knowledge base is codified into standards of care, there are always pleas for a return to the creativity and intuitive practices of earlier times. These tensions are frequently described as a struggle between creativity, client focus, and individuality and wisdom of the therapist and research findings or evidence-based clinical practices. Yet, we suggest that as the profession evolves, so do our notions of what creativity may mean in the field of family psychology.

Sexton and van Dam (2010) took a systemic perspective suggesting that the creativity in FFT takes more than clinical expertise alone. They suggested that creativity and structure are dialectically related and can't be separated. In fact, they argue that it is the structure of the model that provides a set of principles, a specific knowledge base to back up those principles, and research-informed evidence on the validity and reliability of the method, client, therapist, and contextual variables to know/address/include for successful treatment to work in clinical settings. The theoretical models and research findings are the structure within which the expert develops systematic and complex case conceptualizations by providing a reliable and clinically relevant way to understand clients, problems, and context. The core systemic principles of the model are both the knowledge and the procedural structure, which forms the scaffolding of a therapist's expert judgment. It is this scaffolding that shapes the structure within which cases are conceptualized, forms the foundation of how decisions are made, and provides a roadmap of the steps to take to promote successful change process. Theories and research organize the vast array of information we each gain from our clinical experience into meaningful and usable principles that have clinical utility. It is in the praxis of family psychology that the balance between structure and creativity is part of any complex activity. Playing music involves both music theory and the creative application of theory to the mood and context of the moment. Like the musician, first, the family psychologist conceptualizes cases within the knowledge domains of the model and its theoretical principles and assures that the procedural elements adequately represent the model. Only then can he or she bring competence in delivering the model to an individual, couple, or family.

So, family psychology is moving from revolution to evolution (Goldenberg & Goldenberg, 2009). In a teleological sense, we are becoming what we actually have already been, a field defined by both a systems epistemology and a population, a unique perspective on research, teaching, training, and practice with individuals, couples, families, communities, multidisciplinary teams, and organizations. We believe the family systems lens offers a unique voice that combines the best of other models, that is, the pathology model of clinical psychology and the strengths and resources model of counseling psychology, and we believe that family psychology will likely become the dominant roadmap in the field of psychology in the decades to come.

References

Abidin, R. R. (1995). *Parenting stress index* (3rd ed.). Lutz, FL: Psychological Assessment Resources.

Abramson, L. Y., Seligman, M. E., & Teasdale, J. D. (1978). Learned helplessness in humans: Critique and reformulation. *Journal of Abnormal Psychology, 87*(1), 49–74.

Ackerman, M., & Ackerman, M. (1997). Child custody evaluation practices: A survey of experienced professionals (revisited). *Professional Psychology: Research and Practice, 28*(2), 128–135.

Ackerman, N. W. (1972). *The psychodynamics of family life: Diagnosis and treatment of family relationships*. New York: Basic Books.

Ackerman, N. (1973). Some considerations for training in family therapy. In *Career directions* (vol. 2). East Hanover, NJ: Sandoz Pharmaceuticals, D. J. Publications.

Ahrons, C. R. (2011). Commentary on "reconsidering the 'good divorce.'" *Family Relations: Interdisciplinary Journal of Applied Family Studies, 60*(5), 528–532. doi: 10.1111/j.1741–3729.2011.00676.x.

Alexander, J. F., Pugh, C, Parsons, B, F., & Sexton, T. (2000*). Functional family therapy* (Book Three: Vol. II). In D. S. Elliott (Series Ed.). *Blueprints for violence prevention*. Institute of Behavioral Science, Regents of the University of Colorado.

Alexander, J. F., Barton, C., Schaivo, R. S., & Parsons, B. V. (1976). Behavioral intervention of families with delinquents: Therapist characteristics and outcome. *Journal of Clinical and Consulting Psychology, 44*(4), 656–664.

Alexander, J. F., Robbins, M. S., & Sexton, T. L. (2000). Family-based interventions with older, at-risk youth: From promise to proof to practice. *The Journal of Primary Prevention, 21*(2), 185–205. doi: 10.1023/a:1007031219209

Alexander, J. F., Sexton, T. L., & Robbins, M. A. (2003). The developmental status of family therapy in family psychology intervention science. In H. A. Liddle (Ed.), *Family psychology intervention science*. Washington, DC: American Psychological Association Press.

American Board of Professional Psychology (2015). American Board of Forensic Psychology. http://www.abpp.org/i4a/pages/index.cfm?pageid=3313

American Psychological Association. (2002). Ethical principles of psychologists and code of conduct. *American Psychologist, 57*, 1060–1073.

American Psychological Association. (2006). Evidence-based practice in psychology. *American Psychologist, 61*(4), 271–285.

Amundson, B. (2001). America's rural communities as crucibles for clinical reform: Establishing collaborative care teams in rural communities. *Families, Systems & Health, 19*(1), 13–23.

Anderson, D. (2005, April). *Multicultural group counseling and psychotherapy: Converging forces of development and healing*. A workshop and paper presented at a meeting of the American Counseling Association, Atlanta, GA.

Anderson, H. (2009). Collaborative practice: Relationships and conversations that make a difference. In J. Bray & M. Stanton (Eds.), *The Wiley-Blackwell handbook of family psychology* (pp. 300–313). Malden, MA: Blackwell Publishing Ltd.

Anderson, H., & Goolishian, H. (1988). Human systems as linguistic systems: Preliminary and evolving ideas about the implications for clinical theory. *Family Process*, 27 (4), 371 393.

Aos, S., & Barnoski, R. (1998). Watching the bottom line: Cost-effective interventions for reducing crime in Washington. Washington State Institute for Public Policy: RCW 13.40.500.

Ard, B. N. (1973). Providing clinical supervision for marriage counselors: A model for supervisor and supervisee. *Family Coordinator, 22*, 91–97.

Atkins, D. C., Dimidjin, S., & Christensen, A. (2003). Behavioral couple therapy: Past, present, and future. In T. L. Sexton, G. R. Weeks, & M. S. Robbins (Eds.), *Handbook of family therapy: The science and practice of working with families and couples* (pp. 323–347). New York: Brunner-Routledge.

Auerswald, E. H. (1990). Toward epistemological transformation in the education and training of family therapists. In M. Mirkin (Ed.), *The social and political contexts of family therapy* (pp. 19–50). Needham Heights, MA: Allyn & Bacon.

Axelsson, S. B., & Axelsson, R. (2009). From territoriality to altruism in interprofessional collaboration and leadership. *Journal of Interprofessional Care, 23*(4), 320–330.

Ayer, A. J., & O'Grady, J. (1992). *A dictionary of philosophical quotations*. Oxford, UK: Blackwell Publishers, 484.

Barnett, P. A. & Gotlib, I. H. (1988). Psychosocial functioning and depression: Distinguishing among antecedents, concomitants and consequences. *Psychological Bulletin, 104*, 97–126.

Barnoski, R. (2002). Monitoring vital signs: Integrating a standardized assessment into Washington state's juvenile justice system. In R. Corrado, R. Roesch, S. Hart, & J. Gierowski (Eds.), *Multi-problem violent youth: A foundation for comparative research on needs, interventions, and outcomes* (pp. 219–231). Amsterdam, The Netherlands: IOS Press.

Barnoski, R. (2002). Washington state's implementation of Functional Family Therapy for juvenile offenders: Preliminary findings. Washington State Institute for Public Policy, www.wsipp.wa.gov

Barr, H., & Ross, F. (2006). Mainstreaming interprofessional education in the United Kingdom: A position paper. *Journal of Interprofessional Care, 20*(2), 96–104.

Bateson, G. (1972). *Steps to an ecology of mind: Collected essays in anthropology, psychiatry, evolution, and epistemology*. Lanham, MD: Jason Aronson Inc.

Bateson, G. (1979). *Mind and nature. A necessary unity*. New York, NY: E.P. Dutton.

Bateson, G., Jackson, D. D., Haley, J., & Weakland, J. (1956). Towards a theory of schizophrenia. *Behavioral Science, 1*, 251–264.

Baucom, D. H., & Epstein, N. B. (1990). *Cognitive-behavioral marital therapy*. New York: Routledge.

Baucom, D. H., Epstein, N., & LaTaillade, J. J. (2002). Cognitive behavioral couple therapy. In A. S. Gurman & N. D. Jacobson (Eds.), *Clinical handbook of couple therapy* (3rd ed., pp. 26–58). New York: Guilford.

Baucom, D. H., Gordon, K. C., Snyder, D. K., Atkins, D. C., & Christensen, A. (2006).Treating affair couples: Clinical considerations and initial findings. *Journal of Cognitive Psychotherapy: An International Quarterly, 20*, 375–392.

Baucom, K.J.W., Sevier, M., Eldridge, K. A., Doss, B. D., & Christensen, A. (2011). Observed communication in couples two years after integrative and traditional behavioral couple therapy: Outcome and link with five-year follow-up. *Journal of Consulting and Clinical Psychology, 79*(5), 565–576.

Baucom, D. H., Shoham, V., Mueser, K. T., Daiuto, A. D., & Stickle, T. R. (1998). Empirically supported couple and family interventions for marital distress and adult mental health problems. *Journal of Consulting and Clinical Psychology,* (1), 53–88. doi: 10.1037/0022–006X.66.1.53

Beach, S. R. H., Wamboldt, M. Z., Kaslow, N. J., Heyman, R. E., & Reiss, D. (2006). Describing relationship problems in DSM-V: Toward better guidance for research and clinical practice. *Journal of Family Psychology, 20*(3), 359–368.

Beach, S. R. H., & Whisman, M. A. (2012). Affective disorders. *Journal of Marital and Family Therapy, 38*(1), 201–219.

Beavers, R. W. (1985). *Successful marriage: A family systems approach to couples therapy*. New York: W. W. Norton & Co.

Beavers, W. R., Hampson, R. B., & Hulgus, Y. F. (1990). *Beavers Systems Model Manual: 1990 Edition*. Dallas, TX: Southwest Family Institute.

Beck, A. T., Rush, J. A., Shaw, B. F., & Emery, G. (1987). *Cognitive therapy of depression*. New York: The Guilford Press.

Becvar, D. (2003). *In the presence of grief*. New York, NY: Guilford Press.

Belar, C. D., & Perry, N. W. (1992). The national conference on scientist-practitioner education and training for the professional practice of psychology. *American Psychologist, 47*(1), 71–75.

Belsky, J., & Beaver, K. M. (2011). Cumulative-genetic plasticity, parenting and adolescent self-regulation. *Journal of Child Psychology and Psychiatry, 52*, 619–626. doi: 10.1111/j.1469–7610.2010.02327.x

Belsky, J., & Pluess, M. (2009). Beyond diathesis stress: Differential susceptibility to environmental influences. *Psychological Bulletin, 135*, 885–908. doi: 10.1037/a0017376

Bentovim, A., & Kinston, W. (1991). Focal family therapy. In A. S. Gurman & D. P. Kniskern (Eds.), *Handbook of family therapy* (Vol. II, pp. 284–324). New York, NY: Brunner/Mazel.

Berg, I. K., & Miller, S. D. (1992). *Working with the problem drinker: A solution-focused approach.* New York, NY: W. W. Norton & Co.

Bernal, G., Cumba-Avilés, E., & Sáez-Santiago, E. (2006). Cultural and relational processes in depressed Latino adolescents. In S. R. H. Beach, M. Z. Wamboldt, N. J. Kaslow, R. E. Heyman, & M. B. First (Eds.), *Relational processes and DSM-V: Neuroscience, assessment, prevention, and treatment* (pp. 211–224). Washington, DC: American Psychiatric Association.

Bernard, J. M. (1997). The discrimination model. In C. E. Watkins Jr. (Ed.), *Handbook of psychotherapy supervision* (pp. 310–327). New York, NY: Wiley.

Bertalanffy, L. von. (1969). *General system theory.* New York, NY: George Braziller.

Bertalanffy, L. von. (1972). The history and status of general systems theory. *The Academy of Management Journal, 15*(4), 407–426.

Bickman, L. (2005). A common factors approach to improving mental health services. *Mental Health Services Research, 7*(1), 1–4.

Bickman, L, Sexton, T. L., & Kelly, S. (2010). The synergistic effects of FFT and a computer based monitoring system. National Institutes of Mental Health (RO 1 MH087814).

Bion, W. R. (1952). Group dynamics: A review. *International Journal of Psycho-Analysis, 33*(2), 235–247.

Bion, W. R. (1952). Group dynamics: A review. *International Journal of Psycho-Analysis* (Vol. 33). Reprinted in M. Klein, P. Heimann, & R. Money-Kyrle (Eds.), *New directions in psychoanalysis* (pp. 440–477). London, UK: Tavistock Publications. Reprinted in *Experiences in Groups* (1961).

Bird, V., Premkumar, P., Kendall, T., Whittington, C., Mitchell, J., & Kuipers, E. (2010). Early intervention services, cognitive–behavioural therapy and family intervention in early psychosis: Systematic review. *The British Journal of Psychiatry, 197*(5), 350–356.

Blatt, S. J., Auerbach, J. S., & Levy, K. N. (1997). Mental representations in personality development, psychopathology, and the therapeutic process. *Review of General Psychology, 1*(4), 351–374.

Blos, P. (1975). *The second individuation process of adolescence.* New York, NY: International Universities Press.

Bordin, E. S. (1994). Theory and research on the therapeutic working alliance: New directions. In A. O. Horvath & L. S. Greenberg (Eds.), *The working alliance: Theory, research, and practice* (pp. 13–37). Hoboken, NJ: John Wiley & Sons.

Borduin, C. M., Mann, B. J., Cone, L. T., Henggeler, S. W., Fucci, B. R., Blaske, D. M. & Williams, R. A. (1995). Multisystemic treatment of serious juvenile offenders: Long-term prevention of criminality and violence. *Journal of Consulting and Clinical Psychology, 63*(4), 569–578.

Borduin, C. M. & Schaeffer, C. M. (1998). Violent offending in adolescence: Epidemiology, correlates, outcomes, and treatment. In Thomas P. Gullotta, Gerald R. Adams, Raymond Montemayor (Eds.), *Delinquent violent youth: Theory and interventions* (pp. 144–174). New York, NY: Sage Publications.

Bowen, M. (1976). Theory in the practice of psychotherapy. In P. J. Guerin Jr. (Ed.), *Family therapy: Theory and practice* (pp. 42–90). New York, NY: Garner Press.

Bowen, M. (1978). *Family therapy in clinical practice.* New York, NY: Jason Aronson.

Bowers, K. S. (1973). Situationism in psychology—Analysis and a critique. *Psychological Review, 80,* 307–336.

Bowlby, J. (1969). *Attachment and Loss* (Vol. 1). New York, NY: Basic Books.

BPharm, A. K. C. & Victoria Wood, V. (2010). Preparing tomorrow's healthcare providers for interprofessional collaborative patient-centred practice today. *UBCMJ, 1*(2), 22–24.

Bray, J. H., & Stanton, M. (Eds.). (2009). *The Wiley-Blackwell handbook of family psychology.* West Sussex, UK: Blackwell Publishing Ltd.

Bronfenbrenner, U. (1979). *The ecology of human development: Experiments by nature and design.* Boston, MA: Harvard University Press.

Brunhofer, M. O. (2011). Loss and mourning: A life cycle perspective. In Jerrold R. Brandell (Ed.), *Theory and practice in clinical social work* (2nd ed., pp. 665–692). New York, NY: Sage Publications.

Buehlman, K. T., Gottman, J. M., & Katz, L. F. (1992). How a couple views their past predicts their future: Predicting divorce from an oral history interview. *Journal of Family Psychology, 5*(3–4), 295–318. doi: 10.1037 /0893-3200.5.3–4.295

Bullough, V. (1998). Alfred Kinsey and the Kinsey Report: Historical overview and lasting contributions. *Journal of Sex Research, 35,* 127–131.

Burr, W. R., Day, R. D., & Bahr, K. S. (Eds.). (1993). *Research and theory in family science.* Pacific Grove, CA: Brooks/Cole.

Butler, S., Baruch, G., Hickey, N., & Fonagy, P. (2011). A randomized controlled trial of multisystemic therapy and a statutory therapeutic intervention for young offenders. *Journal of the American Academy of Child & Adolescent Psychiatry, 50*(12), 1220–1235.

Campbell, J. P. (1990). The role of theory in industrial and organizational psychology. In M. D. Dunnette & L. M. Hough (Eds.), *Handbook of industrial and organizational psychology* (Vol. 1, 2nd ed., pp. 687–731). Palo Alto, CA: Consulting Psychologists Press.

Campbell, S. B., & Ewing, L. J. (1990). Follow-up of hard-to-manage preschoolers: Adjustment at age 9 and predictors of continuing symptoms. *Child Psychology & Psychiatry & Allied Disciplines, 31*(6), 871–889.

Carlson, C., Kubiszyn, T., & Guli, L. (2004). Consultation with caregivers and families. In R. T. Brown (Ed.), *Handbook of pediatric psychology in school settings* (pp. 617–635). New York, NY: Lawrence Erlbaum Associates Publishers.

Carr, A. (1995). Family therapy and clinical psychology. *Journal of Family Therapy, 17*(4), 435–444.

Carr, A. (2009). The effectiveness of family therapy and systemic interventions for child-focused problems. *Journal of Family Therapy, 31*(1), 3–45.

Carr, A. (2012). *Family therapy: Concepts, process and practice*. West Sussex, UK: Wiley Blackwell.

Carr, A. (2013). *The handbook of adolescent and clinical psychology: A contextual approach* (2nd ed.). London, UK: Routledge.

Carroll, L. (2009). *Alice's adventures in wonderland and through the looking-glass*. Oxford, England: Oxford University Press.

Carson, J. W., Carson, K. M., Gil, K. M., & Baucom, D. H. (2004). Mindfulness based relationship enhancement. *Behavior Therapy, 35*, 471–494.

Carson, R. C. (1969). *Interaction concepts of personality*. Chicago, IL: Aldine.

Carson, R. C. (1991). The social-interactional viewpoint. In M. Hersen, A. Kazdin, & A. Bellack (Eds.), *The clinical psychology handbook* (2nd ed., pp. 185–199). New York, NY: Pergamon.

Carter, B., & McGoldrick, M. (2004). *The expanded family life cycle: Individual, family, and social perspectives* (3rd ed.). Boston, MA: Pearson Allyn & Bacon.

Cedar, B., & Levant, R. F. (1990). A meta-analysis of the effects of parent effectiveness training. *American Journal of Family Therapy, 18*(4), 373–384. doi: 10.1080/01926189008250986

Centre for Mental Health. (2000). *Disaster mental health response handbook*. Vancouver, BC: State Health Publication.

Chambless, D. L., & Hollon, S. D. (1998). Defining empirically supported therapies. *Journal of Consulting and Clinical Psychology, 66*, 7–18.

Chan, A. K., & Wood, V. (2010). Preparing tomorrow's healthcare providers for interprofessional collaborative patient-centered practice today. *UBC Medical Journal, 1*(2), 22–24.

Charles, R. (2001). Is there any empirical support for Bowen's concepts of differentiation of self, triangulation, and fusion? *The American Journal of Family Therapy, 29*, 279–292.

Christensen, A. (1987). Detection of conflict patterns in couples. In K. Hahlweg & M. J. Goldstein (Eds.), *Understanding major mental disorder: The contribution of family interaction research* (pp. 250–265). New York, NY: Family Process Press.

Christensen, A. (2010). *Weekly questionnaire*. Los Angeles, CA: University of California.

Christensen, A., Atkins, D. C., Berns, S., Wheeler, J., Baucom, D.H. & Simpson. L. E. (2005). Traditional versus integrative behavioral couple therapy for significantly and chronically distressed married couples. *Journal of consulting and clinical psychology, 72*(2), 176.

Christensen, A., Atkins, D. C., Yi, J., Baucom, D. H., & George, W. H. (2006). Couple and individual adjustment for two years following a randomized clinical trial comparing traditional versus integrative behavioral couple therapy. *Journal of Consulting and Clinical Psychology, 74*, 1180–1191.

Christensen, A., Atkins, D. C., Baucom, B., & Yi, J. (2010). Marital status and satisfaction five years following a randomized clinical trial comparing traditional versus integrative behavioral couple therapy. *Journal of Consulting and Clinical Psychology, 78*, 225–235.

Christensen, A., Jacobson, N. S. & Babcock, J. C. (1995). Integrative behavioral couples therapy. In N. S. Jacobson & A. S. Gurman (Eds.), *Clinical handbook for couples therapy* (pp. 31–64). New York, NY: Guilford.

Church, A. T., & Katigbak, M. S. (2002). Indigenization of psychology in the Philippines. *International Journal of Psychology, 37*, 129–148. doi: 10.1080/00207590143000315

Claiborn, C. D., & Lichtenberg, J. W. (1989). Interactional counseling. *The Counseling Psychologist, 17*(3), 355–453.

Clark-Stager, W. (1999). Using solution-focused therapy within an integrative behavioral couple therapy framework: An integrative model. *Journal of Family Psychotherapy, 10*(3), 27–47.

Clay, R. A. (2002). An indigenized psychology: Psychologists in India blend Indian traditions and Western psychology. *APA Monitor, 33*(5). Retrieved from http://www.apa.org/monitor/may02/india.aspx

Clothier, P., Manion, L., Gordon, J., & Johnson, S. (2001). Emotionally focused interventions for couples with chronically ill children: A two year follow-up. *Journal of Marital and Family Therapy, 28*, 391–399.

Committee on Ethical Guidelines for Forensic Psychologists. (1991, 2011). Specialty Guidelines for Forensic Psychologists. *Law and Human Behavior, 15*(6), 655–665.

Constantine, L. (1976). Designed experience: A multiple goal-directed training program in family therapy. *Family Process, 15*, 373–396.

Constantine, M. G. (2001). Multicultural training, theoretical orientation, empathy, and multicultural case conceptualization ability in counselors. *Journal of Mental Health Counseling, 23*(4), 357–372.

Constantine, M. G., & Gushue, G. V. (2003). School counselors' ethnic tolerance attitudes and racism attitudes as predictors of their multicultural case conceptualization of an immigrant student. *Journal of Counseling and Development, 81*(2), 185–190.

Cordova, J. V., Jacobson, N. S., & Christensen, A. (1998). Acceptance versus change interventions in behavioral couple therapy: Impact on couples' in-session communication. *Journal of Marriage and Family Counseling, 24*, 437–455.

Cunha, C., Gonçalves, M. M., Hill, C. E., Mendes, I., Ribeiro, A. P., Sousa, I., . . . & Greenberg, L. S. (2012). Therapist interventions and client innovative moments in emotion-focused therapy for depression. *Psychotherapy, 9*(4), 536–548.

Cusinato, M. (1994). Parenting over the family life cycle. In L. L'Abate (Ed.), *Handbook of developmental family psychology and psychopathology* (pp. 83–115). New York, NY: John Wiley & Sons.

Damasia, A. (2005). *Descartes' error: Emotion, reason, and the human brain.* New York, NY: Penguin Books.

Daumit, G. L., Pratt, L. A., Crum, R. M., Powe, N. R., & Ford, D. E. (2002). Characteristics of primary care visits for individuals with severe mental illness in a national sample. *General Hospital Psychiatry, 24*(6), 391–395.

Dawes, R. M., Faust, D., & Meehl, P. E. (1989). Clinical versus actuarial judgment. *Science, 243,* 1668–1674.

De Jong, P., & Berg, I. K. (1998). *Interviewing for Solutions.* Pacific Grove, CA: Brooks/Cole Publishing.

Delisle, G. (2011). *Personality Pathology.* London, UK: Karnac Books Ltd.

Dent-Read, C., & Zukow-Goldring, P. (1997). *Evolving Explanations of Development: Ecological Approaches to Organism-Environment Systems.* Washington, DC: American Psychological Association.

Derogatis, L. R., & Melisaratos, N. (1979). The DSFI: A multidimensional measure of sexual functioning. *Journal of Sex and Marital Therapy, 5,* 244–281.

De Shazer, S. (1991). *Putting difference to work.* New York, NY: Norton.

Diamond, G., & Josephson, A. (2005). Family-based treatment research: A 10-year update. *Journal of the American Academy of Child and Adolescent Psychiatry, 44*(9), 872–887.

Diamond, G., & Liddle, H. A. (1996). Resolving a therapeutic impasse between parents and adolescents in multidimensional family therapy. *Journal of Consulting and Clinical Psychology, 64*(3), 481–488.

Diamond, G. S., Reis, B. F., Diamond, G. M., Siqueland, L., & Isaacs, L. (2002). Attachment-based family therapy for depressed adolescents: A treatment development study. *Journal of the American Academy of Child & Adolescent Psychiatry, 41*(10), 1190–1196. doi: 10.1097/00004583-200210000-00008

Dicks, H. V. (1967). *Marital tensions.* New York, NY: Basic Books.

Dictionary.reference.com (2015). http://dictionary.reference.com/

Dimidjian, S., Martell, C. R., & Christensen, A. (2002). Integrative behavioral couple therapy. In A. S. Gurman & N. S. Jacobson (Eds.), *Clinical handbook of couple therapy* (3rd ed.) (pp. 251–277). New York, NY: Guilford Press.

Dishion, T. J., & McMahon, R. J. (1998). Parental monitoring and the prevention of child and adolescent problem behavior: A conceptual and empirical formulation. *Clinical Child and Family Psychology Review, 1*(1), 61–75.

Dishion, T. J, & Stormshak, E. (2007). *Intervening in children's lives: An ecological, family-centered approach to mental health care.* Washington, DC: American Psychological Association.

Dixon, L. B., & Lehman, A. F. (1995). Family interventions for schizophrenia. *Schizophrenia Bulletin, 21*(4), 631–643.

Doherty, W. J., & Baird, M. A. (1983). *Family therapy and family medicine: Toward the primary care of families.* New York, NY: Guilford Press.

Doss, B. D., Thum, Y. M., Sevier, M., Atkins, D. C., & Christensen, A. (2005). Improving relationships: Mechanisms of change in couple therapy. *Journal of Consulting and Clinical Psychology, 73,* 624–633.

Duncan, B.L., Hubble, M.A., & Miller, S.D. (Eds.). (2010). *The heart & soul of change: Delivering what works in therapy* (2nd ed.). Washington, DC: American Psychological Association.

Duncan, B.L., Miller, S.D., & Sparks, J.A. (2003). Interactional and solution-focused brief therapies: Evolving concepts of change. In T.L. Sexton, G.R. Weeks, & M.S. Robbins (Eds.), *Handbook of family therapy: The science and practice of working with families and couples* (pp. 101–123). New York, NY: Brunner-Routledge.

Dunn, R.L., & Schwebel, A.I. (1995). Meta-analytic review of marital therapy outcome research. *Journal of Family Psychology, 9*(1), 58–68.

Eisler, I. (2005). The empirical and theoretical base of family therapy and multiple family day therapy for adolescent anorexia nervosa. *Journal of Family Therapy, 27*(2), 104–113.

Ellsion, C.R. (2001). A research inquiry into some American women's sexual concerns and problems. In E. Kaschak & L. Tiefer (Eds.), *A new view of women's sexual problems* (pp. 147–159). New York, NY: Haworth Press.

Ellsion, C.R. (2000). *Women's sexualities: Generations of women share intimate secrets of sexual self-acceptance.* Oakland, CA: New Harbinger.

Epstein, N.B., & Baucom, D.H. (2002). *Enhanced cognitive-behavioral therapy for couples: A contextual approach.* Washington, DC: American Psychological Association.

Epstein, N.B., Datillio, F.M. & Baucom, D.H. (in press). Cognitive behavior couple therapy. In T.L. Sexton & J. Lebow (Eds.), *Handbook of family therapy.* New York, NY: Routledge.

Ernest, P., Greer, B., & Sriraman, B. (2009). *Critical issues in mathematics education.* Charlotte, NC: Information Age Publishing.

Eysenck, H.J. (1952). The effects of psychotherapy: An evaluation. *Journal of Consulting Psychology, 16*(5), 319–324.

Fairbairn, W.R.D. (1958). On the nature and aims of psychoanalytic treatment. *International Journal of Psychoanalysis, 39*, 374–385.

Falender, C.A., & Shafranske, E.P. (2004). Clinical supervision: A competency-based approach. Washington, DC: American Psychological Association.

Falicov, C.J. (1988). *Family transitions.* New York, NY: Guilford.

Falicov, C.J. (2003). Culture in family therapy: New variations on a fundamental theme. In T. Sexton, G. Weeks, & M. Robbins (Eds.), *Handbook of family therapy: Theory, research and practice* (pp. 37–55). New York, NY: Brunner-Routledge.

Falicov, C.J. (in press). The multiculturialism and diversity of families. In T.L. Sexton & J. Lebow (Eds.), *Handbook of family therapy.* New York, NY: Routledge.

Farmer, M.A., & Binik, Y.M. (2005). Psychology is from Mars, sexology is from Venus: Can they meet on Earth? *Canadian Psychology/Psychologie canadienne, 46*(1), 46–51.

Ferber, A., & Mendelsohn, M. (1969). Training for family therapy. *Family Process, 8*(1), 25–32.

Ferber, A., Mendelsohn, M. & Napier, A. (Eds.) (1972). *The book of family therapy.* New York, NY: Science House.

Fine, H. (2005). From conflict to partnering. *Journal of Organizational Change Management, 18*(5), 469–481.

Fischer, J., & Corcoran, K. (2007). *Measures for clinical practice and research: A sourcebook* (Vol. 1, 4th ed.). New York, NY: Oxford University Press.

Fisher, C. B. (2003). *Decoding the ethics code: A practical guide for psychologists.* Thousand Oaks, CA: Sage.

Flicker, S. M., Waldron, H. B., Turner, C. W., Brody, J. L., & Hops, H. (2008). Ethnic matching and treatment outcome with Hispanic and Anglo substance-abusing adolescents in family therapy. *Journal of Family Psychology, 22*(3), 439–447.

Fowers, B. J. & Davidov, B. J. (2006). The virtue of multiculturalism: Personal transformation, character, and openness to the other. *American Psychologist, 61,* 581–594.

Framo, J. L. (1965). *Intensive family therapy.* New York, NY: Brunner/Mazel.

Framo, J. L. (1970). Symptoms from a family transactional viewpoint. In N. W. Ackerman (Ed.), *Family therapy in transition.* Boston, MA: Little, Brown & Co.

Frank, J. D. (1971). Therapeutic factors in psychotherapy. *American Journal of Psychotherapy, 25*(3), 350–361.

Frawley-O'Dea, M. G. & Sarnat, J. E. (2001). *The supervisory relationship: A contemporary psychodynamic approach.* New York, NY: Guilford Press.

Fredman, N., & Sherman, R. (1987). *Handbook of measurements for marriage and family therapy.* New York, NY: Brunner / Mazel.

Friedlander, M. L., Escudero, V., Heatherington, L., & Diamond, G. M. (2011). Alliance in couple and family therapy. In J. C. Norcross (Ed.), *Psychotherapy relationships that work: Evidence-based responsiveness* (2nd ed., pp. 92–109). Oxford, England: Oxford University Press.

Friedlander, M. L., Escudero, V., Horvath, A., Heatherington, L., Cabero, A., & Martens, M. (2006). System for observing family therapy alliances: A tool for research and practice. *Journal of Counseling Psychology, 53,* 214–224.

Friedlander, M. L., & Heatherington, L. (1998). Assessing clients' constructions of their problems in family therapy discourse. *Journal of Marital and Family Therapy, 24*(3), 289–303.

Friedlander, M. L., Heatherington, L., Johnson, B., & Skowron, E. A. (1994). Sustaining engagement: A change event in family therapy. *Journal of Counseling Psychology, 41*(4), 438–448.

Friedlander, M. L., Lambert, J. E., Valentín, E., & Cragun, C. (2008). How do therapists enhance family alliances? Sequential analyses of therapist-client behavior in two contrasting cases. *Psychotherapy: Theory, research, practice, training, 45*(1), 75–87.

Friedlander, M. L., Wildman, J., Heatherington, L., & Skowron, E. A. (1994). What we do and don't know about the process of family therapy. *Journal of Family Psychology, 8*(4), 390–416.

Friedman, S. (1993). Possibility therapy with couples: Constructing time-effective solutions. *Journal of Family Psychotherapy, 4,* 35–52.

Friedman, S., & Lipchik, E. (1999). A time-effective, solution-focused approach to couple therapy. In J. M. Donovan (Ed.), *Short-term couple therapy* (pp. 325–359). New York, NY: Guilford Press.

Fuertes, J. N., Miville, M. L., Mohr, J. J., Sedlacek, W. E., & Gretchen, D. (2000). Factor structure and short form of the Miville-Guzman Universality-Diversity Scale. *Measurement and Evaluation in Counseling and Development, 33*, 157–169.

Gardner, F. (2000). Methodological issues in the direct observation of parent-child interaction: Do observational findings reflect the natural behavior of participants? *Clinical Child and Family Psychology Review, 3*, 185–198.

Gauthier, J. (2005). Toward a universal declaration of ethical principles for psychologists: A progress report. In M. J. Stevens & D. Wedding (Eds.), *Psychology: IUPsyS Global Resource* (6th ed.). Hove, UK: Psychology Press.

Gergen, K. J. (1985). The social constructionist movement in modern psychology. *American Psychologist, 40*, 266–275.

Gergen, K. J. (1991). *The saturated self: Dilemmas of identity in contemporary life.* New York, NY: Basic Books.

Gergen, K. J. (1995). The social constructionist movement in modern psychology. *American Psychologist, 40*(3), 266–275.

Gerson, R. (1995). The family life cycle: Phases, stages, and crises. In R. H. Mikesell, D. Lusterman, & S. H. McDaniel (Eds.), *Integrating family therapy: Handbook of family psychology and systems theory* (pp. 91–111). Washington, DC: American Psychological Association.

Glasersfeld, E. von. (1988). The reluctance to change a way of thinking. *The Irish Journal of Psychology, 9*(1), 83–90.

Goldberg, M. (1985). Loss and grief: Major dynamics in the treatment of alcoholism. *Alcoholism Treatment Quarterly, 2*, 1, 37–45.

Goldenberg, H., & Goldenberg, I. (2009). The revolution and evolution of family therapy and family psychology. In J. H. Bray & M. Stanton (Eds.), *The Wiley-Blackwell handbook of family psychology* (pp. 21–36). West Sussex, UK: Blackwell Publishing.

Goldenberg, I., & Goldenberg, H. (2013). *Family therapy: An overview.* Independence, KY: Cengage Learning.

Goldstein, M. J., & Miklowitz, D. J. (1995). The effectiveness of psychoeducational family therapy in the treatment of schizophrenic disorders. *Journal of Marital and Family Therapy, 21*(4), 361–376.

Goodheart, C. D., Kazdin, A. E., & Sternberg, R. J. (2006). *Evidence-based psychotherapy: Where theory and practice meet.* Washington, DC: American Psychological Association.

Gorman-Smith, D., Tolan, P., Henry, D. B., Quintana, E., Lutovsky, K., & Leventhal, A. (2007). Schools and families educating children: A preventive intervention for early elementary school children. In P. Tolan, J. E. Szapocznik, & S. Sambrano (Eds.), *Preventing youth substance abuse: Science-based programs for children and adolescents* (pp. 113–135). Washington, DC: American Psychological Association.

Gotlib, H., & Hammen, C. L. (2014). *Handbook of depression* (3rd ed.). New York, NY: Guilford Press.

Gottlieb, M. C. (1996). Some ethical implications of relational diagnoses. In F. W. Kaslow (Ed.), *Handbook of relational diagnosis and dysfunctional family patterns* (pp. 19–34). Oxford, England: John Wiley & Sons.

Gottman, J. M. (1993). The roles of conflict engagement, escalation, and avoidance in marital interaction: A longitudinal view of five types of couples. *Journal of Consulting and Clinical Psychology, 61*(1), 6–15. doi: 10.1037/0022–006X.61.1.6

Gottman, J. M. (1999). *The marriage clinic: A scientifically based marital therapy.* New York, NY: W. W. Norton & Co.

Graham, C., Carr, A., Rooney, B., Sexton, T., & Satterfield, L. R. (2013). Evaluation of Functional Family Therapy in an Irish Context. *Journal of Family Therapy.* doi: 10.1111/1467-6427.12028

Greenberg, L. S., & Johnson, S. M. (1988). *Emotionally focused therapy for couples.* New York, NY: Guilford Press.

Greenberg, J. R., & Mitchell, S. A. (1983). *Object relations in psychoanalytic theory.* Cambridge, MA: Harvard University Press.

Greenberg, L., & Paivio, S. (1997). *Working with emotion in psychotherapy.* New York, NY: Guilford Press.

Grencavage, L. M., & Norcross, J. C. (1990). Where are the commonalities among the therapeutic common factors? *Professional psychology: Research and practice, 21*(5), 372–378.

Grosz B. J. (1996). Collaborative systems: AAAI presidential address. *AI Magazine, 2*(17), 67–85.

Grovetant, H. D., & Carlson, C. I. (1989). *Family assessment: A guide to methods and measures.* New York, NY: Guilford Press.

Guerin, P. J. (Ed.). (1976). *Family therapy.* New York, NY: Gardner.

Gurman, A. S. (1971). Group marital therapy: Clinical and empirical implications for outcome research. *International Journal of Group Psychotherapy, 21*(2), 174–189.

Gurman, A. S. (1975). Couples' facilitative communication skill as a dimension of marital therapy outcome. *Journal of Marriage and Family Counseling, 1*(2), 163–174.

Gurman, A. S. (2002). Brief integrative marital therapy: A depth-behavioral approach. In A. S. Gurman & N. S. Jacobson (Eds.), *Clinical handbook of couple therapy* (3rd ed., pp. 180–220). New York, NY: Guilford Press.

Gurman, A. S., & Jacobson, N. S. (2002). *Clinical handbook of couple therapy* (3rd ed.). New York, NY: The Guilford Press.

Gurman, A. S., & Kniskern, D. P. (1981). *Handbook of family therapy* (Vol. 2). New York, NY: Brunner/Mazel.

Gurman, A. S., & Kniskern, D. P. (1986). Commentary: Individual marital therapy: Have reports of your death been somewhat exaggerated? *Family Process, 25*(1), 51–62.

Gurman, A. S., & Kniskern, D. P., & Pinsof, W. M. (1986). Research on the process and outcome of marital and family therapy. In S. L. Garfield, & A. E. Bergin (Eds.), *Handbook of psychotherapy and behavior change* (3rd ed., pp. 565–624). New York, NY: Wiley.

Hagen, M. A., & Castagna, N. (2001). The real numbers: Psychological testing in custody evaluations. *Professional Psychology: Research and Practice, 32*(3), 269–271.

Hahlweg, K. & Goldstein, M. J. (Eds.). (1987). *Understanding major mental disorder: The contribution of family interaction research.* New York, NY: Family Process Press.

Halchuk, R., Makinen, J., & Johnson, S. M. (2010). Resolving attachment injuries in couples using emotionally focused therapy: A 3-year follow-up. *Journal of Couple and Relationship Therapy, 9*, 31–47.

Haley, J. (1976). *Problem solving therapy.* San Francisco, CA: Jossey-Bass.

Halford, W., Osgarby, S., & Kelly, A. (1996). Brief behavioral couples therapy: A preliminary evaluation. *Behavioural and Cognitive Psychotherapy, 24*(3), 263–273. doi: 10.1017/S1352465800015113

Halford, W., & Sanders, M. R. (1990). The relationship of cognition and behavior during marital interaction. *Journal of Social and Clinical Psychology, 9*(4), 489–510.

Halperin, S. M. (1991). Counter transference and the developing family therapist: Treatment and supervision issues. *Contemporary Family Therapy, 13*(2), 127–141.

Han, H. R., Kim, M., Lee, H. B., Pistulka, G., & Kim, K. B. (2007). Correlates of depression in the Korean American elderly: Focusing on personal resources of social support. *Journal of Cross-Cultural Gerontology, 22*, 115–127.

Hanna, S. M., & Brown, J. H. (2004). *The practice of family therapy* (3rd ed.). Belmont, CA: Brooks/Cole-Thompson Learning.

Hargrove, David S. (2009). Psychotherapy based on Bowen Family Systems Theory. In J. H. Bray & M. Stanton (Eds.), *The Wiley-Blackwell handbook of family psychology* (pp. 286–299). Malden MA: Wiley Blackwell.

Harpell, J. V., & Andrews, J. (2006). A current review of multisystemic therapy: A social-ecological approach to the treatment of conduct problems among adolescents. *Developmental Disabilities Bulletin, 34*(1–2), 80–106.

Hartman, A. (1995). Diagrammatic assessment of family relationships. *Families in Society, 76*, 111–122. doi: 10.1521/jscp.1990.9.4.489

Hartnett, D., Carr, A., & Sexton, T. (in press). The effectiveness of Functional Family Therapy in reducing adolescent mental health and family adjustment difficulties in and Irish context. *Family Process.*

Hayes, S. C., Luoma, J. B., Bond, F. W., Masuda, A., & Lillis, J. (2006). Acceptance and commitment therapy: Model, processes and outcomes. *Psychology Faculty Publications.* Paper 101. http://scholarworks.gsu.edu/psych_fac pub/101

Hayes, S. H., Strosahl, K., & Wilson, K. G. (1999). *Acceptance and commitment therapy: An experiential approach to behavior change.* New York, NY: Guilford Press.

Hazelrigg, M. D., Cooper, H. M., & Borduin, C. M. (1987). Evaluating the effectiveness of family therapies: An integrative review and analysis. *Psychological Bulletin, 101*(3), 428–442.

Heatherington, L., Friedlander, M. L., & Greenberg, L. (2005). Change process research in couple and family therapy: Methodological challenges and opportunities. *Journal of Family Psychology, 19*(1), 18–27.

Henggeler, S. W., & Lee, T. (2003). Multisystemic treatment of serious clinical problems. In A. E. Kazdin and J. R. Weisz (Eds.), *Evidence-based psychotherapies for children and adolescents* (pp. 301–321). New York, NY: Guilford Press.

Henggeler, S. W., Melton, G. B., & Smith, L. A. (1992). Family preservation using multisystemic therapy: An effective alternative to incarcerating serious juvenile offenders. *Journal of Consulting and Clinical Psychology, 60*(6), 953–961.

Henggeler, S. W., Pickrel, S. G., & Brondino, M. J. (1999). Multisystemic treatment of substance abusing and dependent delinquents: Outcomes, treatment fidelity, and transportability. *Mental Health Services Research, 1*, 171–184.

Henggeler, S. W., Rodick, J. D., Borduin, C. M., Hanson, C. L., Watson, S. M., & Urey, J. R. (1986). Multisystemic treatment of juvenile offenders: Effects on adolescent behavior and family interaction. *Developmental Psychology, 22*, 132–141.

Henggeler, S. W., Rowland, M. D., Randall, J., Ward, D. M., Pickrel, S. G., Conningham, P. B., . . . Stanos, A. B. (1999b). Home-based multisystemic therapy as an alternative to hospitalization of youths in psychiatiric crisis: Clinical outcomes. *Journal of the American Academy of Child and Adolescent Psychiatry, 38*, 1331–1339.

Henggeler, S. W., Schoenwald, S. K., Borduin, C. M., Rowland, M. D., Cunningham, P. B. (1998). *Multisystemic treatment of antisocial behavior in children and adolescents.* New York, NY: Guilford Press.

Hertlein, K., & Weeks, G. (2009). Toward a new paradigm in sex therapy. *Journal of Family Psychotherapy, 20*(2–3), 112–128.

Hess, A. K. (1986). Growth in supervision: Stages of supervisee and supervisor development. *The Clinical Supervisor, 4*, 1–2, 51–67.

Hilgard, E. R., Kelly, E. L., Luckey, B., Sanford, R. N., Shaffer, L. F. & Shakow, D. (1947). Recommended graduate training program in clinical psychology. *American Psychologist, 2*, 539–558.

Hobfoll, S. E. (2002). Social and psychological resources and adaptation. *Review of General Psychology, 6*(4), 307–324.

Hofstadter, D. (1979). *Godel, Escher, Bach: An eternal golden brain.* New York, NY: Basic Books.

Holahan, C. J., & Moos, R. H. (1983). Development of qualitative indices of social support. *British Journal of Clinical Psychology, 22*, 157–162.

Hollon, D., DeRubeis, R. J., Fawcett, J., Amsterdam, J. D., Shelton, R.C., Zajecka, J., . . . Gallop, R. (2014). Effect of cognitive therapy with antidepressant medications vs antidepressants alone on the rate of recovery in major depressive disorder: A randomized clinical trial. *JAMA Psychiatry, 71*, 10, 1157–1164.

Holloway, E. (1995). *Clinical supervision: A systems approach.* Thousand Oaks, CA: Sage.

Hooley, J. M., Phil, D., Miklowitz, D. J., & Beach, S. R. H. (2006). Expressed emotion and DSM-V. In S. R. H. Beach, M. Z. Wamboldt, N. J. Kaslow, R. E. Heyman, M. B. First, L. G. Underwood, & D. Reiss (Eds.), *Relational processes and DSM-V: Neuroscience, assessment, prevention, and treatment* (pp. 175–191). Washington, DC: American Psychiatric Association.

Horner, A. J. (1984). *Object relations and the developing ego in therapy*. New York, NY: Jason Aronson.

Hoyt, M. F., & Berg, I. K. (1998). Solution-focused couple therapy: Helping clients construct self-fulfilling realities. In F. M. Dattilio (Ed.), *Case studies in couple and family therapy: Systemic and cognitive perspectives* (pp. 203–232). New York, NY: Guilford Press.

Hutchings, J., & Lane, E. (2005). Parenting and the development and prevention of child mental health problems. *Current Opinion in Psychiatry, 18*(4), 386–391.

Iliadi, P. (2010). Accountability and collaborative care: How interprofessional education promotes them. *Health Science Journal, 4*(3), 129–135.

Imber-Black, E., Roberts, J., & Whiting, R. A. (Eds.). (2003). *Rituals in families and family therapy*. New York, NY: W. W. Norton & Company.

Ingram, D. (1990). *Critical theory and philosophy*. New York: Paragon House.

Institute of Medicine. (2001). *Crossing the quality chasm: A new health system for the 21st century*. Washington, DC: National Academy Press.

International Council of Psychologists. (2015). *ICP Bylaws*. http://www.icpweb.org/

International Union of Psychological Science. (2014). http://www.iupsys.net/

Islam, G. (2007). Virtue ethics, multiculturalism, and the paradox of cultural dialogue. *American Psychologist, 62*, 704–705.

Jacobson, N. S., & Addis, M. E. (1993). Research on couples and couple therapy: What do we know? Where are we going? *Journal of Consulting and Clinical Psychology, 61*(1), 85–93. doi: 10.1037/0022-006X.61.1.85

Jacobson, N. S., & Christensen, A. (1996). *Acceptance and change in couple therapy*. New York, NY: W. W. Norton & Co.

Jacobson, N. S., Christiansen, A., Prince, S. E., Cordova, J., & Eldridge, K. (2000). Integrative behavioral couple therapy: An acceptance-based, promising new treatment for couple discord. *Journal of Consulting and Clinical Psychology, 68*(2), 351–355.

Jacobson, N. S., & Follette, W. C. (1985). Clinical significance of improvement resulting from two behavioral marital therapy components. *Behavior Therapy, 16*(3), 249–262. doi: 10.1016/S0005-7894(85)80013-7

Jacobson, N. S. and Margoli, G. (1979). *Marital therapy: Strategies based on social learning and behavior exchange principles*. New York, NY: Brunner/Mazel.

Jackson, A. P., & Meadows, F. B. (1991). Getting to the bottom to understand the top. *Journal of Counseling and Development, 70*, 72–74.

Jain Stories. *Blind men and an elephant*. Retrieved August 29, 2006, from JainWorld.com

Johnson, S. M. (1996). *Creating connection: The practice of emotionally focused marital therapy*. New York, NY: Brunner/Mazel.

Johnson, S. M., Hunsley, J., Greenberg, L., & Schindler, D. (1999). Emotionally focused couples therapy: Status and challenges. *Clinical psychology: Science and practice, 6*, 67–79.

Johnson, S. M., & Lebow, J. (2000). The coming of age of couple therapy: A decade review. *Journal of Marital and Family Therapy, 26*, 23–38.

Johnson, S. M., & Talitman, E. (1996). Predictors of success in emotionally focused marital therapy. *Journal of Marital and Family Therapy, 23*, 135–152.

Jones, J. L., & Mehr, S. L. (2007). Foundations and assumptions of the scientist-practitioner model. *American Behavioral Scientist, 50*(6), 766–771.

Jones, E., & Nisbett, R. (1971). *The actor and the observer: Divergent perceptions of the causes of behavior*. New York, NY: General Learning Press.

Kapinus, C. A., & Johnson, M. P. (2003). The utility of family life cycle as a theoretical and empirical tool: Commitment and family life-cycle stage. *Journal of Family Issues, 24*(2), 155–184.

Kaslow, F. W. (1987). Trends in family psychology. *Journal of Family Psychology, 1*(1), 77–90.

Kaslow, F. W. (1988). Trends in family psychology. *Journal of Family Psychology, 1*(1), 77–90.

Kaslow, F. W. (2001). Whither countertransference in couples and family therapy: A systemic perspective. *Journal of Clinical Psychology, 57*, 1029–1040.

Kaslow, N. J., Broth, M. R., Smith, C. O., & Collins, M. H. (2012). Family-based interventions for child and adolescent disorders. *Journal of Marital and Family Therapy, 38*(1), 82–100.

Kaslow, N. J., Celano, M. P., & Stanton, M. (2009). Training in family psychology: A competencies-based approach. In J. H. Bray & M. Stanton (Eds.), *The Wiley-Blackwell handbook of family psychology* (pp. 112–128). West Sussex, UK: Blackwell Publishing.

Kaslow, N. J., Grus, C. L., Campbell, L. F., Fouad, N. A., Hatcher, R. L., & Rodolfa, E. R. (2009). Competency assessment toolkit for professional psychology. *Training and Education in Professional Psychology, 3*, S27–S45. doi:10.1037/a0015833

Katz, J., Beach, S. R. H., & Joiner, T. E. (1999). Contagious depression in dating couples. *Journal of Social & Clinical Psychology, 18*, 1–13.

Kazdin, A. E. (2006). Assessment and evaluation in clinical practice. In C. D. Goodheart, A. E. Kazdin, & R. J. Sternberg (Eds.), *Evidence-based psychotherapy: Where practice and research meet* (pp. 153–177). Washington, DC: American Psychological Association.

Keim, J., & Lappin, J. (2002). Short term couples treatment: A structural/strategic perspective. In A. Gurman & N. Jacobson (Eds.), *Clinical handbook of couple therapy* (3rd ed.). New York, NY: Guilford Press.

Kelley, P. (1996). Metaphorical views of family interaction: A cross-cultural analysis. *Personal Relationships Issues, 3*, 17–23.

Kelley, H. H. (1971). *Attribution in social interaction*. New York, NY: General Learning Press.

Kendler, K. S., Neale, M. C., Kessler, R. C., Heath, A. C., Lindon J., & Eaves, L. J. (1993). Longitudinal twin study of personality and major depression in women. *Archives of General Psychiatry, 50*(11), 853–862.

Kessler, R. C., Sonnega, A., Bromet, E., Hughes, M., & Nelson, C. B. (1995). Posttraumatic stress disorder in the National Comorbidity Survey. *Archives of General Psychiatry, 52*, 1048–1060.

Klimek, D. (1979). *Beneath mate selection and marriage.* New York, NY: Van Nostrand Reinhold Company.

Knobloch-Fedders, L. M., Pinsof, W. M., & Mann, B. J. (2007). Therapeutic alliance and treatment progress in couple psychotherapy. *Journal of Marital and Family Therapy, 33*(2), 245–257.

Knutson, J. F., DeGarmo, D. S., & Reid, J. B. (2004). Social disadvantage and neglectful parenting as precursors to the development of antisocial and aggressive child behavior: Testing a theoretical model. *Aggressive Behavior, 30*(3), 187–205.

Koyama, M. (January 1, 2011). *Interprofessional collaboration in a rehabilitation hospital in Japan. ETD Collection for McMaster University.* Paper AAINR74024; http://digitalcommons.mcmaster.ca/dissertations/AAINR74024

Kral, M. J., Burkhardt, K. J. & Kidd, S. (2002). The new research agenda for a cultural psychology. *Canadian Psychology/Psychologic Canadienne, 43*(3), 154–162.

Kramer, K. P. (2003). *Martin Buber's I and thou: Practicing living dialogue.* Mahwah, NJ: Paulist Press.

Kubie, L. S. (March, 1947). Training in clinical psychology. *Transactions of the First Conference.* New York, NY: Josiah Macy Jr. Foundation.

Kuper, A. (1999). *Culture: The anthropologists' account.* Cambridge, MA: Harvard University Press.

Kvarnström, S. (2008). Difficulties in collaboration: A critical incident study of interprofessional healthcare teamwork. *Journal of Interprofessional Care, 22*(2), 191–203. doi: 10.1080/13561820701760600

Lambert, A. (2011). The process of working ethically with multiple constellations of the family. Unpublished Dissertation, Seattle Pacific University.

Lambo, A. (2000). Constraints on world medical and health progress. In R. Lanza (Ed.), *One world: The health and survival of the human species in the 21st century* (pp. 111–128). Santa Fe, NM: Health Press.

Lambert, E. W., & Guthrie, P. R. (1996). Clinical outcomes of a children's mental health managed care demonstration. *Journal of Mental Health Administration, 23*(1), 51–68.

Laszlo, A., & Krippner, S. (1998). Systems theories: Their origins, foundations, and development. In J. S. Jordan (Ed.), *Systems theories and a priori aspects of perception* (pp. 47–74). Amsterdam, The Netherlands: Elsevier Science.

Leach, M. M., & Harbin, J. J. (1997). Psychological ethics codes: A comparison of twenty-four countries. *International Journal of Psychology, 32*, 181–192.

Leary, T. (1957). *Interpersonal diagnosis of personality.* New York, NY: Ronald Press.

Lebow, J. (2000). What does the research tell us about couple and family therapies? *Journal of Clinical Psychology, 56*, 1083–1094.

Lebow, J. L., Chambers, A., Christensen, A., & Johnson, S. M. (2012). Marital Distress. In D. Sprenkle & R. Chenail (Eds.), *Effectiveness research in marriage and family therapy*. Washington, DC: AAMFT.

Le Grange, D., Crosby, R. D., Rathouz, P. J., & Leventhal, B. L. (2007). A randomized controlled comparison of family-based treatment and supportive psychotherapy for adolescent bulimia nervosa. *Archives of General Psychiatry, 64*(9), 1049–1056.

Lerner, H. (1989). *The dance of intimacy*. New York, NY: Harper and Row.

Levant, R. F. (1997). Editorial: "It's been a hard day's night." *Journal of Family Psychology, 11*(4), 387–390.

Liddle, H. A. (1987). Family psychology: Tasks of an emerging (and emerged) discipline. *Journal of Family Psychology. 1*(1), 5–22.

Liddle, H. A. (1999). Theory development in a family-based therapy for adolescent drug abuse. *Journal of Clinical Child Psychology, 28*(4), 521–532.

Liddle, H. A. (2009). Multidimensional family therapy: A science based treatment system for adolescent drug abuse. In J. Bray & M. Stanton (Eds.), *The Wiley-Blackwell handbook of family psychology* (pp. 341–354). Sussex, UK: Blackwell Publishing.

Liddle, H. A. (2014). Adapting and implementing an evidence-based treatment with justice involved adolescents: The example of multidimensional family therapy. *Family Process, 53*(3), 516–528. doi: 10.1111/famp.12094

Liddle, H. (in press). Multidimensional family therapy. In T. L. Sexton & J. Lebow (Eds.), *Handbook of family therapy*. New York, NY: Routledge.

Liddle, H. A., Bray, J. H., Levant, R. F., & Santisteban, D. A. (2002). Family psychology intervention science: An emerging area of science and practice. In H. A. Liddle, D. A. Santisteban, R. F. Levant, & J. H. Bray (Eds.), *Family psychology: Science-based interventions* (pp. 3–15). Washington, DC: American Psychological Association.

Liddle, H. A., Breunlin, D., & Schwartz, R. (Eds.). (1988). *Handbook of family therapy training and supervision*. New York, NY: The Guilford Press.

Liddle, H. A., & Diamond, G. (1991). Adolescent substance abusers in family therapy: The critical initial phase of treatment. *Family Dynamics of Addiction Quarterly, 1*(1), 55–68.

Liddle, H. A., & Halpin, R. J. (1978). Family therapy training and supervision literature: A comparative review. *Journal of Marriage and Family Counseling, 4*(4), 77–98.

Liddle, H. A., Rowe, C. L., Dakof, G. A., Henderson, C., & Greenbaum, P. (2009). Multidimensional family therapy for early adolescent substance abusers: Twelve month outcomes of a randomized controlled trial. *Journal of Consulting and Clinical Psychology, 77*(1), 12–25. doi: 10.1037/a0014160

Liddle, H. A., & Saba, G. (1983). On contest replication: The isomorphic relationship to training and therapy. *Journal of Strategic and Systemic Therapies, 2*(2) 3–11.

Linehan, M. M., Armstrong, H. E., Suarez, A., Allmon, D., & Heard, H. L. (1991). Cognitive-behavioral treatment of chronically parasuicidal borderline patients. *Archives of General Psychiatry, 48*, 1060–1064.

Litz, B. T., Gray, M. J., Bryant, R. A., & Adler, A. B. (2002). Early interventions for trauma: Current status and future directions. *Clinical Psychology: Science and Practice, 9*(2), 112–134.

Luborsky, L. (1984). *Principles of psychoanalytic psychotherapy.* New York, NY: Basic Books.

Mable, A. L., & Marriott, J. (2002). *Sharing the learning—the health transition fund synthesis series: Primary health care.* Ottawa, ON: Health Canada.

Magnavita, J. J. (2012). Advancing clinical science using system theory as the framework for expanding family psychology with unified psychotherapy. *Couple and Family Psychology: Research and Practice, 1*(1), 3–13. doi: 10.1037/a0027492

Mahler, M., Pine, F., & Bergman, A. (1975). *The psychological birth of the human infant: Symbiosis and individuation.* New York, NY: Basic Books.

Mahrer, A. R., & Boulet, D. B. (1997). The experiential model of on-the-job teaching. In C. Edward Watkins, Jr. (Ed.), *Handbook of psychotherapy supervision* (pp. 164–183). New York: Wiley.

Main, M., Kaplan, N., & Cassidy, J. (1985). Security in infancy, childhood, and adulthood: A move to the level of representation. In I. Bretherton & E. Waters (Eds.), *Monographs of the Society for Research in Child Development, 50*(1–2, Serial No. 209, pp. 66–106).

Maxmen, J. S., & Ward, N. G. (1995). *Essential psychopathology and its treatment.* New York, NY: W. W. Norton & Company.

McDaniel, S. H (August 3, 2010). Personal communication.

McDaniel, S. H., Campbell, T. L., Hepworth, J., & Lorenz, A. (2005). *Family-oriented primary care* (2nd ed.). New York, NY: Springer Publishing.

McDaniel, S. H., Campbell, T. L., & Seaburn, D. B. (1995). Principles for collaboration between health and mental health providers in primary care. *Family Systems Medicine, 13*(3–4), 283–298. doi: 10.1037/h0089075

McDaniel, S., Weber, T., & McKeever, J. (1983). Multiple theoretical approaches to supervision: Choices in family therapy training. *Family Process, 22*, 491–500.

McFarlane, W. R. (2006). Family expressed emotion prior to onset of psychosis. In S. R. H. Beach, M. Z. Wamboldt, N. J. Kaslow, R. E. Heyman, M. B. First, L. G. Underwood, & D. Reiss (Eds.), *Relational processes and DSM-V: Neuroscience, assessment, prevention, and treatment* (pp. 77–88). Washington, DC: American Psychiatric Association.

McFarlane, W. R., Dixon, L., Lukens, E., & Lucksted, A. (2003). Family psychoeducation and schizophrenia: A review of the literature. *Journal of Marital and Family Therapy, 29*(2), 223–245.

McGoldrick, M. A., Carter, B., & Garcia-Preto, N. (2010). *The expanded family life cycle: Individual, family, and social perspectives* (4th ed.). Allyn and Bacon.

McGoldrick, M., Gerson, R., & Petry, S. (2008). *Genograms: Assessment and intervention.* New York, NY: W. W. Norton.

McPherson K., Headrick, L., & Moss, F. (2001). Working and learning together: Good quality care depends on it, but how can we achieve it? *Quality in Health Care, 10,* 46–53.

Melidonis, G. G., & Bry, B. H. (1995). Effects of therapist exceptions questions on blaming and positive statements in families with adolescent behavior problems. *Journal of Family Psychology, 9*(4), 451–457.

Merali, Z. (2005). *Fear still haunts Tsunami survivors.* Retrieved December 22, 2005, from http://www.newscientist.com

Middleberg (2001). Projective identification in common couple dances. *Journal of Marital and Family Therapy, 27*(3), 341–352.

Mikesell, S. G., & Stohner, M. R. (1995). Infertility and pregnancy loss: The role of the family consultant. In R. H. Mikesell, D. Lusterman, & S. H. McDaniel (Eds.), *Integrating family therapy: Handbook of family psychology and systems theory* (pp. 421–436). Washington, DC: American Psychological Association.

Miklowitz, D. J., & Clarkin, J. F. (2003). Diagnosis of family relational disorders. In G. P. Sholevar & L. D. Schwoeri (Eds.), *Textbook of family and couples therapy* (pp. 341–363). Washington, DC: American Psychiatric Publishing, Inc.

Miller, R. B., Anderson, S., & Keala, D. K. (2004). Is Bowen theory valid? A review of basic research. *Journal of Marital and Family Therapy, 30*(4), 453–466.

Miller, S. D., Duncan, B. L., & Hubble, M. A. (1997). *Escape from Babel: Toward a unifying language for psychotherapy practice.* New York, NY: W. W. Norton, Co.

Miller, B. F., Kessler, R., Peek, C. J., & Kallenberg, G. A. (2013). *Establishing the research agenda for collaborative care.* Publication #11–0067. Rockville, MD: Agency for Healthcare Research and Quality. Retrieved from http://www.ahrq.gov/research/findings/final-reports/collaborativecare/collab1.html

Millon, T., Millon, C., Davis, R., & Grossman, S. (2009). *MCMI-III Manual* (4th ed.). Minneapolis, MN: Pearson Education, Inc.

Milne, D. L., & James, I. A. (2002). The observed impact of training on competence in clinical supervision. *British Journal of Clinical Psychology, 41,* 55–72. http://dx.doi.org/10.1348/014466502163796

Minuchin, S. (1974). *Families and family therapy.* Cambridge, MA: Harvard University Press.

Money, J., & Herman, M. (1978). *The handbook of sexology: History and ideology* (Vol. 1). New York, NY: Elsevier.

Monroe, S. M., & Simons, A. D. (1991). Diathesis-stress theories in the context of life stress research: Implications for the depressive disorders. *Psychological Bulletin, 110,* 406–425. doi: 10.1037/0033–2909.110.3.406

Mooney, J. (2011). *Why the time is right for collaborative care.* Retrieved from http://www.kevinmd.com/blog/2011/02/time-collaborative-care.html

Mosak, H. H., & Pietro, R. D. (2006). *Early recollections: Interpretative method and application.* New York, NY: Routledge.

Mpofu, E. (2001). Rehabilitation an international perspective: A Zimbabwean experience. *Disability and Rehabilitation: An International, Multidisciplinary Journal, 23*, 481–489.

Multidimensional Family Therapy. (2015). Prescient, early family therapy's most influential projects. Retrieved from http://www.mdft.org/

Munck, E. (1999). Ethics of sexuality—Ethics of sexology. *Scandinavian Journal of Sexology, 2*, 195–201.

Nadelson, C. C., & Paolino, T. J. (1978). Marital therapy from a psychoanalytic perspective. In T. J. Paolino & B. S. McCrady (Eds.), *Marriage and marital therapy: Psychoanalytic, behavioral, and systems theory perspectives* (pp. 89–164). New York, NY: Brunner/Mazel.

Napier, A. Y., & Whitaker, C. A. (1978). *The family crucible.* New York, NY: Harper & Row.

Nichols, M. P. (1987). *The self in the system: Expanding the limits of family therapy.* New York, NY: Brunner/Mazel Publishers.

Nichols, W. C. (1988). An integrative psychodynamic and systems approach. In H. Liddle, D. Breunlin, & R. Schwartz (Eds.), *Handbook of family therapy training and supervision.* New York, NY: Guilford Press.

Nichols, W. C. (1996). *Treating people in families.* New York, NY: The Guilford Press.

Nichols, M. P. (2013). *Family therapy: Concepts and methods* (10th ed.). Boston, MA: Pearson.

Nichols, M. P., & Schwartz, R. C. (1998). *Family therapy: Concepts and methods.* Boston, MA: Allyn & Bacon.

Nichols, M. P., & Schwartz, R. C. (2001). *Family therapy: Concepts and methods.* Boston, MA: Allyn and Bacon.

Nichols, W. C., & Everett, C. A. (1986). Systemic family therapy: An integrative approach.

New York: Guilford.

Norris, F. H. (2005). Psychosocial consequences of natural disasters in developing countries: What does past research tell us about the potential effects of the 2004 tsunami? Retrieved July 13, 2007, from the National Center for PTSD http://www.redmh.org/research/specialized/tsunami_summary.pdf

Nutt, R. L., & Stanton, M. (2008). Family psychology specialty practice. *Professional psychology: Research and practice, 39*(5), 519–528.

O'Connell, B. (1998). *Solution-focused therapy.* London, UK: Sage Publications.

Okasha, A., Arboleda- Florez, J., & Sartorius, N. (2000). *Ethics, culture, and psychiatry: International perspectives.* Arlington, VA: American Psychiatric Pub.

Orchard C. A., Curran V., & Kabene S. (2005). Creating a culture for interdisciplinary collaborative professional practice. Med Education Online [serial online], 10:11.

Orlinsky, D. E., & Howard, K. I. (1986). In L. S. Greenberg & W. M. Pinsof (Eds.), *The psychotherapeutic process: A research handbook* (pp. 477–501). New York, NY: Guilford Press.

Palmer, P. (1998). *The courage to teach.* San Francisco, CA: Jossey-Bass.

Paolino, T. J., & McCrady, B. S. (1978). *Marriage and marital therapy*. New York, NY: Brunner/Mazel.

Patela, V. L., Cytryna, K. N., Shortliffeb, E. H., & Safranc, C. (1997). The collaborative health care team: The role of individual and group expertise. *Teaching and Learning in Medicine: An International Journal, 12*(3), 117–132.

Patterson, G. R., & Stouthamer-Loeber, M. (1984). The correlation of family management practices and delinquency. *Child Development, 55*(4), 1299–1307.

Patterson, J., Williams, L., Grauf-Grounds, C., & Chamow, L. (1998). *Essential skills in family therapy: From the first interview to termination*. New York, NY: Guilford Press.

Patterson, T. (2009). Ethical and legal considerations in family psychology: The special issue of competence. In J. Bray, & M. Stanton (Eds.) The Wiley-Blackwell handbook of family psychology. UK: Blackwell Publishing, 183–197.

Patterson, T., & Sexton, T. L. (2013). Bridging conceptual frameworks: A systemic heuristic for understanding family diversity. *Couple and Family Psychology: Research and Practice, 2*(4), 237–245.

Paz Pruitt, I. T. (2007). Family treatment approaches for depression in adolescent males. *American Journal of Family Therapy, 35*(1), 69–81.

Pedersen, P. (1994). *A handbook for developing cultural awareness* (2nd ed.). Alexandria, VA: American Association for Counseling and Development.

Pedersen, P. (1995). *The five stages of culture shock: Critical incidents around the world*. Westport, CT: Greenwood Press.

Pelton, S. L., & Hertlein, K. M. (2011). A proposed life cycle for voluntary childfree couples. *Journal of Feminist Family Therapy: An International Forum, 23*(1), 39–53.

Peng, K. & Nisbett, R. E. (1999). Culture, dialectics, and reasoning about contradiction. *American Psychologist, 54*(9), 741–754.

Percevic, R., Lambert, M. J., & Kordy, H. (2004). Computer-supported monitoring of patient treatment response. *Journal of Clinical Psychology, 60*(3), 285–299.

Perlmutter, R. A. (1996). *A family approach to psychiatric disorders*. Washington, DC: American Psychiatric Press, Inc.

Perry, B. L. (2006). Understanding social network disruption: The case of youth in foster care. *Social Problems, 53*, 371–391.

Peterson, B. D., Eifert, G. H., Feingold, T., & Davidson, S. (2009). Using acceptance and commitment therapy to treat distressed couples: A case study with two couples. *Cognitive and Behavioral Practice, 16*, 430–442.

Peterson, Francine K. (1991). Issues of race and ethnicity in supervision: Emphasizing who you are, not what you know. *The Clinical Supervisor, 9*(1), 15–31.

Peterson, R. L., Peterson, D. R., Abrams, J. C., & Stricker, G. (1997). The National Council of

Pettifor, J. L. (2004). Professional ethics across national boundaries. *European Psychologist, 9*, 264–272. doi: 10.1027/1016-9040.9.4.264

Pichot, T., & Dolan, Y. M. (2003). *Solution-focused brief therapy: It's effective use in agency settings*. Binghamton, NY: Haworth Clinical Practice Press.

Pinsof, W. M., & Catherall, D. R. (1986). The integrative psychotherapy alliance: Family, couple and individual therapy scales. *Journal of Marital and Family Therapy, 12*(2), 137–151.

Pinsof, W. M., Goldsmith, J. Z., & Latta, T. A. (2012). Information technology and feedback research can bridge the scientist practitioner gap: A couple therapy example. *Couple and Family Psychology: Research and Practice, 1*, 253–273.

Pinsof, W. M., & Wynne, L. C. (1995). The efficacy of marital and family therapy: An empirical overview, conclusions, and recommendations. *Journal of Marital and Family Therapy, 21*(4), 585–613.

Pinsof, W. M., Zinbarg, R. E., Lebow, J. L., Knobloch-Fedders, L. M., Durbin, E., Chambers, A., & Friedman, G. (2009). Laying the foundation for progress research in family, couple, and individual therapy: The development and psychometric features of the initial systemic therapy inventory of change. *Psychotherapy Research, 19*, 143–156.

Pinto, R. C. (2001). *Argument, inference and dialectic: Collected papers on informal logic.* Vol. 4. Dordrecht, The Netherlands: Kluwer Academic Publishers.

Pittman, F. (1990). Private lies: Infidelity and the betrayal of intimacy. New York, NY: W. W. Norton.

Plato, Emlyn-Jones, C. J. & Preddy, W. (2013). *Republic.* Cambridge, MA: Harvard University Press.

Pupavec, V. (2006). Humanitarian politics and the rise of international disaster psychology. In G. Reyes & G. A. Jacobs (Eds.), *Handbook of international disaster psychology* (pp. 15–34). Westport, CT: Praeger Publishers.

Quick, E. K. (1996). *Doing what works in brief therapy: A strategic solution-focused approach.* San Diego, CA: Academic Press.

Raimy, V. C. (1950). *Training in clinical psychology.* Englewood Cliffs, NJ: Prentice-Hall.

Rait, D. S. (2000). The therapeutic alliance in couples and family therapy. *Journal of Clinical Psychology, 56*(2), 211–224.

Rehman, U. S., Gollan, J., & Mortimer, A. R. (2008). The marital context of depression: Research, limitations, and new directions. *Clinical Psychology Review, 28*, 179–198. doi: 10.1016/j.cpr.2007.04.007.

Riegel, K. F. (1973). Dialectical operations: The final period of cognitive development. *Human Development, 18*, 430–443.

Reiss, I. L. (1993). The future of sex research and the meaning of science. *Journal of Sex Research, 30*, 3–11.

Repetti, R. L., Taylor, S. E., & Seeman, T. E. (2002). Risky families: Family social environments and the mental and physical health of offspring. *Psychological Bulletin, 128*(2), 330–366.

Respect (Def.1). Oxford Advanced Learner's Dictionary Online. Retrieved January, 2, 2015, from http://www.oxforddictionaries.com/us/definition/american_english/respect.

Runions, K. C., & Keating, D. P. (2007). Children's social information processing: Family antecedents and behavioral correlates. *Developmental Psychology, 43*(4), 838–849.

Reyes, G., & Elhai, J. D. (2004). Psychosocial interventions in the early phases of disasters. *Psychotherapy, 41*, 399–411.

Richardson, R, W. (1984). *Family ties that bind: A self-help guide to change through family of origin therapy*. Bellingham, WA: Self-Counsel Press.

Ridely, M. (2003). *Nature via nurture*. New York, NY: HarperCollins.

Robbins, M. S., Alexander, J. F., Newell, R. M., & Turner, C. W. (1996). The immediate effect of reframing on client attitude in family therapy. *Journal of Family Psychology, 10*(1), 28–34.

Robbins, M. S., Alexander, J. F., & Turner, C. W. (2000). Disrupting defensive family interactions in family therapy with delinquent adolescents. *Journal of Family Psychology, 14*(4), 688–701.

Roberts, C., Mazzucchelli, T., Taylor, K., & Reid, R. (2003). Early intervention for behaviour problems in young children with developmental disabilities. *International Journal of Disability, Development and Education, 50*(3), 275–292.

Rogers, C. (1970). *Carl Rogers on Encounter Groups*. New York, NY: HarperCollins.

Rosenzweig, S. (1936). Some implicit common factors in diverse methods of psychotherapy. *American Journal of Orthopsychiatry, 6*, 412–415.

Roth, S., & Epston, D. (1996). Developing externalizing conversations: An exercise. *Journal of Systemic Therapies, 15*(1), 5–12.

Rovelli, C. (1996). Relational quantum mechanics. *International Journal of Theoretical Physics, 35*(8), 1637–1678. doi: 10.1007/BF02302261

Rowe, C. L., Rigter, H., Gantner, A., Mos, K., Nielsen, P., Phan, O., & Henderson, C. (2012). Implementation fidelity of multidimensional family therapy in an international trial. *Journal of Substance Abuse Treatment, 44*(4), 391–399. doi: 10.1016/j.jsat.2012.08.225

Ruddy, N., & McDanile, S. (in press). Couple and family therapy in medical settings. In T. L. Sexton & J. Lebow (Eds.), *Handbook of family therapy*. New York, NY: Routledge.

Ruesch, J., & Bateson, G. (1951). *Communication: The social matrix of psychiatry*. New Brunswick, NJ: Transaction Publishers.

Sackett, D. L., Straus, S. E., Richardson, W. S., Rosenberg, W., & Haynes, R. B. (2000). *Evidence based medicine: How to practice and teach EBM* (2nd ed.). New York, NY: Churchill Livingstone.

Sale, E., Sambrano, S., Springer, J. F., & Turner, C. W. (2003). Risk, protection, and substance use in adolescents: A multi-site model. *Journal of Drug Education, 33*(1), 91–105.

Satir, V. (1972). *Peoplemaking*. Palo Alto, CA: Science and Behavior.

Sattler, D. N. (2007). Tsunamic researchers help rebuild a community. *Observer, 20*(6), 13–17.

Sautz, J. (1995). Collaborative care of Medicaid patients: Lessons from the Oregon Health Plan. *Family Systems Medicine, 13*, 343–349.

Sayre, G. (2002). *The psychosomatic marriage: An empirical study* (Unpublished doctoral dissertation). Seattle Pacific University, Seattle, Washington.

Scaturo, D. J., & McPeak, W. R. (1998). Clinical dilemmas in contemporary psychotherapy: The search for clinical wisdom. *Psychotherapy, 35*, 1–12.

Schaefer, E. S. (1965). Children's reports of parental behavior: An inventory. *Child Development, 32,* 413–424.

Scharff, D. E., & Scharff, J. S. (1987). *Object relations family therapy.* Northvale, NJ: Jason Aronson.

Schmidt, U., Lee, S., Beecham, J., Perkins, S., Treasure, J., Yi, I., . . . Eisler, I. (2007). A randomized controlled trial of family therapy and cognitive behavior therapy guided self-care for adolescents with bulimia nervosa and related disorders. *The American Journal of Psychiatry, 164*(4), 591–598.

Schnarch, D. M. (1997). *Passionate marriage: Sex, love, & intimacy in emotionally committed relationships.* New York, NY: W. W. Norton & Co.

Schoenwald, S. K., Henggeler, S. W., & Rowland, M. D. (in press). Multisystemic therapy. In T. L. Sexton & J. Lebow (Eds.), *Handbook of family therapy.* New York, NY: Routledge.

Schoenwald, S. K., Sheidow, A. S., & Letourneau, E. J. (2004). Toward effective quality assurance in evidence-based practice: Links between expert consultation, therapist fidelity, and child outcomes. *Journal of Child and Adolescent Clinical Psychology, 33,* 94–104.

Schools and Programs of Professional Psychology education model. *Professional Psychology: Research and Practice, 28*(4), 373–386.

Schore, A. (2012). *The science of the art of psychotherapy.* New York, NY: Norton.

Schwartz, R. C. (1988). The trainer-trainee relationship in family therapy training. In H. Liddle, D. Breunlin, & R. Schwartz. (Eds.), *Handbook of family therapy training and supervision.* New York, NY: Guilford Press.

Schwartz, R. C. (2013). *Internal Family Systems Therapy.* New York, NY: Guilford.

Schwartzman, H., & Kneifel, A. (1985). *Families and other systems: The microsystemic context of family therapy.* New York, NY: Guilford Press.

Seedall, R. B. (2009). Enhancing change process in solution-focused brief therapy by utilizing couple enactments. *American Journal of Family Therapy, 37,* 99–113.

Sexton, T. L. (2007). The therapist as a moderator and mediator in successful therapeutic change. *Journal of Family Therapy, 29*(2), 104–110.

Sexton, T. L. (2010). *Functional family therapy in clinical practice: An evidence based treatment model for at risk adolescents.* New York, NY: Routledge.

Sexton, T. L. (in press). Functional family therapy: Evidence based, clinically specific, and creative clinical decision making. In T. L. Sexton & J. Lebow (Eds.), *Handbook of family therapy.* New York, NY: Routledge.

Sexton, T. L., & Alexander, J. F. (2002). Family-based empirically supported interventions. *The Counseling Psychologist, 30*(2), 238–261. doi: 10.1177/0011000002302003

Sexton, T. L., & Alexander, J. F. (2003). Functional family therapy: A mature clinical model. In T. Sexton, G. Weeks, & M. Robbins (Eds.), *Handbook of family therapy.* New York, NY: Brunner/Routledge.

Sexton, T. L., Alexander, J. F., Gilman, L. (2004). *Functional family therapy clinical supervision manual.* Annie E. Casey Foundation, www.aecf.org.

Sexton, T. L., Alexander, J. F., & Mease, A. C. (2003). Levels of evidence for the models and mechanisms of therapeutic change in couple and family therapy. In M. Lambert (Ed.), *Handbook of psychotherapy and behavior change*. New York: Wiley.

Sexton, T. L., Alexander, J. F., & Mease, A. L. (2004). Change models and mechanisms in couple and family therapy. In M. Lambert (Ed.), *Handbook of psychotherapy and behavior change* (pp. 590–646). New York, NY: Wiley & Sons.

Sexton, T. L., Datachi-Phillips, C., Evans, L. E., LaFollette, J., & Wright L. (2012). The effectiveness of couple and family therapy interventions. In M. Lambert (Ed.), *Handbook of psychotherapy and behavior change* (pp. 587–639). New York, NY: Wiley.

Sexton, T. L., & Datchi, C. (2014). The development and evolution of family therapy research: Its impact on practice, current status, and future directions. *Family Process, 53*(3), 415–433.

Sexton, T, Datchi, C., & Patterson, T. (2012). Technological innovations of systematic measurement and clinical feedback: A virtual leap into the future of couple and family psychology. *Couple and Family Psychology: Research and Practice, 1*(4), 285. doi: 10.1037/cfp0000001

Sexton, T. L., & Gordon, K. C. (2009). Science, practice and evidence-based treatments in the clinical practice of family psychology. In J. Bray & M. Stanton (Eds.), *The Wiley-Blackwell handbook of family psychology* (pp. 314–326). West Sussex, UK: Blackwell Publishing.

Sexton, T. L., Gordon, K. C., Gurman, A., Lebow, J., Holtzworth-Munroe, A., & Johnson, S. (2011). Guidelines for classifying evidence based treatments in couple and family psychology. *Family Process, 50*(3), 337–392.

Sexton, T. L., & Griffin, B. L. (1997). *Constructivist thinking in counseling practice, research and training*. New York, NY: Teachers College Press.

Sexton, T. L., Kinser, J. C., & Hanes, C. W. (2008). Beyond a single standard: Levels of evidence approach for evaluating marriage and family therapy research and practice. *Journal of Family Therapy, 30*(4), 386–398.

Sexton, T. L. & LaFollette, J. R. (in press). Criteria for evaluating the research evidence for couple and family therapy interventions. In E. Lawrence (Ed.), *Relationship science*. New York, NY: Cambridge University Press.

Sexton, T. L., & Lebow, J. (2015). *Handbook of family therapy* (4th ed.). New York, NY: Routledge.

Sexton, T. L., Ridley, C. R., & Kleiner, A. J. (2004). Beyond common factors: multilevel-process models of therapeutic change in marriage and family therapy. *Journal of Marital and Family Therapy, 30*(2), 131–149.

Sexton, T. L., Robbins, M. S., Hollimon, A. S., Mease, A. L., & Mayorga, C. C. (2003). Efficacy, effectiveness, and change mechanisms in couple and family therapy. In T. L. Sexton, G. R. Weeks, & M. S. Robbins (Eds.), *Handbook of family therapy: The science and practice of working with families and couples* (pp. 229–261). Philadelphia, PA: Brunner-Routledge.

Sexton, T. L., & Stanton, M. (2015). Systems Theories. In J. Norcoross & G Vandenbos (Eds.), *APA handbook of clinical psychology*. Washington, DC: APA.

Sexton, T. L., & Turner, C. T. (2010). The effectiveness of functional family therapy for youth with behavioral problems in a community practice setting. *Journal of Family Psychology, 24*(3), 339–348.

Sexton, T. L. & van Dam, A. E. (2010). Creativity within the structure: Clinical expertise and evidence-based treatments. *Journal of Contemporary Psychotherapy, 40*(3), 175–180.

Shadish, W. R., & Baldwin, S. A. (2002). Meta-analysis of MFT interventions. In D. H. Sprenkle (Ed.), *Effectiveness research in marriage and family therapy* (pp. 339–370). Washington, DC: American Association for Marriage and Family Therapy.

Shadish, W. R., Montgomery, L. M., Wilson, P., Wilson, M. R., Bright, I., & Okwumabua, T. (1993). Effects of family and marital psychotherapies: A meta-analysis. *Journal of Consulting and Clinical Psychology, 61*(6), 992–1002.

Shadish, W. R., Ragsdale, K., Glaser, R. R., & Montgomery, L. M. (1995). The efficacy and effectiveness of marital and family therapy: A perspective from meta-analysis. *Journal of Marital and Family Therapy, 21*(4), 345–360.

Sheidow, A. J., Henggeler, S. W., & Schoenwald, S. K. (2003). Multisystemic therapy. In T. L. Sexton, G. Weeks, & M. Robbins (Eds.), *Handbook of family therapy: The science and practice of working with families and couples* (pp. 303–322). New York, NY: Brunner-Routledge.

Shields, C. G., Wynne, L. C., McDaniel, S. H., & Gawinski, B. A. (1994). The marginalization of family therapy: A historical and continuing problem. *Journal of Marital and Family Therapy, 20*(2), 117–138.

Siegel, D, J. (2001). Toward an interpersonal neurobiology of the developing mind: Attachment, "mindsight," and neural integration. *Infant Mental Health Journal, 22,* 67–94.

Skowron, E. (in press). Multigenerational family systems. In T. L. Sexton & J. Lebow (Eds.), *Handbook of family therapy.* New York, NY: Routledge.

Skowron, E. A., & Friedlander, M. L. (1998). The differentiation of self inventory: Development and initial validation. *Journal of Counseling Psychology, 45*(3), 235–246.

Skynner, A. C. R. (1976). *Systems of family and marital psychotherapy.* New York, NY: Brunner/Mazel.

Slipp, S. (1984). *Object Relations: A dynamic bridge between individual and family treatment.* New York, NY: Jason Aronson.

Smith M., Glass, G., & Miller, T. (1980). *The benefits of psychotherapy.* Baltimore, MD: John Hopkins University Press.

Snyder, D. K. (1981). *Marital satisfaction inventory.* Los Angeles, CA: Western Psychological Services.

Snyder, D. K. (1999). Affective reconstruction in the context of a pluralistic approach to couple therapy. *Clinical Psychology: Science and Practice, 6*(4), 348–365. doi: 10.1093/clipsy/6.4.348

Snyder, D. K., & Aikman, G. G. (1999). Marital Satisfaction Inventory-Revised. In M. E. Maruish (Ed.), *The use of psychological testing for treatment planning and outcomes assessment* (2nd ed., pp. 1173–1210). Mahwah, NJ: Lawrence Erlbaum Associates Publishers.

Snyder, D. K., Cavell, T. A., & Heffer, R. W. (1995). Marital and family assessment: A multifaceted, multilevel approach. In R. H. Mikesell, D. Lusterman, & S. H. McDaniel (Eds.), *Integrating family therapy: Handbook of family psychology and systems theory* (pp. 163–182). Washington, DC: American Psychological Association.

Snyder, D. K., & Doss, B. D. (2005). Treating infidelity: Clinical and ethical directions. *JCLP/In Session, 61,* 1453–1465.

Snyder, D. K., & Schneider, W. (2002). Affective reconstruction: A pluralistic, developmental approach. In A. S. Gurman & N. S. Jacobson (Eds.), *Clinical handbook of couple therapy* (3rd ed., pp. 151–179). New York, NY: Guilford Press.

Snyder, D. K., & Wills, R. M. (1989). Behavioral versus insight-oriented marital therapy: Effects on individual and interspousal functioning. *Journal of Consulting and Clinical Psychology, 57*(1), 39–46. doi: 10.1037/0022–006X.57.1.39

Snyder, D. K., Wills, R. M., & Grady-Fletcher, A. (1991). Long-term effectiveness of behavioral versus insight-oriented marital therapy: A 4-year follow-up study. *Journal of Consulting and Clinical Psychology, 59*(1), 138–141. doi: 10.1037/0022–006X.59.1.138

Spanier, G. B. (1976). Measuring dyadic adjustment: New scales for assessing the quality of marriage and similar dyads. *Journal of Marriage and the Family, 38*(1), 15–28. doi: 10.2307/350547

Sue, D. W., Arredondo, P., & McDavis, R. J. (1992). Multicultural counseling competencies and standards: A call to the profession. *Journal of Counseling and Development, 70,* 477–483.

Sperry, L., & Carlson, J. (1991). *Marital therapy: Integrating theory and technique.* Denver, CO: Love Publishing Company.

Sprenkle, D. H. (2012). Intervention research in couple and family therapy: A methodological and substantive review and an introduction to the special issue. *Journal of Marital and Family Therapy, 38*(1), 3–29.

Sprenkle, D. H., Blow, A. J., & Dickey, M. H. (1999). Common factors and other nontechnique variables in marriage and family therapy. In M. A. Hubble, B. L. Duncan, & S. D. Miller (Eds.), *The heart and soul of change: What works in therapy.* Washington, DC: American Psychological Association.

Sprenkle, D. H., Davis, D. D., & Lebow, J. L. (2009). *Common factors in couple and family therapy: The overlooked foundation for effective practice.* New York, NY: Guilford.

Stanton, M. (2009). The systemic epistemology of the specialty of family psychology. In J. H. Bray & M. Stanton (Eds.), *The Wiley-Blackwell handbook of family psychology* (pp. 5–20). West Sussex, UK: Wiley-Blackwell. doi: 10.1002/9781444310238.ch

Stanton, M. (2012). Introduction to couple and family psychology: Research and practice. *Couple and Family Psychology: Research and Practice, 1*(1), 1–2.

Stanton, M., & Welsh, R. (2012). Systemic thinking in couple and family psychology research and practice. *Couple and Family Psychology: Research and Practice, 1*(1), 14–30.

Steinglass, P. (1991). An editorial: Finding a place for the individual in family therapy. *Family Process, 30*(3), 267–269.

Sternberg, R. J. (1986) A triangular theory of love. *Psychological Review, 93,* 119–135.

Stone, M. H., & Hoffman, N. M. (2005). Borderline states and individual psychology. In A. Freeman, M. H. Stone, & D. Martin. (Eds.), *Comparative treatments for borderline personality disorder* (pp. 133–149). New York, NY: Springer Publishing Co.

Storm, C. L., Todd, T. C., Sprenkle, D. H., & Morgan, M. M. (2001). Gaps between MFT supervision assumptions and common practice: Suggested best practices. *Journal of Marital and Family Therapy, 27,* 227–239.

Stricker, G., & Healey, B. J. (1990). Projective assessment of object relations: A review of the empirical literature. *Journal of Consulting and Clinical Psychology, 2*(3), 219–230.

Stricker, G., & Trierweiler, S. J. (1995). The local clinical scientist: A bridge between science and practice. *American Psychologist, 50*(12), 995–1002.

Strong, S. R., & Clairborn, C. D. (1982). Change through interaction: Social psychological processes of counseling and psychotherapy. New York, NY: Wiley.

Sue, D. W., & Sue, D. (2012). *Counseling the culturally diverse: theory and practice.* New York, NY: John Wiley & Sons.

Sullivan, H. S. (1954). *The psychiatric interview.* New York, NY: W. W. Norton.

Taylor, S. E., Fiske, S. T., Etcoff, N. L., & Ruderman, A. J. (1978). Categorical and contextual bases of person memory and stereotyping. *Journal of Personality and Social Psychology, 36*(7), 778–793.

Terman, L. M., Buttenwieser, P., Ferguson, L. W., Johnson, W. B., & Wilson, D. P. (1938). *Psychological factors in marital happiness.* New York, NY: McGraw-Hill.

Thibaut, J. W., & Kelley, H. H. (1959). *The social psychology of groups.* Oxford, England: John Wiley.

Thoburn, J. W., Bentley, J. A., Ahmad, Z. S., & Jones, K. C. (2012). International disaster psychology ethics: A social justice model imbedded in a systems paradigm. *Traumatology, 18*(4), 79–85.

Thoburn, J. W., Cecchet, S., Oliver, T., Jones, K. C., & Sanchez, O. (2011). Where do we go from here? The development of a family psychology identity. *The Family Psychologist, 27*(1), 6–10.

Thoburn, J. W. & Hammond-Meyer, A. (2004). Eating disorders. In F. Kline, & L. B. Silver (Eds.) *The educator's guide to mental health issues in the classroom.* (pp. 141–170). Baltimore: Brookes Publishing.

Thoburn, J. W., Hoffman-Robinson, G., Shelley, L., & Sayre, G. (2009). Collaborative treatment for the psychosomatic couple. *The Family Journal: Counseling and Therapy for Couples and Families, 17*(1), 6–13.

Thoburn, J. W., Hoffman-Robinson, G., Shelly, L. & Hagen, A. (2009). Clinical practice in family psychology. In J. Bray, & M. Stanton (Eds.), The Wiley-Blackwell handbook of family psychology. UK: Blackwell Publishing, 198–211.

Thoburn, J. W., Mauseth, K., McGuire, T., Adams, K., & Cecchet, S. (2015). The Health Support Team: The development of an indigenous community volunteer mental health training program in Haiti. Unpublished manuscript.

Thomas, F. N., & McKenzie, P. N. (1986). Prolific writers in marital and family therapy: A research note. *Journal of Marital and Family Therapy, 12*(2), 175–180.

Tiefer, L. (1994). The social construction and social effects of sex research: The sexological model of sexuality. In C. B. Travis & J. W. White (Eds.), *Sexuality, society, and feminism.* Washington, DC: American Psychological Association.

Todd, T., & Storm, C. (1997). *The complete systemic supervisor.* Boston, MA: Allyn & Bacon.

Trowell, J., Joffe, I., Campbell, J., Clemente, C., Almqvist, F., Soininen, . . . Tsiantis, J. (2007). Childhood depression: A place for psychotherapy. An outcome study comparing individual psychodynamic psychotherapy and family therapy. *European Child & Adolescent Psychiatry, 16*(3), 157–167.

Tyler, F. B., Tyler, S. L., Echeverry, J. J., & Zea, M. C. (1991). Making it on the streets in Bogota: A psychosocial study of street youth. *Genetic, Social and General Psychology Monographs, 117*(4), 395–417.

United Kingdom Central Council for Nursing, Midwifery and Health Visiting (UKCC). (1994). *The Midwife's Code of Practice.* London, UK: UKCC.

United States Census Bureau (2014). *United States Census Bureau.* Retrieved October 22, 2014.

Varela, J. G., & Conroy, M. A. (2012). Professional competencies in forensic psychology. *Professional Psychology: Research and Practice, 43*(5), 410–421.

Vaughn, M. G., & Howard, M. O. (2004). Adolescent substance abuse treatment: A synthesis of controlled evaluations. *Research on Social Work Practice, 14,* 325–335.

Visser, C. F. (2013). The origin of the Solution-Focused approach. *International Journal of Solution-Focused Practices, 1*(1), 10–17.

Wagner, E. H., Austin, B. T., & von Korff, M. (1996). Organizing care for patients with chronic illness. *Milbank Quarterly, 74*(4), 551–544.

Waldron, H. B., & Turner, C. W. (2008). Evidence-based psychosocial treatments for adolescent substance abuse. *Journal of Clinical Child and Adolescent Psychology, 37*(1), 238–261.

Walker, B. B., & London, S. (2007). Novel tools and resources for evidence-based practice in psychology. *Journal of Clinical Psychology, 63*(7), 633–642.

Wall, T. (September, 16, 2007). Personal communication.

Walter, J. L., & Peller, J. E. (1992). *Becoming solution focused in brief therapy.* New York, NY: Brunner/Mazel.

Wampold, B. E. (1997). Methodological problems in identifying efficacious psychotherapies. *Psychotherapy Research, 7*(1), 21–43.

Wampold, B. E. (2003). Bashing positivism and revering a medical model under the guise of evidence. *The Counseling Psychologist, 31*(5), 539–545.

Wampold, B. E., & Bhati, K. S. (2004). Attending to the omissions: A historical examination of evidence based practice movements. *Professional Psychology: Research and Practice, 35*, 563–570.

Wanlass, J., & Scarff, D. E., (in press). Psychodynamic approaches to couple and family therapy. In T. L. Sexton & J. Lebow (Eds.), *Handbook of family therapy*. New York, NY: Routledge.

Waters D. B., & Lawrence, E. C. (1993). *Competence, courage, and change: An approach to family therapy*. New York, NY: W. W. Norton & Co.

Watkins, E. C. (1992). Psychotherapy supervision and the separation-individuation process: Autonomy versus dependency issues. *Clinical supervisor, 10*(1), 111–121.

Watzlawick, P., Beavin-Bavelas, J., & Jackson, D. (1967). *Pragmatics of human communication—A study of interactional patterns, pathologies and paradoxes*. New York, NY: W. W. Norton.

Watzlawick, P., Weakland, J., & Fisch, R. (1974). *Change: Principles of problem formation and problem resolution*. New York, NY: Norton.

Webster-Stratton, C. H. (1990). Stress: A potential disruptor of parent perceptions and family interactions. *Journal of Clinical Child Psychology, 19*(4), 1302–1312.

Webster-Stratton, C. H. (1996). Early intervention with videotape modeling: Programs for families of children with oppositional defiant disorder or conduct disorder. In E. D. Hibbs & P. S. Jensen (Eds.), *Psychosocial treatments for child and adolescent disorders: Empirically based strategies for clinical practice* (pp. 435–474). Washington, DC: American Psychological Association.

Weeks, G. R., & Nixon, G. F. (1991). Family psychology: The specialty statement of an evolving field. *The Family Psychologist, 7*(4), 9–18.

Weisner, T. S., & Fiese, B. H. (2011). Introduction to special section of the Journal of Family Psychology, advances in mixed methods in family psychology: Integrative and applied solutions for family science. *Journal of Family Psychology, 25*(6), 795–798.

Weiss, R. L., & Heyman, R. E. (1990). Marital distress. In A. S. Bellack, M. Hersen, & A. E. Kazdin (Eds.), *International handbook of behavior modification and therapy* (2nd ed., pp. 475–501). New York, NY: Plenum Press. doi: 10.1007/978-1-4613-0523-1_23

Weiss, R. L., Hops, H., & Patterson, G. R. (1993). A framework for conceptualizing marital conflict: A technology for altering it, some data for evaluating it. In L. D. Handy & E. L. Mash (Eds.), *Behavior change: Methodology concepts and practice* (pp. 309–342). Champaign, IL: Research Press.

Welsh, R., Greenberg, L., & Graham-Howard, M. (2009). Family forensic psychology. In J. Bray & M. Stanton (Eds.), *The Wiley-Blackwell handbook of family psychology* (pp. 702–717). West Sussex, UK: Wiley-Blackwell.

Wessells, M. (2009). Do no harm: Toward contextually appropriate psychosocial support in international emergencies. *American Psychologist, 64*, 842–854.

Weston, W. W. (2005). Patient-centered medicine: A guide to the biopsychosocial model. *Families, Systems, & Health*, 23(4), 387–392.

Whisman, M. A., Johnson, D. P., Be, D., & Li, A. (2012). Couple-based interventions for depression. *Couple and Family Psychology: Research and Practice*, *1*(3), 185–198.

White, M. (1989). *Selected papers*. Adelaide, Australia: Dulwich Centre Pub.

White, J. M., & Klein, D. M. (2007). *Family theories* (3rd ed.). New York, NY: Sage Publications.

Whitley, B. E. Jr., & Kite, M. E. (2006). *The psychology of prejudice and discrimination*. Belmont, CA: Thompson Wadsworth.WHO (2013). *Japan Inter Professional Working and Education Network*. Global Health Workforce Alliance. Retrieved from http://www.who.int/workforcealliance/members_partners/member_list/jipwen/en/index.html

Wiener, N, (1948). *Cybernetics: Or control and communication in the animal and the machine*. Cambridge, MA: MIT Press.

Williams, B., Kaslow, F., & Grossman, N. S. (1994). Guidelines for the development of postdoctoral programs in family psychology. Unpublished manuscript.

Wilson, G. T., & Fairburn, C. G. (2007). Treatments for eating disorders. In P. E. Nathan & J. M. Gorman (Eds.), *A guide to treatments that work* (3rd ed., pp. 579–609). London, UK: Oxford University Press.

Wimberly, J. D. (1998). An outcome study of integrative couples therapy delivered in a group format. *Dissertation Abstracts International, 58*(12-B), 6832.

Wincze, J. P., & Carey, M. P. (2001). *Sexual Dysfunction*. New York, NY: Guilford Press.

Winnicott, D. W. (1965). *The maturational processes and the facilitating environment*. New York, NY: International Universities Press.

Wittgenstein, L. (1965). *Philosophical Investigations*. New York: The Macmillan Company.

Wood, L. F., & Jacobson, N. S. (1985). Marital distress. In D. H. Barlow (Ed.), *Clinical handbook of psychological disorders* (pp. 344–416). New York, NY: Guilford Press.

Index

Acceptance and commitment therapy (ACT): about, 151, 162; clinical assessment, 163–64; clinical process and interventions, 163–65; goals of treatment, 163; theoretical foundations, 162–63

Accommodation/joining stage, 130

Adolescents, 76, 77

Affect, developmental, 156

Alignments, 128–29

Alliance: defined, 128; therapeutic, 77, 96–99; within system, 101–2

Alliance-based motivation, 139

Ambiguity, acceptance of, 15–17

American Board of Forensic Psychology, 188

American Psychological Association Ethics Code, 204–5

Anorexia, 76

Anxiety, 131, 180–81

Apprenticeship, 197

Aristotelian philosophy, 24

Art, 18–19

Assessment. See Clinical assessment

Attachment, 154

Attachment-based family therapy, 76

Attitudes, family psychologist, 13–17

Bateson, G., 32, 33, 40–41

Behavior: childhood/adolescent problems, 76; complementary patterns, 33; influences on, 27; social bases of, 193–94; symmetrical patterns, 33. See also Cognitive behavioral couples therapy

Behavior change phase, 141

Beliefs, 56–57

Biological foundations, 193

Blame, reducing, 78, 103

Blind men describing elephant metaphor, 6

Bloch, Iwan, 178

Bordin, E. S., 96–97

Bowen, Murray, 131–32. See also Multigenerational models

Bowen family therapy, 133, 180–81. See also Multigenerational models

Breakout sessions, 209

Bridging model, 90

Bronfenbrenner, U., 29

Bulimia, 76

Carr, A., 54

Case planning, 112–13, 117–18

Causality, 31–32

CBCT. *See* Cognitive behavioral couples therapy

Change: consolidating and maintaining, 106; expectation of positive, 96; first-order, 34; process of, 104–6; second-order, 34; solution-focused therapy, 158; stability *versus*, 31; as systems characteristic, 32. *See also* Therapeutic change, mapping territory of

Change mechanisms research, 67

Children, 76, 189

Circularity, 31–32

Claiborn, C. D., 57

Client, determining, 92, 204–6

Client populations, 9

Clinical action, mechanisms of, 70–71

Clinical assessment: about, 109–11; acceptance and commitment therapy, 163–64; characteristics, 111; clinical intake session, 119–22; closing the loop, 123; cognitive behavioral couples therapy, 165–66; diagnosis, 122–23; diagnostic assessment, 113–14; domains, 113–17; dyadic relationship assessment, 120; family assessment, 111–12; family relational systems assessment, 120–21; FFT Clinical Feedback System, 116; FFT Clinical Measurement Inventory, 116; functional family therapy, 115–16; individual assessment, 111–12, 119–20; outcome assessment, 117; praxis in family psychology, 118–23; process assessment, 114–16; referral, 118–19; research and, 110; sex therapy, 180; systemic perspective and, 112–13; Systemic Therapy Inventory of Change, 115; training in, 194–95; treatment plan development, 123

Clinical intake session, 119–22

Clinical intervention models. *See* Couple-focused clinical intervention models; Family-focused clinical intervention models

Clinical interventions: about, 99; common factors, 93–95, 100–104; defined, 68, 99; efficacy of, 74–78; replicable and identifiable, 68–69. *See also* Process and clinical interventions

Clinical outcomes, comprehensive, 71

Clinical practice, mapping territory of: about, 87–88; change, process of, 104–6; client, identifying, 92; clinical interventions: common or specific factors, 93–95; clinical interventions in family psychology, 99–104; relational components of change, 95–96; therapeutic alliance, 96–99; therapeutic change, mapping territory of, 88–99; therapeutic relationship, 92–93; therapist, role of, 91–92

Clinical problems, 54–58, 70, 105

Clinical profile (CP), 115

Clinical trial studies, 65, 69–70

Coalitions, 128–29

Cognitive behavioral couples therapy (CBCT): about, 165–66; clinical assessment, 165–66; goals of treatment, 166; process and interventions, 166–67; research foundations, 169–70; sex therapy and, 181; therapist, role of, 167

Collaboration, 147

Collaborative health care, 184–88

Common factors model, 93–95, 100–104

Communication, 167

Comparison trial studies, 66

Competence, 35–36, 195, 198

Complementary behavior patterns, 33

Confidentiality: disclosure and, 206–7; secrets and, 208–10

Confucianism, 39

Congruence, 96

Constructivism, 34

Consultant, therapist as, 161

Context, 3–4, 35–40, 122
Contextual and historical influences, 57
Contextual variables, 67, 200–201
Contingent, supervision as, 201
Corrective emotional experience, 157
Countertransference, 156–57
Couple-focused clinical intervention models: about, 149–52; acceptance and commitment therapy, 151, 162–65; cognitive behavioral couples therapy and Integrative Behavioral Couples Therapy, 151, 165–70; Emotionally Focused Therapy, 151, 170–73; evidence-based approaches, 165–73; psychoanalytic/psychodynamic models, 151, 152–57; risk and protective factors, 150; solution-focused therapy, 151, 157–61; theoretically based, 152–65
Couples: characteristics/context, 52–54; defined, 51
CP (clinical profile), 115
Creativity, 18–19, 214–15
Cultural competence, 35–36
Culture, 35–40, 53–54, 187
Curiosity, 14–15
Current context, 122
Cybernetics, 30

Data-based, evidence-based supervision as, 204
Decisions, purpose and intention in, 14
Decision trees, 209
Depression, 22–23, 72
Descriptive research, 64, 65
Detour triangulation, 129
Development, 42
Developmental, supervision as, 202–3
Developmental affect, 156
Developmental history of the family, 121–22
Diagnosis, 122–23
Diagnostic assessment, 113–14

Dialectic: about, 5; ambiguity and, 16–17; culture/diversity and, 38–40; Hegelian, 38–39, 82, 201; research-practice, 81–83; supervision and, 201–2; as unifying thread of family psychology, 43–44, 107
Differences, individual, 194
Differentiation, 132–33
Disclosure, 206–7
Diversity, 35–40, 70, 78
Doss, B. D., 205–6, 208
Double bind theory, 32
Dyadic relationship assessment, 120
Dynamism, 42, 63–64, 111

Ecology, 42, 107
Education, in collaborative health care, 186–87
Effectiveness studies, 66, 69
Efficacy studies, 66, 69
Emotional cut off, 132
Emotionally Focused Therapy (EFT): about, 151, 170; research foundations, 172–73; theoretical foundations, 170–71; therapy goals and interventions, 171–72
Emotions, secondary *versus* primary, 171
Empathic joining, 164–65
Empathy, 95
Encourager, therapist as, 161
Ending treatment, 106
Engagement and motivation phase, 140–41
Enlightenment, 24
Epistemology, defined, 6. *See also* Systemic epistemology of family psychology
Equifinality, 34
Ethics in family psychology: about, 192; client, determining, 204–6; confidentiality and disclosure, 206–7; confidentiality and secrets, 208–10
Ethnicity, 53–54

Evidence, 69
Evidence-based clinical intervention
    models: cognitive behavioral
    couples therapy and Integrative
    Behavioral Couples Therapy, 151,
    165–70; couple-focused, 165–73;
    Emotionally Focused Therapy, 151,
    170–73; family-focused, 134–47;
    functional family therapy, 126,
    138–44; Multidimensional Family
    Therapy, 126, 144–47; Multisystemic
    Family Therapy, 126, 134–38
Evidence-based supervision, 203–4
Evidence-based treatment, 89–90
Exception questions, 160–61
Expectations, 56–57, 96
Experiential family therapy, 49–50
Externalizing, 103

Facilitator, therapist as, 161
Falicov, C. J., 54
Families/couples: characteristics/
    context, 52–54; defined, 51
Family assessment, 111–12
Family diversity, 53–54
Family-focused clinical intervention
    models: about, 125–27; evidence-
    based, 134–47; functional family
    therapy, 126, 138–44; as lenses,
    126–27; Multidimensional
    Family Therapy, 126, 144–47;
    multigenerational models, 126,
    131–34; Multisystemic Family
    Therapy, 126, 134–38; structural/
    strategic clinical models, 126,
    127–31; theoretically based, 127–34
Family forensic psychology (FFP),
    188–89
Family life cycle, 53
Family-of-origin work, 196
Family-oriented psychologists, 26
Family projection, 131–32
Family psychoeducation (FPE), 75–76
Family psychologists: attitudes, 13–17;
    characteristics, core, 95–96; dilemmas,

19–20; scientist-practitioner-based,
    78–81; as system psychologists, 7–8;
    training of, 13, 191–98
Family psychology: client populations,
    9; ethics in, 192, 204–10; evolution
    of, 215; family therapy *versus*, 9–11;
    international, 181–83; praxis of,
    11–13; settings, 8–9; specialty areas
    of, 177–90; systemic epistemology
    of, 21–44, 71–74, 107; systems
    epistemology as core of, 27–28;
    today, 7–9; traditional psychology
    versus, 22–23; training in, 13,
    191–98; unifying threads of, 40–44.
    See also specific topics
Family psychology research. *See*
    Research
Family relational patterns, 55–56
Family relational systems assessment,
    120–21
Family therapy, 9–11
Family therapy movement, 25–26
FEAR (acronym), 151, 152–57
Feedback, 32–33, 112
FFP (family forensic psychology),
    188–89
FFT. *See* Functional family therapy
FFT–Care4, 142
FFT Clinical Feedback System
    (FFT–CFS), 116
FFT Clinical Measurement Inventory
    (FFT–CMI), 116, 142
First-order change, 34
FPE (family psychoeducation), 75–76
Functional approach, 37–38
Functional family therapy (FFT):
    about, 126, 138; behavior change
    phase, 141; clinical assessment,
    115–16; effectiveness of, 78;
    engagement and motivation phase,
    140–41; generalization phase,
    141–42; process and interventions,
    140–42; research support, 143–44;
    theoretical foundations, 139–40;
    therapist, role of, 142–43

Functionality, 42–43, 107
Fusion/undifferentiation, 132

Generalization phase, 141–42
General System Theory, 26, 29
Goals of treatment: acceptance
 and commitment therapy, 163;
 cognitive behavioral couples
 therapy, 166; Emotionally Focused
 Therapy, 171–72; formulating, 105;
 functional family therapy, 140;
 multigenerational models, 133;
 Multisystemic Family Therapy, 136;
 psychoanalytic/psychodynamic
 models, 154–55; solution-focused
 therapy, 159; structural/strategic
 clinical models, 129

Hegelian dialectic, 38–39, 82, 201
Hermeneutics, 30–31
Historical influences, 57
History and systems, 194
Hope, 96
Human sexuality, 177–78

IAFP (International Academy of
 Family Psychology), 183
IBCT (Integrative Behavioral Couples
 Therapy), 151, 167–70. See also
 Cognitive behavioral couples
 therapy
ICP (International Council of
 Psychologists), 182
Ideographic, clinical assessment as,
 111
Individual assessment, 111–12,
 119–20
Individual breakout sessions, 209
Individual differences, 194
Infidelity, 208–9
Intake session, clinical, 119–22
Integrative Behavioral Couples
 Therapy (IBCT), 151, 167–70. See
 also Cognitive behavioral couples
 therapy

Internal systems, 28, 52
International Academy of Family
 Psychology (IAFP), 183
International Council of Psychologists
 (ICP), 182
International family psychology,
 181–83
International Union of Psychological
 Science (IUPsyS), 182–83
Internships, 195–96
Interpersonal, supervision as, 201
Interpersonal competencies, 102–3
Interpersonal family therapy, 50
Interpersonal theory, 25
Interpretations, 155
Interprofessional health care, 184–88
Intersystems sex therapy model,
 179–80
Intervention research, 64–65
Isomorphism, 200
IUPsyS (International Union of
 Psychological Science), 182–83

Jones, J. L., 79
Judicial system, 188–89

Language, 30–31
Legal issues, 188–89
Lenses, 18, 126–27
Level of evidence approach, 80, 81
Lichtenberg, J. W., 57
Life cycle, family, 53
Live supervision, 196–97
Local clinical scientist mind-set, 17

Maintenance of change stage, 131
Map metaphor, 87–88
Maps, 18
Marriage and family therapists, 205
MDFT. See Multidimensional Family
 Therapy
Meaning among patterns, 34
Meanings, shared, 39–40
Mediators, 66–67
Medical history of the family, 121–22

Medical settings, 9
Mehr, S. L., 79
Mental illness, vulnerability to, 72
Meta-analytic research reviews,
    67–68
Metaphors, 6, 87–88
Minors, 207
Minuchin, Salvador, 48, 127–28
Miracle question, 159–60
Model focused, evidence-based
    supervision as, 203–4
Moderators, 66–67
Moderator studies, 66
Motivation: alliance-based, 139;
    functional family therapy, 140–41;
    therapeutic, 112–13
MST. See Multisystemic Family
    Therapy; Multisystemic therapy
Multiculturalism, 35–40
Multidimensional-ecosystemic-
    comparative approach, 54
Multidimensional Family Therapy
    (MDFT): about, 126, 144; process
    and interventions, 145–46;
    research support, 147; theoretical
    foundations, 144–45; therapist, role
    of, 146–47
Multidisciplinary health care, 184–88
Multigenerational models: about,
    126, 131; goals of treatment, 133;
    process and interventions, 133–34;
    theoretical foundations, 131–33;
    therapist, role of, 134
Multisystemic Family Therapy (MST):
    about, 126, 134–35; goals, primary,
    136; process and interventions,
    136–37; research support, 137–38;
    theoretical foundations, 135–36
Multisystemic process, 111, 204
Multisystemic therapy (MST), 78

Narrative, 30–31
Negativity, reducing, 78, 103
Nomothetic, clinical assessment as,
    111

Object relations, 50–51, 154
Openness, 14–15
Outcome assessment, 117
Outcome studies, 65–66

Patient and patient family roles, in
    collaborative health care, 186
Pattern-based relationships, 33
Patterns: complementary behavior,
    33; family relational, 55–56;
    meaning among, 34; recursive, 128;
    symmetrical behavior, 33
Patterson, J., 122–23
Patterson, T., 208
Phasic, evidence-based supervision
    as, 204
Platonic philosophy, 24
Positive regard, 95
Postdoctoral fellowships, 197–98
Practice, 11–12
Practice guidelines, 16
Practicum, internship, and
    postdoctoral fellowships, 195–98
Pragmatism, 34
Praxis: of clinical assessment, 118–23;
    of family psychology, 11–13
Primary emotions, 171
Problem attributions, 56–57
Problem-solving skills, 166
Process and clinical interventions:
    acceptance and commitment
    therapy, 163–65; cognitive
    behavioral couples therapy,
    166–67; Emotionally Focused
    Therapy, 171–72; functional
    family therapy, 140–42;
    Multidimensional Family Therapy,
    145–46; multigenerational models,
    133–34; Multisystemic Family
    Therapy, 136–37; psychoanalytic/
    psychodynamic models, 155–57;
    solution-focused therapy, 159–61;
    structural/strategic clinical models,
    129–31
Process assessment, 114–16

Processes: family, 52; of relational systems, 29–31
Process-to-outcome studies, 66–67
Projection, family, 131–32
Psychiatric, developmental, and medical history of the family, 121–22
Psychoanalysis, 25
Psychoanalytic/psychodynamic models: about, 151, 152; goals of treatment, 154–55; theoretical foundations, 152–54; therapist, role of, 157; treatment process and clinical interventions, 155–57
Psychodynamic, defined, 153
Psychoeducation, 167
Psychology, traditional, 22–23
Psychosocial history of the family, 121
Purpose and intention in decisions, 14
Purposeful interventions, 89

Questioner, therapist as, 161
Questions, 159–61

Race, 53–54
Radical constructivism, 34
Randomized clinical trials (RCTs), 65, 69–70
Records for each person, separate, 208
Recursive patterns, 128
Referral, 118–19
Reframing, 101, 139–40
Relapse prevention, 103–4
Relational, evidence-based supervision as, 204
Relational components of change, 95–96
Relational factors, in therapeutic change, 89
Relational process, clinical assessment as, 111
Relational structures, changing, 102
Relational systems, 28–31, 51–54
Relational triads, 56

Research: about, 61–62; change mechanisms, 67; clinical assessment and, 110; clinical interventions, efficacy of, 74–78; cognitive behavioral couples therapy, 169–70; criteria for, 68–71; descriptive, 64, 65; domains, 64–65; as dynamic process, 63–64; Emotionally Focused Therapy, 172–73; epistemological perspective, support for, 71–74; functional family therapy, 143–44; intervention, 64–65; methodologies, 69–70; Multidimensional Family Therapy, 147; Multisystemic Family Therapy, 137–38; in praxis of family psychology, 11; research-practice dialectic, 81–83; science and the scientific method, 62–64; scientist-practitioner-based family psychologists, 78–81; systemic approach to, 63; types, 65–68
Research-practice dialectic, 81–83
Respect, 96
Restructuring the family stage, 130
Risk and protective factors, 57–58, 73, 102–3, 150
Rituals, family, 52
Rogers, C., 95–96
Roles, in collaborative health care, 185–87

Satir, Virginia, 49–50
Scaffolds, 113
Scaling questions, 160
Schemas, 154
Schizmogenesis, 33
Schizophrenia, 75–76
Science and the scientific method, 62–64
Scientific foundations of family psychology. See Research
Scientist-practitioner-based family psychologists, 78–81
Secondary emotions, 171

Second-order change, 34
Secrets, 208–10
Semantics, 30–31
Sequences, 156
Session plans, 118
Settings, 8–9
Setting the stage, 155
Sexology, 177–78
Sex therapy, 177–81
Sexton, T. L., 100–101
SFT. *See* Solution-focused therapy;
   Structural family therapy
Snyder, D. K., 205–6, 208
Social bases of behavior, 193–94
Social constructivism, 34
Social relationship skills, 166
Solution-focused therapy (SFT):
   about, 151, 157–58; goals of
   treatment, 159; process and clinical
   interventions, 159–61; theoretical
   foundations, 158; therapist, role of,
   161
Specialty areas of family psychology:
   about, 177, 189–90; collaborative
   health care, 184–88; family forensic
   psychology, 188–89; international
   family psychology, 181–83; sex
   therapy, 177–81
Stability *versus* change, 31
STIC (Systemic Therapy Inventory of
   Change), 115
Strategic family therapy, 48–49
Structural and relational factors, 58
Structural family therapy (SFT),
   48, 102, 128, 129, 146. *See also*
   Structural/strategic clinical models
Structural/strategic clinical
   models: about, 126, 127–28;
   accommodation/joining stage, 130;
   goals of clinical treatment, 129;
   maintenance of change stage, 131;
   process and interventions, 129–31;
   restructuring the family stage, 130;
   theoretical foundations, 128–29;
   understanding/assessment stage,
   130

Structures of relational systems,
   28–29
Subpoenas, 207
Substance abuse, adolescent, 77. *See
   also* Multidimensional Family
   Therapy
Supervision: contextual variables
   in, 200–201; as contingent,
   201; as data-based, 204; as
   developmental, 202–3; dialectic in,
   201–2; evidence-based, 203–4; as
   interpersonal, 201; as isomorphic,
   200; live, 196–97; as model
   focused, 203–4; as multisystem,
   204; as phasic, 204; as relational,
   204; as systemic, 199–200
Symmetrical behavior patterns, 33
Systematic case studies, 67
Systematic inquiry, 14–15
Systemic epistemology of family
   psychology: about, 21–24; culture
   and diversity in systemic thinking,
   35–40; research support for,
   71–74; revolution and evolution,
   24–26; structures and processes of
   relational systems, 28–31; systems
   characteristics, 31–34; systems
   epistemology as core of family
   psychology, 27–28; unifying threads
   of family psychology, 40–44, 107
Systemic perspective: on clinical
   assessment, 112–13; of clinical
   problems, 54–58; as core of family
   psychology, 27–28; culture and
   diversity in, 35–40; difficulty
   of taking, 6; on research, 63; on
   supervision, 199–200
Systemic Therapy Inventory of
   Change (STIC), 115
System psychologists, 7–8
Systems: characteristics, 31–34;
   defined, 27; internal, 28, 52;
   relational, 28–31, 51–54; as unifying
   thread of family psychology, 42
Systems integrative family therapy, 76
Systems thinking, 3–5, 19, 28

Team leadership, in collaborative health care, 185

Techniques, defined, 68, 99

Terman, L. M., 178

Themes, 156

Theoretical foundations: acceptance and commitment therapy, 162–63; Emotionally Focused Therapy, 170–71; functional family therapy, 139–40; Multidimensional Family Therapy, 144–45; multigenerational models, 131–33; Multisystemic Family Therapy, 135–36; psychoanalytic/psychodynamic models, 152–54; solution-focused therapy, 158; structural/strategic clinical models, 128–29

Theoretically based clinical intervention models: acceptance and commitment therapy, 151, 162–65; couple-focused, 152–65; family-focused, 127–34; multigenerational models, 126, 131–34; psychoanalytic/ psychodynamic models, 151, 152–57; solution-focused therapy, 151, 157–61; structural/strategic clinical models, 126, 127–31

Theories: about, 45–46; basis of, 47; of family psychology, 47–51; in praxis of family psychology, 11; role of, 46–47. See also specific theories

Therapeutic alliance, 77, 96–99

Therapeutic change, mapping territory of: client, identifying, 92; clinical interventions: common or specific factors, 93–95; relational components of change, 95–96; therapeutic alliance, 96–99; therapeutic relationship, 92–93; therapist, role of, 91–92

Therapeutic motivation, 112–13

Therapeutic relationship, 92–93

Therapist, role of: cognitive behavioral couples therapy, 167; functional family therapy, 142–43; Multidimensional Family Therapy, 146–47; multigenerational models, 134; psychoanalytic/ psychodynamic models, 157; solution-focused therapy, 161; therapeutic change, 91–92. See also Family psychologists

Tiefer, L., 178

Traditional psychology, 22–23

Training in family psychology: about, 13, 191–93; assessment, 194–95; biological foundations, 193; competency in family psychology, 195; history and systems, 194; individual differences, 194; practicum, internship, and postdoctoral fellowships, 195–98; social bases of behavior, 193–94

Transference, 156–57

Transportability and implementation studies, 67

Treatment goals. See Goals of treatment

Treatment interventions, defined, 68

Treatment planning, 112, 117–18, 123

Treatment process. See Process and clinical interventions

Treatment programs/models, defined, 68, 99

Triads, relational, 56

Triangulation, 56, 129

Understanding/assessment stage, 130

Undifferentiation, 132

Unifying threads of family psychology, 40–44

Variables, contextual, 67, 200–201

Whitaker, Carl, 49

Within system alliance, 101–2

Youth development, 73

About the Authors

JOHN W. THOBURN is professor of clinical psychology at Seattle Pacific University. He is a licensed psychologist and licensed marriage and family therapist in the state of Washington and is board certified in couple and family psychology by the American Board of Professional Psychology and he is a Fellow of the American Psychological Association. Dr. Thoburn is past president of the Society for Family Psychology, Division 43 of the American Psychological Association, is past president of the American Academy of Couple and Family Psychology and is currently president of the International Academy of Family Psychology. Dr. Thoburn has been the recipient of the Society for Family Psychology's Family Psychologist of the Year Award, the Florence W. Kaslow Award for Distinguished Contributions to International Psychology, the American Board of Professional Psychology's award for Significant Contributions to the Field of Family Psychology and the American Psychological Association's International Humanitarian Award. He is coeditor of the book, *Clergy Sexual Misconduct: A Systems Approach to Prevention, Intervention, and Oversight.*

THOMAS L. SEXTON is professor emeritus at Indiana University. He is one of the model developers of Functional Family Therapy (FFT) and presents workshops on FFT and consults with mental health systems integrating evidence-based practices both nationally and internationally. He is the author of *Functional Family Therapy in Clinical Practice* (2010) and the *Handbook of Family Therapy* (2003 and 2015). His interest in family psychology and psychotherapy research has resulted in more than 60 journal articles, 35 book chapters, and 4 books. He is a member of the APA Treatment Guidelines Steering Committee and writes extensively about evidence-based practices, particularly in family psychology. Dr. Sexton is a licensed psychologist (IN), a Fellow of the American Psychological

Association, and a board-certified family psychologist (ABPP). He is the past president of the Society for Family Psychology, the editor of *Couple and Family Psychology: Research and Practice*, and the past president of the Diplomate Board for Couple and Family Psychology, and he was the 2011 Family Psychologist of the Year.